Where the Paths Meet

Bringing the Bible together to reveal God's plan of salvation

Does not wisdom call out? Does not understanding raise her voice? On the heights along the way, where the paths meet, she takes her stand; beside the gates leading into the city, at the entrances, she cries aloud. (Proverbs 8:1-3)

Dr. Charles R. Vogan Jr.

Copyright © 2001 Charles R. Vogan Jr.
All rights reserved

ISBN 978-0-6151-3928-9

Scripture taken from the HOLY BIBLE, NEW INTERNATIONAL VERSION, Copyright © 1973, 1978, 1984 International Bible Society. Used by permission of Zondervan Bible Publishers.

Ravenbrook Publishers

A subsidiary of
Shenandoah Bible Ministries

www.shenbible.org

Contents

Introduction	3

The Old Testament

What the Old Testament is all about	11
Creation	26
The Covenant	69
The Law	93
David	125
The Prophets	149

The New Testament

What the New Testament is all about	179
Jesus Christ the New Man	192
The Apostles	219

Conclusion	267

This book arose out of the work of several previous works, including the following books as well as numerous unpublished manuscripts and studies:

The Bible Describes Creation

Eight Fundamentals of the Christian Faith

Ten Keys to the Bible

The Witness

Mystery Revealed: A Beginner's Bible Survey

A New Model

Introduction

The Bible is a big book. Perhaps that's the reason that so many people don't know what the Bible is about. Where does one start? How do we make sense of the hundreds of unrelated stories and teachings in its two thousand pages? It seems easier to use it simply as a reference, pulling a few good sayings and principles from stories here and there, or possibly focusing on one or two great themes and ignoring the rest.

But one gets the sense that this doesn't do justice to the book when we read passages such as the following:

> He answered, "Then I beg you, father, send Lazarus to my father's house, for I have five brothers. Let him warn them, so that they will not also come to this place of torment." Abraham replied, "They have Moses and the Prophets; let them listen to them." "No, father Abraham," he said, "but if someone from the dead goes to them, they will repent." He said to him, "If they do not listen to Moses and the Prophets, they will not be convinced even if someone rises from the dead." (Luke 16:27-31)

Keep in mind that this is from the *New* Testament, not the Old; that *Jesus* said it to teach a point; that it's saying that we will learn what we need to be *saved* (isn't this what we thought the New Testament teaches?) from the part of the Bible we usually associate with the Law!

When I first started studying the Bible years ago, I did what probably everyone else does: read the Bible from cover to cover. From that I learned that the Bible is a collection of stories and ideas that had apparently little connection with each other. Teachers helped me see a few "scarlet threads" here and there to connect Old Testament pictures to their New Testament fulfillment, but not much more.

Introduction

Over the years I started understanding concepts that were important to each Testament – such as the Law of Moses, and King David's reign, and the birth of the Church – and their influence throughout the Bible. Even so, at this point I was only learning the Bible by regions and traveling the local roads.

When these different roads started *meeting together*, I began to see the story, the point, of the entire Bible. The Bible's lessons are not unrelated stories or doctrines. I stumbled onto the superhighways, so to speak, that connect the regions of the Bible together. What is especially exciting is how these superhighways cross back and forth between Old and New Testaments. Now I understand that the Old Testament concepts weren't just for the Jews in those particular days, but for all of God's people in whatever era they live.

To see this network of roads and the interdependence and sharing of information between different sections of the Bible, we have to back up far enough to see the big picture. Individual details won't help us much at this point – they will only confuse us since we don't see yet the overall fabric into which they fit. For instance, we could stop on many passages that say "you *must* do this!" and lose the flow of the story. It's true that the Israelites, for example, were told to keep *all* the Law that came through Moses – for "*that* will be our righteousness." (Deuteronomy 6:25) And if they would have kept it perfectly, they *would* have been righteous! But they didn't. And that's why the story goes on, as God arranges an alternate method of becoming righteous that will still satisfy the Law.

So we're going to look at the main roads in Scripture – the very roads that the Bible itself often travels – and see where they all lead us.

The **<u>Old Testament</u>** is after something – it's putting a picture together. We aren't very clear about what that picture might be until we get to the New Testament and it tells us to go back and look for it: the Old Testament *describes Christ* in a unique way.

Creation shows us our God in his first great work. We learn the methods he used to make the world, and throughout the rest of the Bible we will see him use these

Introduction

same methods as he works on earth on our behalf. We will also see the role that Christ played at Creation and why – and what that means for the rest of time and eternity. And we will learn why the Fall was so devastating to Creation and why God reacted so violently against the perpetrator, man.

The *Covenant* is God's great answer to the problem of sin and death. God made a covenant with Abraham and his descendants. Those four promises guide the history of the people of God through the rest of the Old Testament. But the Covenant is also the Gospel – whatever Christians get from God even now is entirely due to the Covenant with Abraham our father.

When God gave the *Law* to Israel through Moses, he was giving them a precious gift that no other nation enjoyed. The Law is perfect and eternal; it's a description of God's righteous Kingdom. If we could keep it, we would be perfectly righteous. But the Jews misunderstood the purpose of the Law and, by the time Jesus came, had so confused and complicated the Law that they had no idea how to benefit by it. The point is that only a Christian can satisfy the Law. But not by tackling it directly – there's another way.

David came at just the right time. Israel was at the lowest point in her history, and God needed a leader to take care of the needs of his people. David did five things during his reign that set the nation back on its feet. This provided a standard by which all kings following him were judged – including his most illustrious descendant Jesus Christ.

The *Prophets* played multiple roles in Israel's history. It was through them that the people of God felt the hand of their King ruling over them, and heard his edicts. But most importantly the Prophets pointed to the day when the problems inherent in the physical system of the Jews

Introduction

would be permanently solved through the spiritual Kingdom of the Messiah.

The **_New Testament_** presents us with a staggering concept. Paul called it a *mystery*. We learn in this book about the New Man – the Second Adam, the New Creation – that God had in mind to make ever since the ruin of his first Creation. This is the ultimate solution of sin and death, a solution that will be perfect and eternal. Jesus himself is that New Man, and we can take part in the process of the New Creation by becoming one with him through his Spirit.

God made the world through _Jesus Christ_ – for good reason. Christ not only has the authority to rule the world, but he himself leads the way to a new Creation that will fix all the problems that the first Creation fell into. He also kept the Law perfectly, something that God has wanted to see a *man* do for a long time! As the Son of David, he came to put together a Kingdom according to the Mosaic pattern and also according to the program of his father David. And he is the fulfillment of the Covenant with Abraham, so much so that if we are united with him we become heirs of that same Covenant, on its highest level. During his ministry he successfully lifted the people of God out of the physical system of the Old Testament into the new spiritual kingdom that will last forever.

The _Apostles_ – the eyewitnesses of Christ – laid the foundation for the entire Church. They saw and understood the spiritual work and nature of Christ and revealed that to the rest of the Church through their writings. They focus on what it's like to live by the Spirit, which is the key to being one with Christ and enjoying the rich inheritance of Heaven.

If you need to learn the facts of the Bible first, this book isn't the place to start. You need to begin reading the Bible book by book, and perhaps work through a Bible survey to learn its 2000 years of history. Read about the Creation, and Abraham and Moses, the Judges,

Introduction

Kings David and Solomon, the Prophets, the Gospels, and the Letters of the Apostles. This will give you the background material you will need to come back here and start thinking about how it all comes together.

Hopefully as you read this study and think about the great themes of the Bible, you will begin to see the paths coming together. At their *juncture* is wisdom. When you see how the different pieces fit together, you're starting to understand God's great plan of salvation.

The Old Testament

What the Old Testament is all about

To Christians, the Old Testament is perhaps the more confusing book of the two Testaments. There are many reasons for that.

First, it's always been a Jewish book, since the books in it were written by Jews for the Jews. It deals with the Temple, its sacrificial system, Israelite history, Jewish leaders and Jewish sins. Judaism is a different religion from Christianity; though our faith started there, we feel that we don't need it anymore, and it seems a waste of time to study it now.

> **Answer**: We're going to address this point in a minute. The Old Testament is very much a book for Christians; God intended it to be so from the beginning of time.

Second, the Old Testament simply isn't taught much in the Church today. Pastors themselves aren't comfortable with it, because they don't understand it very well either. So we only hear some of the more well-known stories like David and Goliath, and Noah's Ark, and Jonah and the great fish. Most of our time is spent in the New Testament with the life of Christ and Paul's missionary journeys.

> **Answer**: Seminaries and Bible colleges are largely responsible for this, since their courses on the Old Testament don't make it very appealing or understandable. Hopefully, once people start getting a grip on the Old Testament and seeing its plain lessons and how integral it is with the lessons

of the New, we will start hearing more from it in our churches.

Third, the Old Testament seems to be a confusing collection of stories that don't relate very well. It's obviously a history of the Jewish people. But beyond that, it's difficult to pick out any common theme through all the books. It's especially confusing to get into the wisdom literature, or the prophets, and see how that ties in with everything else. It's almost as if it's just a random collection of literature – stories, wise sayings, history, prophecies, law – that the Jews simply collected over the centuries and stuck into one book.

> **Answer**: It's only random to those who haven't seen the connecting links yet. It *does* make sense once you back up far enough to see the overall picture. The picture is startlingly clear!

Fourth, the Old Testament is full of a culture that's so foreign to us now. Culture is the *way* a people live: the Israelites lived in a world that's strange to us modern Americans. Their way of solving problems wasn't the way we do things now. And what they valued is also often strange to us. For example, they wouldn't have dreamed of letting a stranger pass through town without offering him hospitality; it would have been a shame on the entire community. We, however, live to ourselves and let strangers fend for themselves. So when we read their Scriptures, we often don't understand what's going on because of the unspoken assumptions about their kind of world.

> **Answer**: Fortunately culture plays a minor role in the Bible. The Israelites did have a different way of living from ours, but the spiritual lessons of the Bible never depend on their culture. What God taught them

about his eternal Kingdom is the same thing he wants *us* to learn, we who live thousands of years later in cultures all over the world.

Fifth, the most serious problem that Christians have with the Old Testament is the fact that God seemed to be different then than he is now. If we have the same God that the Israelites had (and we *have* to believe that, or we get into serious doctrinal troubles!) then how are we to account for the fact that God seems to have changed by the time the New Testament was written? Jesus Christ came to reveal God to us, and it *appears* that he reveals a God who has dramatically changed since the time of Moses and the prophets. If he hasn't actually changed, then the picture in the New Testament is more like a clear photograph, whereas the Old Testament picture is a rough crayon drawing in comparison. If this is true, can we rely on the Old Testament? Shouldn't we just put it aside and stick to the New Testament alone for a full revelation of God? If you believe this, you are in a large company. Many Christians have had this problem with the Old Testament for 2000 years, and they will continue to have it until the Lord comes back. And it's a serious problem; it's not an issue that can be thrown aside as unimportant. If indeed our understanding of God has changed then the Old Testament is only partially useful to us Christians at best; and if God himself has changed then we have a lot of work to do rewriting our theology books!

> **Answer**: This charge only comes up because people don't really understand the Old Testament. The God of the Israelites is our Christian God. We will find that the way God worked in their day is the *same* way he works now. In fact, we have often been blinded to the God of the New Testament and can't understand the way he works there because we haven't been alerted to his ways

in the Old Testament. Learn the Old Testament lessons about God, and you will start seeing the same God at work, using the same methods, in the Apostles' work and the birth of the Church.

These are standard objections that people use for not studying the Old Testament. But there are just as compelling reasons to take the Old Testament seriously.

First, the same themes are in both the Old and New Testaments. They both talk about the Covenant, they both talk about the Law, they both talk about the Temple. The Christian themes that we hold so precious to our faith are first described and believed by the saints in the Old Testament – faith, forgiveness of sins, a sacrifice for sins, holiness, the glory of God, and many more. The Old Testament themes that we usually think were appropriate only for the Israelites in their day are still topics to grapple with in the Church: the Law of Moses describes what sin and righteousness are; the Prophets described the Messianic Kingdom that we live in now; the Creation introduced us to a God who is presently building a second Creation, using the same methods; the Temple was a shadow of the Temple in Heaven where we are commanded to worship in our day.

Second, the New Testament constantly quotes from the Old Testament. According to one list, there are more than 350 direct and indirect quotes from the Old Testament in the pages of the New. Jesus and the Apostles reached back to the Old when they were telling people about God, about sin and salvation, about righteousness and holiness, and about getting ready for Heaven. Think about it: until there was such a thing as the New Testament, the Apostles had only the Old Testament to use in their preaching. Paul proved to the Jews repeatedly that Jesus was the Christ *from their own Scriptures*. (Acts 17:2-3)

Third, there are clues that there's always been a Christian side to the Old Testament message; it's not just a Jewish book. God had Jesus and Christian salvation in mind from the very beginning of the story of the Israelites. It's not as if God tried to work with the Jews and, after failing repeatedly, finally switched to the modern methods he's using in the Church. He introduced our Gospel to his people at the beginning of the story.

> The Scripture foresaw that God would justify the Gentiles by faith, and *announced the gospel in advance to Abraham*: "All nations will be blessed through you." So those who have faith are blessed along with Abraham, the man of faith. (Galatians 3:8-9)

> Your father Abraham rejoiced at the thought of seeing *my day*; he saw it and was glad. (John 8:56)

> All inhabitants of the earth will worship the beast – all whose names have not been written in the book of life belonging to *the Lamb that was slain from the creation of the world*. (Revelation 13:8)

> But as for you, continue in what you have learned and have become convinced of, because you know those from whom you learned it, and how from infancy you have known the holy Scriptures [**and for Paul, that was the Old Testament**], *which are able to make you wise for salvation through faith in Christ Jesus.* (2 Timothy 3:14-15)

> These were all commended for their faith, yet none of them received what had been promised. God had planned something better for us so that *only together with us* would they be made perfect. (Hebrews 11:39-40)

Fourth, there are many concepts that we Christians believe that are found only in the Old Testament. The account of Creation is found only in Genesis, yet it describes the methods that God uses to build his Church – the new, second Creation. Knowing those methods helps us understand how he works in our day. Another example is the story of King David. Once we learn what God called him to do in Israel, then we can take that information to the New Testament and figure out what and why Jesus did what he did in the Gospels (being the Son of David and assuming David's throne). The point is that the Apostles don't go over the same information that the Old Testament did; why should they, if we've studied it first? The New *builds on* the Old, it doesn't replace or ignore or repeat the Old.

Preparation for Christ

The point of the Old Testament is Jesus Christ. The New Testament isn't the only part of the Bible that deals with him. The entire Bible explains him, according to Christ's own testimony about himself:

> You diligently study the Scriptures because you think that by them you possess eternal life. *These are the Scriptures that testify about me*, yet you refuse to come to me to have life. (John 5:39-40)

> He said to them, "This is what I told you while I was still with you: Everything must be fulfilled that is written about me in the Law of Moses, the Prophets and

What the Old Testament is all about

the Psalms." Then he opened their minds so they could understand the Scriptures. (Luke 24:44-45)

And the reason that both Testaments deal specifically with Jesus is that he's such a huge subject! Most people think that Jesus is mainly useful only for "getting saved." But the Bible reveals an amazing scope and depth to Christ that it would take an eternity to explore thoroughly. For instance, here's a short list of the aspects of Christ that we find in the Bible:

- *God made the world through Christ (Colossians 1:16)*
- *Christ is the Logos who controls the world (John 1:1-5)*
- *The solution to sin – Christ's death and resurrection – was first worked out before sin ever happened (Revelation 13:8)*
- *The covenant with Abraham was to him and his Seed – that is, Christ (Galatians 3:16)*
- *In Joseph we see the plan first worked out to save God's people*
- *Jesus is the King of his people, and that kingdom was described both at Mt. Sinai with the giving of the Law, and the reign of King David*
- *The Temple and its sacrificial systems describe what Christ does now for his people in Heaven (Hebrews 8:5)*
- *The Names of God all through the Bible describe the nature and work of Christ*
- *The Prophets predict the coming Kingdom of Christ*
- *Jesus came and worked in humility so that we might see him in faith (Matthew 16:16-17)*
- *Jesus laid the foundation of the Church in his apostles (Ephesians 2:19-20)*

What the Old Testament is all about

- *The Church was a direct result of Christ on his throne, sending his Spirit (John 16:7)*
- *The day is coming when Christ will end the first step – the physical world – and unveil the new Kingdom that he's been working on (Revelation 21:1-5)*

As you can see, the story of Jesus extends from the beginning of the Bible to the end. It's *all* about him. We can't take the low road and say that Jesus is only for getting us saved. That salvation involved millions of people, over thousands of years, and was the result of long planning and complex historical processes. By the time we get to the New Testament, if we've been watching carefully, we realize that the coming of Christ wasn't a surprise element in a Jewish religion – he came to push forward the plan he'd been working on all along in the Old Testament.

So, in light of how complex this subject is, in mercy God gave us a way to approach the subject of Christ slowly, a way that enables us to see clearly what's going on. The human mind can only take in so much information before it experiences data overload. In most human endeavors, we approach complex problems in the same way: we break the problem down into separate steps or areas, then we master each step so that we understand it thoroughly. Then when we fully understand the steps, we put them together into a whole. For example, the space shuttle is a grand experience to witness, but only the engineers and scientists who make it happen know how complex the project is. It involves government agencies and hundreds of companies, with thousands of people, across many states and over many years. Only by breaking down the task into thousands of smaller steps can they hope to achieve their goal. In the same way, in order to understand and fully take advantage of who Christ is, we first have to break the problem down into smaller manageable pieces.

If we had waited until the New Testament to learn about Christ, we would have been overwhelmed by the experience and missed his significance entirely. And in fact that's what happens in many churches today. They aren't grounded in the Old Testament, so the only information that people get about Jesus is basically what they learn about him in the Gospels and the Apostles' letters (of which they get little enough as it is!). This is like jumping into calculus without first going through basic math and algebra! It's no wonder that Christians have learned phrases about Jesus without really understanding what they mean. They say that they believe in Jesus, but they don't know what they believe *about* him. Knowing him has little or no effect on their lives, except providing them a social outlet with others who claim to know him.

That's where the Old Testament comes in. It takes the subject of Jesus and breaks it down into thousands of manageable pieces for us. Though we aren't often told there that it's dealing with some aspect of Jesus, we just can't forget what Jesus himself and his apostles said about the Old Testament. It was given to the Church so that we will understand who *Christ* is.

Most Christians know that the Old Testament talks about Christ in some way. They know about the prophecies of Christ, for example, like the one about Christ being born to the virgin Mary. (Isaiah 7:14) They know that the New Testament keeps quoting Old Testament prophecies. And some of the more obvious "types" (physical symbols of spiritual realities) like Joseph and David are pretty well known. But they still see the Old Testament as a separate book with its own theme (or themes), which happens to have a few forward references to Christ in it. They fail to see that the purpose of the Old Testament is to *describe Christ*. It has no other main theme.

The world of God

When a person is converted, Jesus brings that person into a huge world, much bigger than one can learn about in a short study. Imagine yourself entering the United States for the first time. There are thousands of laws to learn, thousands of new places to see, millions of items to buy, an entire culture to learn (not to mention English, one of the most difficult and extensive languages on the planet!), thousands of schools offering almost unlimited opportunities to learn – there's just no end to what one can learn about our country. No native of the US, let alone a foreigner, can take it all in – it's just too much for a single lifetime.

What the Old Testament is all about

This is what the Kingdom of God is like. Just by becoming a Christian we have entered a new world that would make our country pale by comparison. God's world is forever; it's full of unlimited treasures and opportunities. Just to give you an idea of the potential of God's Kingdom, keep in mind that the same mind and power that created the universe (which, by the way, is scheduled for destruction because it will have outlived its usefulness!) prepared Heaven for his people to enjoy *forever*. What can God fill this new world with when he has a mind to richly bless us? What can his creativity come up with when he makes a world that will never wear out, never grow old, never need replacing – a world that millions of people can explore and enjoy forever without finding its end? If we could step into that new world right now, it would be totally overwhelming. Imagine this scene:

> But you have come to Mount Zion, to the Heavenly Jerusalem, the city of the living God. You have come to thousands upon thousands of angels in joyful assembly, to the church of the firstborn, whose names are written in Heaven. You have come to God, the judge of all men, to the spirits of righteous men made perfect, to Jesus the mediator of a new covenant, and to the sprinkled blood that speaks a better word than the blood of Abel. (Hebrews 12:22-24)

That's only a glimpse of what is open to you as a child of God, an heir of Heaven – all this is waiting for your arrival. It would be a help if we got some information first, *before* we arrive, as to what to expect when we get there! Plus, as we communicate with God regularly through his Word and prayer, he's going to keep referring to his spiritual world and how it works. So we need to understand what he's talking about, so that we can take advantage of that information and respond to him accordingly with faith, hope and love.

So the Old Testament is an attempt to cover the important highlights of this new world of God that Jesus has brought us into – like an orientation course for new college students. It does it in simple terms, on a simpler level than just dropping us into eternity without any preparation beforehand. The Israelites were the first to learn about it.

The Lord taught them these things on a physical level, using "shadows" for the time being to get them used to living with God in an easy way. But everything that the Israelites enjoyed, everything they learned about and lived in, was a preview of a Christian living in God's Kingdom, and that's now what we have in Jesus. They were the pioneers who first walked through and experienced the world that God has for his people. The thing to remember, however, is that everything that they learned about is a description of what it's like to live with God. This is the life that God has prepared for Jesus and his new family.

> For no matter how many promises God has made, they are "Yes" in Christ. And so through him the "Amen" is spoken by us to the glory of God. (2 Corinthians 1:20)

We can say it this way:

The Old Testament is a description of Christ, and our relationship to God the Father through him.

The Old Testament is rich for the Christian. It prepares us for Heaven, for living with God in his house. It trains us on *how* to live with this God; it teaches us ahead of time about the kinds of things that will be expected of us there. Here's a short list of subjects that the Old Testament deals with:

- ***The things we can expect from God*** – wisdom and understanding, salvation and redemption, rule and Law, covenant blessings, land flowing with milk and honey, eternal treasures and an inheritance.

- ***The things Jesus does for us*** – priest, prophet, protection, king, prosperity, rebuking and correcting, salvation.

- ***The ways that God works with us*** – does miracles, commands us, reveals through his Word, works over time, deals gently with forbearance and sometimes harshly with the wicked.

- ***The roles that Jesus plays in the Kingdom of God*** – prophet, king, warrior, judge, priest, temple, sacrifice, salvation, father, counselor – in other words, all the Names of Christ that describe his many functions in the Kingdom for his people's sake.

- ***Our place in the Kingdom*** – subjects to the King, the army of God, blessed people in the Promised Land, heirs, witnesses.

- ***What Jesus enables us to do*** – know God and come into his presence, defeat our enemies, worship, live in holiness, serve God.

As you can see, the Old Testament is, from front to back, a very detailed account of what it's like to live with God. When we get to the New Testament, another message is waiting for us there – that is, how we can *enter* this new world that God has prepared for us. But it assumes that you've already read about God's Kingdom in the Old Testament and really want to go *there*!

Making it simple

God is a wise teacher. Since we're such children compared to his infinite intellect, he has to water down the message a great deal and present it very plainly if we are to understand it. So what God did was work out the lessons of Christ on a physical level first, before going on to the more advanced levels of the Spirit. We are going to find the Old Testament dealing with physical realities that symbolize the spiritual realities that the New Testament will deal with later.

The physical dominates the Old Testament. For example, here are some of the events we find there:

- *The covenant promises to Abraham dealt with physical realities – his son Isaac, the land of Canaan, the nation of Israel, and the Temple and its sacrifices*

- *Joseph saved his family and Egypt from famine*

- *The Israelites were slaves in physical bondage in Egypt*
- *The Exodus consisted of ten plagues and the crossing of the Red Sea*
- *The Law was given at Mt. Sinai on stone tablets*
- *The Israelites learned about God's ways through desert wanderings and hardships*
- *The Judges fought against and defeated physical enemies like the Philistines*
- *David captured Jerusalem and reigned over Israel from Dan to Beersheba*
- *Solomon built a physical Temple, and offered the blood of bulls and goats for sins*
- *The Lord killed much of Sennacherib's army when it threatened Jerusalem*
- *Elijah challenged the prophets of Baal on Mt. Carmel with a burnt sacrifice*
- *The Israelites were exiled to Babylon for their idol worship*
- *Nehemiah and Ezra led the Israelites in the rebuilding of Jerusalem and its walls and Temple*
- *Malachi rebuked the Jews about failing God in the way they offered their sacrifices, including the tithe*

These are stories dealing with *this* world, not the next world. Christians have only a reader's interest in the stories of Palestine, because we know that's not what God promised his people for eternity. We're looking forward to Heavenly treasures, a Heavenly city. (Hebrews 11:16)

But the reason that God focused on the physical level in the Old Testament is because that's what we understand the easiest. It's always been tough on God's people to coexist with other peoples in this world, because whereas they can show us their gods (gods of silver or stone, sitting on shelves at home or in temples) we can't show anybody our God. Our God isn't an idol, nor are we allowed to represent him with anything physical. Remember the commandment!

> You shall not make for yourself an idol in the form of anything in Heaven above or on the earth beneath or in the waters below. You shall not bow down to them or worship them; for I, the LORD your God, am a jealous God, punishing the children for the sin of the fathers to the third and fourth generation of those who hate me, but showing love to a thousand generations of those who love me and keep my commandments. (Exodus 20:4-6)

So it's going to be difficult at first trying to understand a God we can't see or hear with our physical senses. To accommodate us, therefore, God started out simple – he worked out the fundamentals of our faith using physical realities. This is something we can easily grasp and understand. Not that God intended to *stay* on that level forever – the lessons in the Old Testament were temporary, and only intended to teach us what would have been too much to handle on a purely spiritual level. As Paul tells us, the Law was a schoolmaster that was given to the young student to teach him about Christ; we start at an easy level, and work up from there.

> So the Law was put in charge to lead us to Christ that we might be justified by faith. Now that faith has come, we are no longer under the supervision of the Law. (Galatians 3:24-25)

Jesus is like a diamond. He has different facets, or polished faces, that we need to turn slowly and examine carefully. The Old Testament offers us this approach. Here we can watch the King at work and learn all about him. Here we can watch the Judge and what exactly he does with the hearts of men. Here we learn about the Redeemer, and all the complex requirements for satisfying the Law. At this pace we have a chance to fully understand and appreciate what Jesus is and did. We can move from facet to facet at our own pace. Then we can return to the New Testament and keep up with the story without missing any of the details and assumptions that it makes of him there.

We need this slow approach to get the correct understanding of Christ before we get to the New Testament. When we read the stories in the New Testament we find that there are many things going on even in the simplest of stories. Jesus wears many hats, so to speak. He is King and Judge, Redeemer and Creator, Friend and Brother, Bread and Shepherd, and many more spiritual realities all at the same time. And the New Testament writers don't often slow down to explain what's going on – they assume that we've already done our homework in the Old Testament and therefore don't need any explanations. For example, did you know that when Jesus called his disciples together at the beginning of his ministry (Matthew 4:18-22), he was making a strategic move for the building of the Church that is exactly what David did when he took over the rule of Israel? In this way he was "doing as his father David had done," a standard that all the kings of Israel were judged by.

But if we haven't first learned the basics of our faith in the Old Testament, the fast-paced and condensed lessons of the New Testament will leave us wondering what's really going on. Somehow we first need a slower approach to him where we can learn about each role separately, before we get into the rush of the New Testament presentation. Didn't the writer of Hebrews get frustrated over how ignorant his students were about the basics? (Hebrews 5:11-14) That's where the Old Testament comes in.

When we get to the New Testament, the writers are going to assume that you have done this study already for yourself. They will say things like "take off your old selves," "put on Christ," "set your eyes on things above." They don't go into much detail about how to do those things, however! They are high and proper goals for every Christian; but it can be frustrating for a child of God to know what the ideal is and not be able to reach it. The Old Testament gives us practical case studies on how to know the ideals that God calls us to, and how to reach them.

Creation

Creation is one of the most important concepts that the Bible teaches us about. So much of the world, and so much of the Bible, can only be understood correctly in light of the Creation story. For example, ethics and morality come directly out of Creation. Our calling in life, the very meaning of life, redemption from sin, the purpose of the material universe – we get answers to these and many more questions only in Genesis. So we have to fully understand *what* God did in the beginning, and *how* he did it. What you believe about the process of Creation will determine how you look at the rest of the Bible.

Unfortunately, very few people of our generation understand what the Bible is telling us about it – or why it's so important to believe it just as it's written in Genesis. The question boils down to this: did God make the world in six literal days, simply by speaking things into existence out of nothing? Or did the universe come into existence over long eons of time – through evolution and the normal laws of physics that are still in force today? If the first is true then we are definitely in God's hands, at his mercy at every moment, and the world could just as easily end as quickly as it started. If evolution is true, then God and the Bible need to be reinterpreted in the light of modern science. God would be further away, more predictable, and less necessary in ordinary life than we were led to believe by the Bible stories. If evolution is true, then scientists, not theologians, have the secrets of life.

Modern Creationists are doing a good job at showing the unscientific nature of the argument of evolution. They are also showing that Christians can do good science and still believe in the Bible – the Bible and scientific principles do not contradict each other, since the same God wrote them both. But Creationists aren't going far enough. By presenting physical evidence and interpreting it in the light of the Bible's history, they aren't really convincing anybody except those who want to be convinced. The evolutionists use that same evidence for *their* arguments! Physical evidence doesn't prove much at all; it's only useful as a supporting argument at best, since evidence can be used by either side.

What is needed is to expand the Biblical argument. Genesis 1-3 isn't the only passage that deals with Creation – the entire Bible supports a literal interpretation of the Creation account. When we do this, we will have an iron-clad argument that will stand up in court – and it will be something that evolutionists and unbelievers can't disprove. Creationists have the answer for Creation in the Bible that any court of law would accept as fact.

God used three primary methods to create the world: through his **Word**, by **miracle**, and by **command**. The reason this is important to understand is that he used *the same three methods* all during Israel's history as he formed his Kingdom among them; and Jesus used these *same methods* when he came to build the new spiritual Kingdom. Creation's account of *how* God works introduces us to all the rest of his works in Scripture.

There are two problems that make it difficult for us to find out exactly what happened at the beginning of the universe: *first*, none of us were there. We like to see things for ourselves before we believe them. Since no human being was there at the Creation, we naturally wonder whether the account that we have in Genesis is really reliable; that's why many people prefer the scientific answer, since its realism and familiar principles appeal to us more than the amazing miracles that Genesis claims happened.

Second, and this is a more difficult problem, even if we would have been there, we wouldn't have been able to tell exactly what was going on. It was such a complex spiritual event that most of it would have been way beyond our abilities to follow and understand. A miracle is something that we humans can't understand; we can see the beginning, and we can see the result, but how in the world it happened is a mystery to us. And the Creation would have been just as much a mystery to us if we would have been there and watched it happen.

Evolution has its own explanation for what happened at the beginning. The problem is that they weren't there at the beginning and therefore can never know for sure. Scientists can tell you how the world works *now*, but they don't have any idea of how the world was *first made*.

So, if we want any hope of understanding what went on, we have to look inside the architect's record. God has provided a source of information for us so that we can know exactly what happened at the beginning. Using the two concepts of revelation and faith, we can easily see how God made the world.

Through his Word - Revelation

We tend to underestimate the vast distance between the Creator and his creatures. Followers of other religions can't accept the fact that the universe itself isn't God. To them, all of existence, including whatever gods one cares to believe in, are part of a continuous span between the gross physical and the purely spiritual. Everything is part of God to them – and if it is, then *they* are also part of God.

Christianity, however, teaches that before the world was made, God existed alone, needing nothing but himself to exist. When he made the universe, therefore, it was *out of nothing*; he used nothing *of* himself, the universe is in no way part of himself, and it can just as easily be annihilated without any effect upon himself. This total and complete separation of identity between God and the world is basic to our Christian faith. We need to accept this truth if we really want to understand the true nature of many of his works in the world – not the least being the Incarnation of Christ.

The Creation event also depended on this separation. The world is not God. This means that we can understand the world we are a part of, but we have no way of knowing God himself unless he comes in to us from the outside and reveals himself to us. He is not *in* the Creation, in the sense of being an integral part of its makeup; therefore we must look *outside* the universe – in a spiritual world – in order to find him. Or should I say, our only hope is if he comes in from the outside and finds us.

Creation

The meaning of the word "revelation" is to uncover, to take away the veil. What this means in respect to God is that he is *completely* hidden from our view until he himself pulls the veil away. The Scripture says that "clouds and thick darkness surround him" (Psalm 97:2). We can't easily know God as long as we are so limited by the physical world we are a part of. It's like being in a fog: we need the strong rays of the sun (or Son, as Hebrews 1:3 tells us) to penetrate the fog and clear away the confusion. So, if we are to learn anything about God, we can only wait until he has mercy on us and reveals himself to us.

There are two ways in which we can know God, and both of them depend on his self-revelation: first, through natural theology, which is a careful analysis of God's Creation looking for the telltale signs that he really did make the world. And the Bible does say that the created world tells us something of his nature and the way he works –

> … what may be known about God is plain to them, because God has made it plain to them. For since the creation of the world God's invisible qualities — his eternal power and divine nature — have been clearly seen, being understood from what has been made, so that men are without excuse. (Romans 1:19-20)

But the problem is that our sin prevents us from learning about God in nature. Natural theology is useful up to a point, but its main shortcoming is that it deals only with the physical evidence of Creation, which can be interpreted in various ways, depending on the theological persuasion of the investigator. An atheist will see design as part of the process of evolution, and modern scientists are developing sophisticated theories that can, on paper at least, explain how the world got to its present state using only math, physics and chemistry – and they willingly ignore the God in the process. Therefore, the only way that man can know the truth about God now, in a way that there can be no confusion or debate, is if God deliberately reveals himself through his Word and rips away the veil in our minds (which have been corrupted by sin and mortality) so that we *can* see him.

Creation

The Bible is the primary source and method of the revelation of God. In fact, that's the primary purpose of the Bible – *to reveal God*. We show our ignorance of its purpose when we use it for everything except that! If knowing God is, literally, eternal life (John 17:3), then we need a completely reliable source that reveals him to us so that we can live and not die. Only the Bible can do that for us.

Without revelation we are at a complete loss to know the truth about God. Notice how many theories about God have come from false religions as well as various philosophies throughout history, though they each claim to know the truth about God. Besides the fact that they can't all be right when no two of them agree with one other, their account of God doesn't fit the facts. They talk about a God they don't know, have never met, and he can't fulfill their most basic needs. As the prophets of Baal discovered, Baal will not – and cannot – answer when there is real work to be done. (1 Kings 18:16-40)

If we expect God to send rain and sunshine and other natural processes of the world, which the Baal worshippers were careful to do, then it's easy to attribute whatever happens in the world to Baal. But when we need a miracle, an event that is contrary to the way this world works and can't possibly happen except by divine intervention, then false gods can't help us. And revelation shows us that the God of the Bible is fully capable of helping us, as well as very willing, by using impossible miracles.

Now let's apply the principle of revelation to the Creation account. All through Genesis 1 we are told that God started every creative act through his Word:

"And God said ..."

We cannot overestimate how important this phrase is. If God wanted to create the entire universe in an instant, he could have easily done that. But rather than leave us guessing about how he did it, he slowed the process down and described it to us. In other words, he deliberately revealed his steps to us so that we wouldn't miss what was going on. Now, since he's giving us a chance to follow him, we learn that he created the world from nothing, by miracle, by means of command, in the presence of the Spirit, and so on. We would have missed all of this if he hadn't taken the time to reveal the steps to us.

What is critical to grasp here is that *unless God shows us, we can't possibly know what really happened.* It's not a matter of training, as if we would eventually know what happened, given the time and scientific expertise; that's what evolution claims with its scientific theories. The Bible, however, is showing us what we can never discover on our own. Things happened in that event that no amount of instruments or scientific training will uncover. It was a spiritual event, performed by Someone who refuses to use any natural means to accomplish his will. There was *nothing there except him* in the beginning! No matter or energy, laws of physics, chemical formulas, *nothing.*

How does one take a picture of nothing? How can we imagine a spiritual event? How can we know the steps of that event, and understand what happened, unless the Creator himself shows us what he was doing and interprets it for us? How can created beings possibly know their beginning when that beginning was a miracle? In other words, even the best scientists with the most sophisticated instruments would never be able to discover that God made the world through command. That reality doesn't fit into any scientific categories. We needed this revelation of Genesis 1 to show us this – because a lot about life and judgment will depend on this very real foundation stone of the Creation. Command is there, in the fabric of the universe, though the only place we learn about it is in God's account of what happened at the beginning of the world.

Physicists are aware of the very real limitation of the human mind when grappling with the question of origins. They keep backing up their explanation of the evolution of the universe to the moment of the Big Bang – even to the trillionth of a second after the Big Bang; but they are at a loss to know what lies precisely *before* that beginning moment of existence. They need a revelation just as much as anybody, because their equations can't give them the answers they are looking for and they just can't handle the idea of *nothingness.* But they can't bring themselves to accept the Bible's revelation of that moment when there was nothing, and the action that God took to bring matter into existence.

The revelation of Genesis 1-3 unveils the King at work, making a kingdom of subjects, and making the Kingdom *his* way – through miracles. It shows how utterly dependent we are on him — if he can command and make a world, he can also command and destroy the world just as easily. This isn't the solid, never-ending universe that evolution claims! What Genesis shows us is information about our world that is *not* what we expected when we use science alone to examine the evidence.

The Bible shows us that same foundation and relationship between us and our Creator everywhere we read it, not only in Genesis. Notice that many times, when man and God had dealings with each other, we find the same Creation themes at work. For example, when God opened up the Red Sea so that the Israelites could cross it and escape the Egyptians, we are told plainly how that event happened. God did it by means of a *miracle* (not a natural event!), and he did it by *command*. Unless the Bible would have told us this very plainly, however, we wouldn't have accepted the story as it stands. Human reason rebels at the thought of the impossible happening.

In order to see and understand the truth about God and Creation, we don't need to be scientific experts. The only thing we need is God's revelation: he can show this truth to anybody who has an open mind and a humble heart. Scientists feel that they are the only ones who can understand how the world was made, but they make a serious mistake. God reveals this knowledge to his children, to those who are willing to listen to him. We can and should pursue scientific research in other areas, but on the issue of Creation we will only know the truth if we use the only thing that can clearly show us what really happened: the Bible.

God works through miracles

Everyone knows that the Bible contains stories of miracles. What most people may not realize, however, is that this is the key for understanding the works of God. He prefers to work through miracles when he has important work to do. He always has, and the Biblical record shows that.

A miracle is both completely mysterious and simple to understand. We will never know *how* God does a miracle, but we can easily know *what* it is. **A miracle is when God does something by his own hand, apart from natural means.** In other words, in order to achieve his goal, he purposely avoids the normal processes that we would use to reach those goals; he goes around the physical laws and does what he wants out of nothing and without going through intermediate steps.

An example will suffice to show the difference between his miracles and our work. When we want bread, we know that there are certain steps that we must go through to get it: plow the ground, sow the seed, kill the weeds and insects, harvest the grain, grind the grain and make the bread, and distribute it through the food service channels so that people can buy it at the store. We can't leave out any of the steps because we are bound by the limitations of our physical circumstances; we must obey the world's physical laws.

When God wants to make bread, however, he skips all the intermediate steps. He isn't bound by physical laws as we are. He simply reaches out and creates it out of nothing — and in a way that defies the natural order of things. For example, he rained down manna on the Israelites in the desert. There was nothing in the world that could explain such an event; in fact, the recipe was and still is unknown to man! We can't do what God did, nor can we understand how he did it. In order to understand something and duplicate it, we need to see the steps between the initial idea and the finished result. But, by definition, God skips all the steps in between when he works a miracle. Jesus did the same thing twice when he fed the multitudes with a few fish and loaves of bread. Although he started with something small, he fed thousands with it — a feat of miracle that we can't duplicate ourselves, with all our scientific knowledge.

If you study the miracles of God in the Bible, you will notice this fact about every one of them. He just sidesteps the physical limitations, eliminating all the steps in between that you and I would need to accomplish the same thing, and does it directly.

Of course science can't grasp such an event. Science deals with laws, with cause and effect, with process and step-by-step procedure. Science is at a complete loss to explain an event that skips the intermediate steps. It can't understand a process that ignores natural laws and has no need for raw materials. *Science can do nothing to help us understand the works of God.* It is simply out of its depth here, and always will be.

The miracles that God did stagger the imagination. They were not sleights of hand that could be eventually understood and explained (not even by sophisticated twentieth century science!), but monumental "violations" of natural law that cannot be explained in any way. God raised the dead, split apart rivers and seas, brought the walls of cities down in sudden collapse, flooded the entire earth, rained down fire and destruction from the sky, turned water into wine, made people able to walk on water, healed lepers instantly with a word — the list goes on and on.

These events impressed the people who saw them because they were so *impossible*. They were entirely different than the modern "magic" that scientists can do. It's true that our scientific gizmos would also amaze people from ancient times; they might (if brought into our age) even consider our science to be miracles as well. But the difference is that we can explain *how* we do what we do; but God does things that *can't* be explained or understood, nor can we duplicate them. Remember the definition of a miracle: God *skips* the steps that we need to accomplish the same thing. Our science, on the other hand, *depends* on those steps. And because we have to go through the steps, we require resources to accomplish our goals; God, on the other hand, requires nothing to do a miracle. The events that are recorded in the Bible were the genuine article. They are miracles for which he provided witnesses. The Bible doesn't bother us with situations that our modern science would be able to explain away.

Providence, on the other hand, is when God works *through* the natural processes of the world to do his will. All the steps are there, and scientists can tell us exactly what happened; but knowing God's intentions is the only way we can know *why* it happened. Providence is tricky to interpret since we are imposing a spiritual meaning on physical events. We all have stories about how we were "miraculously" saved from some disaster, or our circumstances led to our being able to reach our goals, and we are convinced that it was for a "purpose" (which may be true!). But since God worked that out through the normal processes of life that we can observe and describe, we call it Providence — not, technically, a miracle. And although it may be true, the evidence that God was really involved isn't nearly so convincing as for a bona fide miracle.

Creation was obviously a miracle, if we take the Genesis account as it stands. The Bible presents it *as a miracle*. It offers no scientific explanation for what happened, and it doesn't leave any opening for a scientist to gain a foothold. The way it presents the event is with a child-like simplicity, assuming that God did what he said he did. There is no hint in the text that the writer expected us to take it in any other way than what it plainly says.

Every single piece of information in the account is a separate miracle. Let's look at them all together, and you will see that it certainly isn't a natural way of starting a universe, and none of it agrees with our modern scientific explanations!

- There was **nothing** except God before the world was made.
- God **commanded**, and all things came into being.
- Different parts were created on different **days**.
- The whole work took **six days**.
- He **blessed** each living thing to make it prolific.
- The Lord rested on the seventh day, making it **holy**.
- There were two special **trees**: the tree of the knowledge of good and evil, and the tree of life.
- Man was formed from the **dust** of the ground.
- Man and woman were made **righteous**.
- Woman was taken out of the **side** of man to be his helper.
- The devil, in the form of a **serpent**, deceived Eve.

- When Eve ate of the tree of the knowledge of good and evil, her eyes were *opened* and she knew she was naked. Adam experienced the same thing.
- In the day they ate the fruit, they *died spiritually* and were doomed to *die physically*.
- The two were *expelled* from the Garden of Eden and the way to the Tree of Life was *barred* by an angel.

There is no way that a modern, scientifically-minded atheist would accept any of these details as they stand. They are miracles contrary to the natural world; they assume huge spiritual realities that science knows nothing about. In order to accept that such things really happened, one would have to have a faith born in Heaven, with a perspective that can see bigger things going on than science can provide.

Obviously the Bible expects us to believe in the reality of spiritual principles, spiritual powers at work that override and guide physical events: the reality of God, the reality of sin and death, the reality of holiness and of pleasing God, the reality of dark powers who work against God, and so on. The Bible expects us to take hold of the entire picture, all of the parts of the story, not just the physical laws that scientists would primarily be interested in. This is what makes Christians believe that there are greater issues being discussed here than just how the physical world began.

Furthermore, other Biblical passages assume and depend on the fact that Creation was a miracle. For example,

> For in six days the LORD made the Heavens and the earth, the sea, and all that is in them, but he rested on the seventh day. (Exodus 20:11)

> For in six days the LORD made the Heavens and the earth, and on the seventh day he abstained from work and rested. (Exodus 31:17)

> For he spoke, and it came to be; he commanded, and it stood firm. (Psalm 33:9)

> By faith we understand that the universe was formed at God's command, so that what is seen was not made out of what was visible. (Hebrews 11:3)

> But they deliberately forget that long ago by God's Word the Heavens existed and the earth was formed out of water and by water. (2 Peter 3:5)

As you can see, the Bible never gives us any reason to believe that Creation didn't happen exactly as it says in Genesis. The reason that the Bible never questions the "how" of Creation is that the miracle described in Genesis is not only probable, but *necessary*. If we eliminate the possibility of miracles, the entire Kingdom of God would collapse – since all of God's creative works were done through miracles. Creation *had* to be a miracle, because events that followed it depended on the world being made, for instance, by means of *command* – clearly a miraculous method.

For example, a literal six-day creation is the very foundation of the Sabbath laws. The point of the Sabbath is to take one day out of seven to rest, as God did after Creation. This Law is part of the Decalogue and is of supreme importance to God's people. It would have been a devious interpretation, and a dangerous example, to invent a Sabbath ordinance like this from a creation that supposedly took eons. If the Creation took only six days, however, this Law is perfectly understandable and fitting. And since the Christian Sabbath is the spiritual extension of the original Law (Hebrews 4:9-11), it would behoove us to step carefully here: the Law, and our salvation in Christ, literally depends on the foundation of Creation and *how* it was done.

Another area that would suffer seriously if the miraculous element of Creation were removed is the way that God worked in other instances recorded in the Bible. If we can't accept the fact that he created the world as Genesis literally claims, then that would throw all other miracles of the Bible into question. These other miracles are actually lesser displays of his power than the first creative act.

Creation

When God used Moses to inflict the plagues upon Egypt, Pharaoh's magicians recognized that they were dealing with a power that was above, and therefore overruling, natural or earthly powers: "This is the finger of God." (Exodus 8:19) They knew what they were up against: a person *can* know how the physical universe works, if given enough time and resources; he *can't* know how God does his miraculous works, no matter how much time he works to understand it, because God bypasses the forces and material of this world and creates out of nothing. The Egyptians had never seen this kind of power and strategy before; they knew they were looking at the Creator's work, not the work of any earthly power. Man just can't fathom a miracle.

> As you do not know the path of the wind, or how the body is formed in a mother's womb, so you cannot understand the work of God, the Maker of all things. (Ecclesiastes 11:5)

At this point we need to compare the two models of miracle and evolution, and it will become evident that they are two entirely different ways of looking at things – they simply can't coexist. In Figure 1 is the classic understanding of the process of evolution:

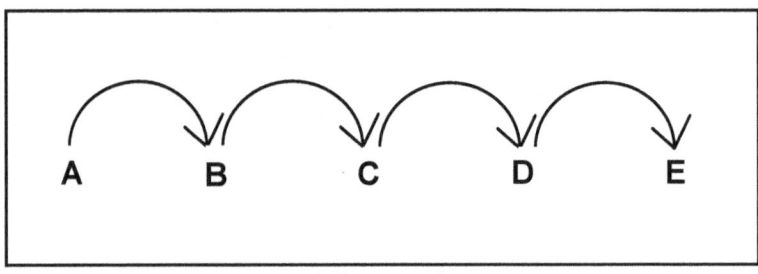

Figure 1

The main characteristic of evolution is that each step leads, naturally and logically, to the next step. A grows into B, and B grows into C, and so on. One can trace the steps that an organism took to go from the beginning of its existence (A) to its present form (E). The only way to account, for example, for Step B is to assume that there was a previous Step A that *could* bring about Step B with its peculiar characteristics. A moth's coloring, for instance, could change from white to dark because its genes have the capability of dark coloring under the right circumstances. There's no place for miracle here.

Figure 2 is a diagram of creating by miracle.

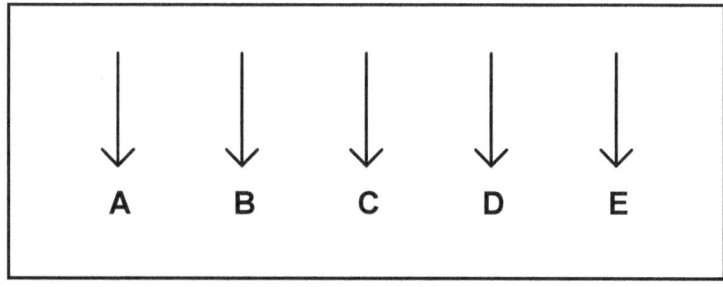

Figure 2

In this model, every step came about by a direct Divine act that brings it into existence. For example, God made the dog, the horse, the elephant, the giraffe, and the cat. The five creatures share the same world – like pieces to a puzzle forming a coherent picture – but there is no reason to believe that one creature changed into one of the others, (just because they share common characteristics doesn't logically lead to the conclusion that one changed into the other! – there *are* other logically acceptable options, especially when we have evidence that says so). Nor do we *have* to believe that they all descended from a common ancestor just because they share characteristics (especially when nobody can produce the ancestor!).

Since a miracle doesn't follow natural steps — since God skips the natural means and does the work directly with his own hand — obviously miracles and evolution are not the same thing. Either one or the other happened, but not both.

By command

One of the most obvious things of the Creation account is the fact that God *commanded* each step of the process. The phrase "Let there be …" is not a wish or desire, but an authoritative intent that such a thing *shall be*, by decree. The miracles were the act of carrying out God's *command*.

Other passages in the Bible also spell out the fact that God used commands when he created the universe:

> For he spoke, and it came to be; he *commanded*, and it stood firm. (Psalm 33:9)

> Let them praise the name of the LORD,
>   for he *commanded* and they were created.
> He set them in place for ever and ever;
>   he gave a decree that will never pass away.
>   (Psalm 148:5-6)

> When he gave the sea its boundary so the waters would not overstep his *command*, and when he marked out the foundations of the earth ... (Proverbs 8:29)

> By faith we understand that the universe was formed at God's *command*, so that what is seen was not made out of what was visible. (Hebrews 11:3)

We could go on looking at passages that show God as King, but any open-minded reader of the Bible will see for himself that God does things with authority; that's his nature. Now let's take this concept back to the Creation event. Knowing what we do about the Lord of Heaven and earth from the rest of the Bible, what do the commands in Genesis teach us about Creation?

- ***The Word of God is the foundation of the world.*** God spoke first, then the world came to be. This is always the order of things in God's world. His Word forms the foundation of all his works because it expresses his will, his intentions, his purposes; it outlines the way he wants things to exist and operate; it serves as the standard against which all things must measure up; it will form the basis for Judgment Day when God determines the worth and effectiveness of all things at the end of time. When the king speaks, his word is always his will for his kingdom and must be executed. In God's case we call this the "oracles" of the Lord.

- ***The origin of all things is outside the universe.*** No one can say that God is the world and the world is God! God's command came *before* anything else existed; it was the First Cause, and will always be the power which creates and upholds the universe. It stands outside time and space; it caused time and space and gave scientific laws their form and expression.

- ***Everything was made according to the will of God.*** Since he commanded things to exist, we have to assume that these weren't the ordinary words or wishes of an ordinary person. God is the Master, the Lord, the King; when he commands, things happen exactly as he wishes them to happen. When man commands, he hopes (or expects) others to carry out his wishes. But in God's case, he himself fulfills his own word. As the old saying goes, if you want something done right, you must do it yourself. So he carried out his own commands so that the result would perfectly fit his expectations.

Note that after he commanded each part of Creation to exist, he looked at it and pronounced it "good." He found it pleasing to him because it was exactly as he wanted it to be. It fit his purposes; he knew that it would serve his eternal plans to be made thus. Whatever God does, he does to perfection and excellence, and the results must please *him*.

- ***The world is his Kingdom.*** Perhaps the most striking truth to come out of the Genesis account is that we are a part of a Kingdom, made to serve God with all of our being. If he brought us into existence with a command, this means that the rest of our lives will (at least it ought to, by design!) consist of *obeying this King*.

The Creative command reveals an overall plan, a goal, a purpose for the universe. We may not know the entire plan until it unwinds through the rest of history, but we are, nevertheless, a part of something bigger than our own personal lives and interests. The plan, if you haven't seen it yet, was to build a universal Kingdom with God at its head. So it shouldn't be any surprise to you that in God's kingdom there are such things as responsibility, accountability, Law, guilt and punishment, right and wrong, reward, justice, community and relationships, and obedience. A Kingdom needs things like these to run smoothly. God's original command created this kind of world in which *obedience to the King in all forms* is our primary concern in life.

- ***There has to be a Judgment Day.*** One must know God in order to appreciate the way he does things. He is holy, righteous, and good. He himself doesn't do anything unjust. He creates things to please himself, to fulfill his wishes – but also to make a harmonious and complex whole that will effectively glorify his Name, his wisdom and power. We should expect to find, in his Creation, everything that will bring about all these desirable results.

But human history hasn't proceeded according to the original pattern. Through no fault of his own, God has had to deal with a race of rebels. Man has attempted to ruin God's plans and his creation. If it were up to us, things would *not* go in the direction that God had planned from the beginning.

But God's wisdom is bigger than our rebellion, and he had already laid plans – before Creation – to undo the effects of our wickedness before it happened. Not only does he constantly frustrate the plans of sinners – the wicked can't win, he'll see to that! – he plans to demand a full accounting from us on the Last Day. On that day, a day in which he will bring our works to an end and fully reveal his works, he will finally reveal himself as the King and Judge that he claims to be. All works of sin will be destroyed, all sinners punished, all the righteous rewarded, the old Heavens and earth destroyed and new ones set up eternally in their place. Everything that we have done "while in the body" (2 Corinthians 5:10) will be judged, destroyed, rectified, or accepted – according to the will of the King who has power and authority to do so. Then, if man has not yet been convinced of it, he will realize that God was serious when he commanded us to obey him in *all things*.

Note that God's command is not the same as one of our commands. When we order someone to do something, we issue the order and then can only hope that they do it. We also expect them to obey us because we know that they have the ability to do what we say. When God commands, however, it's a different situation. What he says to do, usually, is *impossible* for his subject to perform. The thing or person that he commands is unable to do what he expects of them. The reason for that is this: what God desires is more than this world can do; his standards and powers are much higher than ours, so we have no hope of doing something that would please him.

He is building an *eternal* kingdom, and bringing about *spiritual* perfection on earth – and both of these things are impossible in earthly terms and capabilities. We use whatever materials are at hand when we do our own work, but God has to provide his own materials for his special work among us, because none of ours will suit his purposes. How can you use stones and cement, or even silver and gold, to build a house for God that will hold him? Solomon knew this when he built the Temple; he knew that only God's Name can dwell there:

> But will God really dwell on earth with men? The Heavens, even the highest Heavens, cannot contain you. How much less this temple I have built! (2 Chronicles 6:18)

Creation

When God issues a command, therefore, he has to provide his own power and materials to make sure the job gets done to his satisfaction. We call this his *creative command*:

> As the rain and the snow
> come down from Heaven,
> and do not return to it
> without watering the earth
> and making it bud and flourish,
> so that it yields seed for the sower and bread for the eater,
> *so is my word that goes out from my mouth:*
> *It will not return to me empty,*
> *but will accomplish what I desire*
> *and achieve the purpose for which I sent it.* (Isaiah 55:10-11)

Since God knows that what he wants from us is beyond our ability to do, he intends to do it himself – even as he issues the command to us. In other words, he sends the power to obey him along with the command. Jesus demonstrated this principle in an amazing miracle:

> Jesus said in a loud voice, "Lazarus, come out!" The dead man came out, his hands and feet wrapped with strips of linen, and a cloth around his face. (John 11:43-44)

The man couldn't do it himself; so Jesus empowered him to do it. And, even though Jesus knew the man couldn't do it, yet he commanded him. That command reveals the deep relationship of Master and subject, between Creator and Creation, built into the world from the beginning.

If God knows very well that we can't obey his commands, and he intends to do it himself anyway, why does he bother to make it a command? Why didn't he just wave his hand over the abyss of nothingness and create a universe without bothering with commands?

Creation

We can turn to Psalm 33 for the answer.

> Let all the earth *fear* the LORD;
>   let all the people of the world *revere* him.
> For he spoke, and it came to be;
>   he commanded, and it stood firm.
>   (Psalm 33:8-9)

Notice that all the earth is told to *fear* the Lord and all the people *revere* him. The word "for" tells us the reason: because he *commanded* the earth into existence. In other words, he used commands to create the world because he wanted a **kingdom**, a world that would forever fear and serve him. The means that he used determined what the outcome would look like. *We were made to be servants of God and nothing else.* That's what the command of creation teaches us.

This explains the assumption, every time we read about God relating to men, that he's the Master and they simply *must* do what he wants upon penalty of punishment. All the world was *made* to obey God.

The basic relationship of King-servant that God established at the beginning with the entire universe explains many things about our lives and the way the world works:

- ***This is a kingdom.*** There are many aspects about a kingdom, things that we modern readers may not be familiar with until we think about it. *First*, obviously there is a king. His word is law. He is the center of the kingdom around whom the people rally in loyalty and pledge their support. *Second*, he forms the government by which the people regulate their lives. They follow his laws, his sentences, his justice. This system of government holds the kingdom together in peace and harmony. *Third*, he provides economic stability and makes it possible for the people to work and prosper. *Fourth*, he provides protection from their enemies, sometimes gathering an army and leading it into battle to defend their homes.

God is like this in all these ways. When he made the world through command, he assumed the title of King over all the earth – along with all the responsibilities that come with that position. He is a good and caring King. For example, he makes sure that each of his creatures get something to eat every day:

Your kingdom is an everlasting kingdom,
  and your dominion endures through all generations.
The LORD is faithful to all his promises
  and loving toward all he has made.
The LORD upholds all those who fall
  and lifts up all who are bowed down.
The eyes of all look to you,
  and you give them their food at the proper time.
You open your hand
  and satisfy the desires of every living thing.
(Psalm 145:13-16)

His justice is proverbial. His wisdom guides and governs the entire earth. He defends and protects his people from their enemies. (Psalm 23:3-5)

But the other side of the coin is that we are bound to obey him according to the Law that he set down for us. He gave us a conscience along with our minds, so that we feel the sting of disobedience when we don't do what we *know* he wants us to do. His moral government is impossible to escape completely, even in the most depraved of civilizations.

- ***We will never be other than what he made us*.** It's not surprising that God built a certain amount of flexibility into his creation. Evolutionists have long pointed out that creatures do change somewhat to fit into their surrounding environment (though scientists have yet to prove that creatures change from one distinct "kind" to another!). We can appreciate God's wisdom of forethought that he would make the world able to change and conform to changing physical circumstances.

There is only a certain amount of change possible, however, and that's because of the command of Creation. When God commanded the trees to exist, bear fruit, and generate more trees after their kind, *he meant it*. No tree has ever done anything other than carry out that command (barring other circumstances, of course). None of us creatures are free to be what God doesn't want us to be.

> "Should you not fear me?" declares the LORD. "Should you not tremble in my presence? I made the sand a boundary for the sea, an everlasting barrier it cannot cross. The waves may roll, but they cannot prevail; they may roar, but they cannot cross it." (Jeremiah 5:22)

Not only that, we *can't* be other than what he commanded us to be. If we try to change, we will more than likely pervert and ruin ourselves in the process. You can see examples of this when scientists tinker around making different kinds of animals by experimenting with their genes (they often end up with ugly monsters!), or by making hybrid garden plants that promise to overproduce but can't go on to reproduce themselves. Such tinkering strays from the original design, and that will rarely be beneficial or as efficient in the long run – only God's original, perfect designs work well in all respects.

- **_To change what God made is to destroy it._** The last point leads to this one. If we try to "improve" on what God commanded to exist, and make it do what it wasn't supposed to do, we will ruin it. For some unknown reason, though God certainly has the power to stop us if he wanted to, he will let us twist and turn things to suit ourselves even when it means ruining things. And the worst mistake we ever made was to do that very thing to our own spiritual nature.

We were made to obey him, and to glorify him in our actions on earth. When we turned away from that calling, we turned away from what we were designed to do, and that could only result in death. Our purpose is not to live for ourselves but for God. No wonder, then, as a result of our daily fixation on ourselves, that we carelessly murder our fellow men in many creative ways, that God doesn't get the glory he deserves, and that we fail at everything we do when we don't depend on our Creator, who is the only source of all good things.

We also see the results of our rebellion in the world that we constantly twist and ruin to suit our own fancy. Instead of working on and taking care of the earth as God's stewards (Genesis 2:15), we changed it according to our own design – we created a new world in which sinners can ignore God's moral requirements and get away with it. Daily we invent ways to avoid depending on the Lord for our needs. It's no wonder that, as we face problems with our environment and struggle to survive against disease, death, and the lack of material necessities, we build up a civilization full of machinery and chemicals and atomic waste and city expansion, destroy whole forests, wipe out hundreds of species of animals and plants, and pollute our farmland and water sources with agricultural chemicals and waste materials. We made the world that we want, but we are ruining the earth and ourselves in the long run. The world was not made for such mindless destruction.

- ***We are not free agents.*** When God made man, he gave him a direct order:

> Be fruitful and increase in number; fill the earth and subdue it. Rule over the fish of the sea and the birds of the air and over every living creature that moves on the ground. (Genesis 1:28)

This fits into the general picture of a well-balanced, prosperous kingdom that we have already looked at. Man was God's vice-regent who would make such a kingdom a reality on earth. This would require dedication, wisdom, skill, motivation, and responsibility. This would only work, however, if the vice-regent would get all his orders from the King of kings – man has to find out *from God* how to rule God's world. It's not surprising that man would not be permitted to do things his own way; he was only free to obey God and do things God's way – to build God's earth and maintain the order that God intended.

- ***Sin is a disaster in the system.*** Adam decided that instead of following God's command, he would act according to his own will. He used his own senses and judgment to determine what was right and wrong. He turned his back on his high calling and accepted the deceitful promises held out to him by the Devil. Instead of depending on God's provision and God's command, he sought counsel in his own heart and depended on his own efforts for provision.

In a world that was so finely balanced, so perfect, so capable of fulfilling all of God's expectations, the least disturbance to the system would throw everything out of joint. So when the vice-regent himself rebelled, the whole world fell into ruin! It was a disaster, a deep-rooted catastrophe that, on the surface, couldn't possibly be fixed. It was directly contrary to everything that God had in mind for it.

Sin is never a small issue with God. We can only truly understand it when we remember that the world is God's Kingdom. Sin has ruined the entire structure of that Kingdom. And once we realize how catastrophic sin is to God's world, we will begin to realize the need for a drastic and effective solution to sin. Punishment is not out of order here; it's not cruel and unusual for God to punish sinners. If we don't understand his method of solving the problem of sin (in other words, someone has to die for it!), it's because we don't yet realize the enormity of our crime against God and his world.

- **_We are responsible to him._** A command implies responsibility. In man's case, the responsibility that God laid upon him reflects the specific type of work that he has been given to do. Although most people don't know exactly what Adam's responsibility actually was, on Judgment Day there will be a reckoning, there *must* be a reckoning, of accounts. Then God will make it very clear to us what it was that he called us to do.

And it will also be very clear at that time whether we actually measured up to his expectations. Right now the confusion of life, and our mistaken opinions of ourselves, make us think that we're a real asset in God's Kingdom! But all the confusion will be swept away on Judgment Day, in order to reveal whether we have built the foundation of God's dwelling using "gold, silver, costly stones" or "wood, hay or straw." (1 Corinthians 3:12)

We can expect God to apply a very penetrating analysis to our work on Judgment Day: *first*, we will then see the depth of our calling, the wide scope of activity that God expected us to work on. He gave each of us far more to do than we are usually willing to admit. ***Second***, we will then see the degree that we *could* have met his expectations – indeed, what we *should* have done, apart from all excuses and the confusion of circumstances. ***Third***, we will also see that his demands of us were perfectly reasonable. He never gave us more than we could do. Considering the abilities and opportunities that we've had, he has every right to expect a certain success rate from us. ***Finally***, in light of these revelations, we will also be forced to admit that his punishment of the wicked, and the rewards to the righteous, are fair and just – considering what they are and have done.

> As the weeds are pulled up and burned in the fire, so it will be at the end of the age. The Son of Man will send out his angels, and they will weed out of his kingdom everything that causes sin and all who do evil. They will throw them into the fiery furnace, where there will be weeping and gnashing of teeth. Then the righteous will shine like the sun in the kingdom of their Father. He who has ears, let him hear. (Matthew 13:37-43)

When God separates the wicked and the righteous like this, he's only doing what a good king would do to preserve order and justice in his Kingdom.

A legal document

The Bible is *not* a scientific textbook, and both sides know this. Creationists know that the Bible doesn't deny science, or prevent us from doing good science. But they need to leave science at the door when they enter the realm of origins. The works of God are holy ground, and we will only take away from his glory if we try to understand his works through a scientific mentality.

Besides, it's obvious that the Bible itself doesn't approach the subject from a scientific viewpoint. That's a framework that we moderns try to fit over the story, and it doesn't work. Science claims to be able to do so much, and has actually accomplished a great deal, in our lifetimes, and it's not surprising that we tend to look at it as a wonderful panacea that will explain anything. In fact, science can help us understand and use the world *as it stands now* — which is its proper domain. But it can't explain the miraculous beginning of the universe, because it was an unnatural origin. The birth of the universe has no likeness at all to the processes and principles that describe the world today.

No, the Bible is actually a *legal* document, not a scientific treatise. It's a collection of affidavits — sworn statements — by eyewitnesses who testified to what they saw and heard. It isn't asking for a scientific judgment from us, because this isn't a matter for science; it's a legal and moral issue.

If, in all of our actions and thoughts and studying and seeking for truth, we limit our scope to what Ecclesiastes calls "everything under the sun," then we will never find God. *That* is the great mystery that man has wondered about since the beginning of his existence. It's always been a nagging thought in the back of his mind that there just may be a God. If there is a God, then we are suddenly faced with enormous implications for our lives. So people everywhere, in all times and places, have searched for the answer to this mystery of God.

The Bible claims to have the answer to this question. It provides us with eyewitnesses to the real God: they testify that they *have* seen him and his works; *they were there* on the scene when God revealed himself; and there was no doubt that it was God. So the witnesses who testify in the Bible are dealing, fundamentally, with *the reality of God* — something that we have to learn the truth about. For example, here are some well-known passages concerning the witnesses of the Bible:

> John *testifies* concerning him. (John 1:15)

> I tell you the truth, we speak of *what we know*, and we *testify* to what we have seen, but still you people do not accept our *testimony*. (John 3:11)

Creation

> That which was from the beginning, which *we have heard*, which *we have seen with our eyes*, which *we have looked at* and *our hands have touched* — this we *proclaim* concerning the Word of life. The life appeared; *we have seen it* and *testify* to it, and we *proclaim* to you the eternal life, which was with the Father and *has appeared to us*. We *proclaim* to you what *we have seen and heard*, so that you also may have fellowship with us. And *our fellowship is with the Father and with his Son, Jesus Christ*. We write this to make our joy complete. (1 John 1:1-4)

> But you will receive power when the Holy Spirit comes on you; and you will be my *witnesses* in Jerusalem, and in all Judea and Samaria, and to the ends of the earth. (Acts 1:8)

> Therefore, since we are surrounded by such a great cloud of *witnesses*, let us throw off everything that hinders and the sin that so easily entangles, and let us run with perseverance the race marked out for us. (Hebrews 12:1)

This is just a sampling, some of the better known passages. Actually the entire Bible testifies to the reality of God, in many ways. God created the world, he made it for our benefit, he demands and gets glory, he guides the history of men and nations, he condemns sinners and rewards the righteous, he decides when and where people will live (Acts 17:26), he created a vast spiritual structure for our salvation and has planned an eternity of unimaginable life for his people, making this world only an introduction by comparison. We of course can see none of this work of God on our own; the entire superstructure is a matter for faith. That's the business of the Bible: to provide testimony of eyewitnesses from history who verified that it is all true and quite real, and we are expected to believe them. And since these spiritual realities have tremendous implications for us, the Bible works those out for us as well. One of the areas that it spends a great deal of time on is the subject of miracles.

Creation

There is something important going on in the Genesis passage that we mustn't miss. The topic of Creation is an issue that divides even Christians in our day, let alone the battle between Creationists and atheistic evolutionists. But this account of Creation contains elements that will go a long way to solving the problem of what really happened.

The Lord used, in the Bible, an effective strategy of dealing with man's natural unbelief when he resorted to the use of eyewitnesses. The entire Bible is actually a collection of eyewitness testimonies given to prove one point: ***there really is a God, and he's just as the Bible describes him.*** According to their testimony, they *saw* him work in this world through miracles, set up his Kingdom, destroy the wicked and make his people righteous according to the strict requirements of his Law, and so on. Though people through all ages will naturally be skeptical that God would do such things, we have the testimony of reliable witnesses who have assured us that it's all very true.

A witness is one of the most effective and conclusive ways to make your case in court. It's the judge's (in our American system it's usually the jury's) job to find out the facts about what really happened. He reviews the evidence and listens to the arguments of the prosecutor and the defendant. Physical evidence can be helpful, but everyone knows how either side through clever arguments can manipulate evidence. But when an eyewitness comes in and claims to have seen what actually happened – he was there on the scene – then the case is made. The court decides according to his testimony.

In order to overturn the eyewitness' testimony, it's not enough to say that you don't like the sound of it and choose not to believe it. He claims to have been there when it happened! What you have to do, in order to satisfy the court that you have a real argument, is present your own witness to challenge the first one's testimony. Personal opinions aren't a good enough argument. So in order to successfully challenge an eyewitness you actually have to call him a *liar*. And that's a charge that the court is going to take very seriously – you had better have your facts ready and convincing.

Creation

The Lord knew that people wouldn't believe the Genesis account of Creation. It's just too full of astonishing miracles for the modern, scientific mind to accept. So he preempted us by having an eyewitness on hand to testify to what really happened: the **Holy Spirit**:

> And the Spirit of God was hovering over the waters.
> (Genesis 1:2)

The Spirit of God was the perfect witness to have on hand, for several reasons:

- **First**, the Spirit is absolutely faithful to the truth. He is called the "Spirit of truth" (John 14:17) because he never lies. He takes of what is Christ's and faithfully gives it to us, unchanged. It's the Spirit's business to make sure we understand God as he really is, not according to opinions and lies and false philosophies. Whatever the Spirit tells us about God and his works is not only true, but it's the *only* and *best* way to say it! Truth is what God sees, not what man thinks up with his limited senses, experience and reason.

- **Second**, the Spirit can see what's really going on. The Spirit is the only one who really knows God (1 Corinthians 2:10-11). He can see spiritual realities that we can't see. God did more at Creation than make physical objects; he built a spiritual superstructure that all of the physical universe rests on. And without the Spirit showing us this spiritual world, we would never see it. In fact, the Spirit is the key to *all* the witnesses of God in the Bible. They couldn't see or know God themselves without the Spirit making it possible.

- **Third**, in order to reject the testimony of Genesis, one would have to call the Spirit of God a *liar*. I'd like to meet the foolish person who would do that. On Judgment Day, God will call each of us to his throne and demand why we didn't believe the testimony that he gave through his faithful witness. Our lives will hang in the balance

Creation

according to our answer! The Spirit of God is the most reliable witness who ever testified to God's works; a stupid answer like "I didn't want to believe it" won't hold water in God's court.

> And it is the Spirit who testifies, because the Spirit is the truth. For there are three that testify: the Spirit, the water and the blood; and the three are in agreement. We accept man's testimony, but God's testimony is greater because it is the testimony of God, which he has given about his Son. Anyone who believes in the Son of God has this testimony in his heart. *Anyone who does not believe God has made him out to be a liar*, because he has not believed the testimony God has given about his Son. (1 John 5:7-10)

The prophets wrote the Old Testament. Moses is generally accredited by tradition as well as the rest of the Biblical writers for having written Genesis through Deuteronomy. And in Deuteronomy we read that Moses was the greatest of the Old Testament prophets. He spoke with God, and God spoke with him.

> Since then, no prophet has risen in Israel like Moses, whom the Lord knew face to face, who did all those miraculous signs and wonders the Lord sent him to do in Egypt – to Pharaoh and to all his officials and to his whole land. For no one has ever shown the mighty power or performed the awesome deeds that Moses did in the sight of all Israel. (Deuteronomy 34:10-12)

And Peter tells us how the prophets knew what to write:

> Above all, you must understand that no prophecy of Scripture came about by the prophet's own interpretation. For prophecy never had its origin in the will of man, but men spoke from God *as they*

> *were carried along by the Holy Spirit.* (2 Peter 1:20-21)

This means, then, that when Moses wrote the book of Genesis, he didn't write his own opinions. He wrote what the Holy Spirit told him to write. And since the Spirit was the eyewitness of Creation, Moses gave us an *eyewitness account* of the Creation event from the only one who *could* tell us the truth of what happened.

Through Faith

Faith is such a characteristic feature of God's people that we find it from beginning to end in the Bible, from Abraham the "father" of the faithful to the Church of the faithful in Christ found in Revelation. But though faith is a universal characteristic among Christians, this doesn't mean that it's something easily understood or easily had. Faith is a gift from God (Ephesians 2:8) and is beyond the natural ability of human beings, especially because of our sin.

Faith is always the way we have to approach all matters of the Spirit, because none of our physical senses can enable us to know the certainty of the world of God. This is because faith is a special spiritual skill that makes the impossible happen: it gives us a vision, an understanding, of God's world. Without faith we can't understand the truth even if we are looking straight at it!

Faith, as Hebrews tells us, is "being sure of what we hope for and certain of what we do not see." (Hebrews 11:1) What faith gives us is **the ability to see God's spiritual world**. Though our physical senses can't know God, our souls can – when the Spirit makes our dead souls alive so that we *can* see God. The Spirit reveals God – this is his job among us – so that we can see and know the truth about God. Without the Spirit we can see nothing; but because of the Spirit, a light from Heaven shines down on us and we can know God personally.

> The Spirit searches all things, even the deep things of God. For who among men knows the thoughts of a man except the man's spirit within him? In the same way no one knows the thoughts of God except the Spirit

of God. We have not received the spirit of the world but the Spirit who is from God, that we may understand what God has freely given us. This is what we speak, not in words taught us by human wisdom but in words taught by the Spirit, expressing spiritual truths in spiritual words. The man without the Spirit does not accept the things that come from the Spirit of God, for they are foolishness to him, and he cannot understand them, because they are spiritually discerned. (1 Corinthians 2:10-14)

In order to do this, the Spirit has to take us outside this physical world, beyond where our normal senses operate, and show us the spiritual world in a way that we will know for certain that such things are true. This is the root of true faith. Abraham, the "father of the faithful," first experienced this when God gave him the promise of a son:

> Abram believed the Lord, and he credited it to him as righteousness. (Genesis 15:6)

The promise was clearly incredible; he and especially his wife Sarah were too old to have a son. But something in what Abraham saw, through his faith, convinced him that God's promise would most certainly happen in spite of its impossibility:

> Against all hope, Abraham in hope believed and so became the father of many nations, just as it had been said to him, "So shall your offspring be." Without weakening in his faith, he faced the fact that his body was as good as dead — since he was about a hundred years old — and that Sarah's womb was also dead. Yet he did not waver through unbelief regarding the promise of God, but was strengthened in his faith and gave glory to God, being fully persuaded that God had power to do what he had promised. This is why "it was credited to him as righteousness." (Romans 4:18-22)

Creation

Faith – our awareness and certainty of spiritual realities – keeps us in touch with God and serves us in an important way: it makes the things of God so real that we change our lives to fit what we know, much to the surprise of those who don't see what we see! We live in God's presence, we live for God's Heavenly rewards, we live in the fear of God and his commands, we don't fear the world anymore, we don't yield to temptations, we hate our spiritual enemies, we love our brothers and sisters in the Lord. None of this makes sense to an unspiritual man, but it makes perfect sense to a Christian who has seen the reality of this new world of which he is now a citizen.

Life here becomes a parallel existence, so to speak: our physical senses tell us about the physical world we live in, and our awakened spiritual senses tell us about the world of God that we live in. We become "strangers and aliens" in this world while we make our way toward the place where we know that we have our eternal citizenship. (Hebrews 11:13-16) We are actually living in two worlds, and can see both of them: our physical eyes for this world, and our spiritual eyes, or faith, for the world of God.

We find, at all the critical junctures in Biblical history, that faith was the only way to truly understand the work that God was doing. Each event required a special skill of discernment that reason or senses couldn't provide. For example, only by faith could the disciples know who Jesus really was. According to physical senses, he was only the carpenter's son; the Jews in general were completely confused about him:

> When Jesus came to the region of Caesarea Philippi, he asked his disciples, "Who do people say the Son of Man is?" They replied, "Some say John the Baptist; others say Elijah; and still others, Jeremiah or one of the prophets." "But what about you?" he asked. "Who do you say I am?" Simon Peter answered, "You are the Christ, the Son of the living God." Jesus replied, "Blessed are you, Simon son of Jonah, for this was not revealed to you by man, but by my Father in Heaven." (Matthew 16:13-17)

That special revelation that was given to Peter was light from Heaven, unveiling the real glory that was behind the outward humility of Christ. Only in that way could the disciples know the truth about him.

Faith is necessary to understand many other spiritual works recorded in the Bible: for example, David in his battle against Goliath, the truth about Christ's birth, the prophecies of the Old Testament, the forgiveness found in the Temple worship in Jerusalem. Without faith we would form a wrong interpretation of what is really going on – we will miss the fact that this is really God working, doing things in ways peculiar to himself. For example, Paul was thankful that the Thessalonians could see the true nature of his preaching:

> And we also thank God continually because, when you received the word of God, which you heard from us, you accepted it not as the word of men, *but as it actually is*, the word of God, which is at work in you who believe. (1 Thessalonians 2:13)

When we rely on faith so heavily to understand God's works, we naturally find ourselves in a predicament. It's natural for unbelievers to assume that, since faith deals with the invisible world and with what our senses can't help us understand, we Christians are dealing therefore with the non-existent and unimportant. If nobody can see God, and we have to accept the Bible's explanation that God really was involved in Creation (though nobody saw him at work!), then why do we need to believe in something we can't see? This is the charge that unbelievers will inevitably make against Christians whenever we fall back on "faith" to interpret Creation. If we deliberately point to the unseen to explain the visible, why then resort to it at all?

The reason is this: the God who is above and beyond Creation, who is in no way a part of this world, is responsible for making this world what it is. We have to look outside the system to explain the system. Evolution looks within the system, hoping that the world will explain itself (which it can't, because there are many things that can't be accounted for by using only evolution). The only explanation that works, the only truth that fully accounts for the world we live in, is that a spiritual God made it all out of nothing for his purposes. Only faith can see that, so only faith finds the truth.

Faith is the *only* way we will know God or understand his works. So, let's take this truth back to the Genesis account of Creation and apply it. Let's not continue to stumble over the incredible nature of the account and substitute a "reasonable" scientific answer. Our ability to reason depends on our senses and what we know about *this* world; but our faith reaches beyond this world to a God who says he can – and did – make the world through miracle.

Only someone who truly knows God – that is, who sees God in faith – will be convinced. Faith can easily see that a miracle-working, holy King who does his will by creative command, by means of the power of the Spirit, would not have made the world in any other way except what the Genesis account states very clearly.

The Genesis account *requires* faith. It makes no sense unless we can see the greater spiritual forces at work behind the making of the universe. We read there that God spoke and the whole universe came into being immediately. "*By faith* we understand that the universe was formed at God's command, so that what is seen was not made out of what was visible." (Hebrews 11:3) Our senses can't explain that truth, scientific instruments can't explain it to us, our reason and rational minds can't explain it – the only "instrument" capable of grasping the nature of what happened and how it happened is this *spiritual* sense of faith that God gives his people.

This is so fundamental a truth that we can claim without hesitation this fact: if someone with all the scientific training in the world were there at Creation when it happened, he would have come away from the event having no understanding of what he saw, even though he might have had all the data and recording instruments he could have wished for, and plenty of time to analyze the data. Evolution only requires mathematics, physics, chemistry, and various instruments to be understood. But the skill needed – indeed, required – to understand *this kind* of Creation recorded in Genesis is faith.

If we use anything less than faith, however, we will be completely blind to the tremendous spiritual work going on in it. Without faith the event becomes too fantastic to believe; so we fall back on what we can learn with our senses, and of course we then miss out on the hand of God working his will into his world. We will never believe in a miracle-working God without faith; we will never bend our knees in humble fear and submission to the King who commands. Without faith, "it is impossible to please God, because anyone who comes to him must believe that he exists and that he rewards those who earnestly seek him." (Hebrews 11:6)

A strictly scientific viewpoint of Creation can't please God, because there's no faith in it. Neither can a hybrid version of Creation and evolution please him because such a position substitutes rational scientific answers for the impossible miracles. What this Genesis account is designed to do is make a *believer* out of you, a humble *servant* of the King, ready and willing to receive Heavenly treasures for your life on earth. At the end of time, those who approached God with faith will be rewarded.

> These have come so that your faith — of greater worth than gold, which perishes even though refined by fire — may be proved genuine and may result in praise, glory and honor when Jesus Christ is revealed. Though you have not seen him, you love him; and even though you do not see him now, you believe in him and are filled with an inexpressible and glorious joy, for you are receiving the goal of your faith, the salvation of your souls. (1 Peter 1:7-9)

There is one more truth about the Creation account that we mustn't overlook. Since the entire Bible is a book that requires faith, we would expect its introductory chapters to set the tone for what is to come. We see miracles here, we see the impossible happen, we are introduced to a unique God, who intends to do the same kinds of things for his people across all ages. We see the world spring into a state of servanthood at its very beginning; we see a power that nothing in the universe can copy. All the elements for historic Judaism and Christianity are in this story of Creation. It's as if this account is an archway spanning the entrance into the rest of God's Word: written across it, in unmistakable letters, is the message, "All who enter here must enter with *faith*."

How The Biblical Writers Used The Creation Account

The people of God in Bible times read the Genesis account only one way: the literal way. You can tell that they did, because when they needed the God who made the world in a certain way then they prayed to him for the same kinds of things. In other words, when they needed immediate miracles from the King in whose hands are all things, they turned to the Creator who made the world through miracles, by command, in six days.

Hezekiah - When Sennacherib, the Assyrian army commander, surrounded Jerusalem and threatened to destroy it, he told the people in the city that no god – not even Israel's God – could protect them. They may as well give up quietly. But Hezekiah couldn't accept this. He immediately went to pray to the Lord. Notice, however, which God he calls on: *the God who made Heaven and earth*. He realized that he needed the Creator for this crisis. It's true that other gods couldn't stop Sennacherib, because they were empty hopes of false religions. But Israel's God was real; he was so real that everything and everybody on earth were in his hands – he could do what he wanted with them. What Hezekiah was asking for, therefore, was the kind of power that could stop the enemy in his tracks. In other words, he was asking for a miracle from the only God who could do such a thing.

What we need to learn here is that Hezekiah knew what to ask for: he wanted the *same kind* of power and wisdom that created the world, because only that kind of answer would fulfill his present needs. If he had gotten a *natural* answer – destruction of the enemy by disease, success for his soldiers, boredom on Sennacherib's part as he prolonged his siege – then it would have taken much longer to solve the problem (if ever!), which wasn't what Hezekiah needed at this moment. He needed a full-scale miracle, immediately, and he got one. Any other "solution" would have made people wonder whether God were really in charge. (*2 Kings 19:14-19*)

Nehemiah – When the Israelites returned from Exile, they faced the daunting task of rebuilding the city and the Temple – while holding off enemies who wanted to tear down their work. Naturally they turned to their God for help. Notice that they immediately call on the God who *made the Heavens, even the highest Heavens, and all their starry host, the earth and all that is on it, the seas and all that is in them.* In other words, they want the ear of the Creator. Why is that?

Read the rest of the prayer and you will find out why. The priests retold some of the history of the Israelites – when they were enslaved in Egypt, and God rescued them from Pharaoh's hand by means of *miracles*. They remembered that God fed the Israelites bread, meat and water in the middle of the desert – again through *miracles*. They remembered that God rescued them from their enemies and drove out the Canaanites from Palestine, all through *miracles*. Time and time again the Israelites rebelled against God, and he allowed them to fall into the hands of oppressive nations – but then he relented over and over and rescued them by means of *miracles*.

Is the pattern becoming plain? When the Jews found themselves in trouble, surrounded by enemies, faced with the possibility of destruction just when they had arrived home to build things up again – they called on the Creator who continually uses miracles to protect them. They knew that they needed nothing less than the power of Heaven to protect them.

They knew that the Creator does miracles, that it was the Creator who provided for their ancestors and protected them along the way. No other god works like this; no other god (or force or principle of science) *can* work like this. Also, the fact that Israel's God used miracles in their day was, to them, the natural thing for him to do. How else *would* the Creator solve their problems? He simply wouldn't use any method other than miracles, because that's how he first created the world – and the result, remember, was *very good*. He works the same way in all ages when there's a need that's impossible for the world to supply. (***Nehemiah 9:6***)

The Apostles - When the new Church was spreading the Gospel of Christ throughout Jerusalem, Christians naturally ran into trouble with unbelievers. The Apostles began to experience persecution at the hands of the Jews for their new faith in Christ. Their response was to immediately go to God in prayer for help. It's revealing to see *which God* they called on – the God who *made the Heaven and the earth and the sea, and everything in them*.

They wanted the Creator's help, and they homed in on several of his characteristics: **first**, his *power*, since they needed that kind of power to counteract the forces of darkness and persecution that were arrayed against them.

Second, they needed the *authority* of the Lord of Heaven and earth – one who would command his subjects, even those who refused to obey him, to submit to him whether willing or not. Remember the Command of Creation? They knew that if this God commanded their enemies to back off, they wouldn't be able to resist his command.

Third, they specifically asked for *healings* and *miraculous signs and wonders* to support their ministry. They wanted positive proofs in their ministry that would convince people that here was the real God, the God who could do the impossible for his people. They needed a miracle-working God to go before them, and naturally the One that came to mind was the One who first created all things – *through miracles*!

Only the One who performs miracles, who regularly turns to miracles to do the impossible in the face of great need, could answer this prayer. In other words, they knew their God; they knew how to use the information in Genesis to their advantage when presenting their requests to him. They didn't disappoint him with doubts of his abilities, but asked for what he could do, and what he had already proven (at Creation) that he could do. Their prayer was answered immediately in a way that showed the hand of the Creator. (*Acts 4:24-30*)

Peter – There is an amazing passage in 2 Peter that makes the entire issue very plain.

> First of all, you must understand that in the last days scoffers will come, scoffing and following their own evil desires. They will say, "Where is this 'coming' he promised? Ever since our fathers died, everything goes on as it has since the beginning of creation." But they deliberately forget that long ago by God's word the Heavens existed and the earth was formed out of water and by water. By these waters also the world of that time was deluged and destroyed. By the same word the present Heavens and earth are reserved for fire, being kept for the day of judgment and destruction of ungodly men. (*2 Peter 3:3-7*)

What Peter is saying is that the *very thing* that unbelievers reject – the *way* the world was made (by miracle, in six days) and the Great Flood in Noah's day (*world-wide*, not a local flood) will be the *same methods* that God will use to destroy the world in the end – another doctrine which they also reject.

Are we part of the faithful?

Not only have we seen undeniable proof that the saints of the Bible believed Genesis to be literally true, we also have been presented with a challenge. The challenge is this: are we part of the people of God? The answer to that is in whether we believe the same things about God that these Biblical saints believed. If we do, we are a part of them; if not, then they stand apart from us and condemn us for our *unbelief.*

The glory of God is at stake here. Genesis is the introduction to all of God's works in this world. The same miracles that created the world also uphold the world. The same commands that set the parameters of life in the beginning continue to rule over us. Jesus in his ministry merely emphasized the point when he used the powers of the Creator to rule over his environment and begin building a new world. If we throw away these important truths of Genesis, we have cut ourselves off from God and the way he works.

There is no point for us to pray as the saints in the Bible prayed if we don't believe that Genesis is true as it stands. They asked for what the Creation account showed them about God and the way he works; it's plain to see that they believed in the very things that modern evolutionary scientists refuse to believe in. If we don't believe it, then we have broken faith with our spiritual forefathers. We don't share their faith in *this* God, that he would do *these* kinds of things in our day. If we change the account in any way at all, by reading in evolution and cutting out the miracles and commands, then we have left the historic faith and are literally creating a new god who works in different ways from the ways that the Prophets and Apostles believed about their God. The Church consists of people who have the *same* faith in the *same* Biblical God. If we don't believe in that God, we have no right to claim spiritual descent from these spiritual giants of the faith. Nor should we expect the Creator God to answer our prayers with his unique wisdom and power.

The Covenant

The idea of *covenant* is much more important in the Bible than you might imagine. It spans the entire book, from Genesis to Revelation. It not only has to do with the covenant people Israel but with the covenant people of the Church.

The covenant is not only a running theme throughout the Bible, it is the only reason that anybody, Jew or Gentile, gets anything at all from the Lord. Most people hope that the Lord will do something good for them; but only those who are "heir to the covenant" have the legal rights to the good things of God. "Therefore, the promise comes by faith, so that it may be by grace and may be guaranteed to all Abraham's offspring — not only to those who are of the Law but also to those who are of the faith of Abraham. He is the father of us all." (Romans 4:16)

What is a covenant?

In our day we use contracts and lawyers and courts to make agreements with each other, and we have all sorts of ways to make the other party keep their side of the bargain. But in the days of Abraham they had none of these things; so they had to use a different system for making agreements.

The word "covenant" referred to a legally binding agreement between two people. In it they agreed to do certain things for each other. But the Hebrew word for "covenant" is *berith* (Hebrew ברית) which is usually used along with the word "to cut." There is an amazing reason for this. When two people wanted to make this kind of agreement, they would get some animals and, with a sword, cut them into halves and lay the halves out on the ground, making a path down between them. Then one person would walk down the path between the animal halves and declare what he agreed to do for the other person.

The Covenant

The idea was that if he failed to do as he agreed, the offended party would have the legal right to take a sword and do to him what was done to the animals! Then when he was finished making his promise, the other person would do the same. As you can imagine, people didn't enter into an agreement like this unless they were serious about it!

Now turn to Genesis 15 for an example of how a covenant was done. In it the Lord instructed Abraham to cut a heifer, a goat and a ram into halves and lay them out on the ground in two rows. Then when Abraham was put into a deep sleep (so that he could see the Lord come down in a vision), the Lord himself walked down through the animal halves and declared his agreement with Abraham.

> When the sun had set and darkness had fallen, a smoking firepot with a blazing torch appeared and passed between the pieces. On that day the LORD made a covenant with Abram and said, "To your descendants I give this land, from the river of Egypt to the great river, the Euphrates — the land of the Kenites, Kenizzites, Kadmonites, Hittites, Perizzites, Rephaites, Amorites, Canaanites, Girgashites and Jebusites." (Genesis 15:17)

What is truly amazing is that the Lord was submitting himself to the hands of Abraham in this agreement; he (the Author of life!) was putting his life on the line. He would keep the terms of this agreement or willingly forfeit his life. This should show you how seriously he took the covenant with Abraham. There was absolutely no question that the Lord was going to do what he promised.

The second amazing thing about this story is that God did *not* require Abraham to walk down between the animal halves. Normally they would both do it; but in this case the Lord knew that Abraham and his descendants would surely put the covenant in jeopardy if it depended on them in any way. So God took it upon himself to keep both sides of the bargain. Not that he was allowing Abraham to get away with sin in the future. But he knew that Abraham *would* sin — and since the covenant was tremendously important to the Lord, he was acting now to protect it from any future threats to its fulfillment.

The Covenant with Abraham

What was this covenant that the Lord made with Abraham? There had been a covenant made before this time with Noah; but Abraham was the first important step in the process of salvation. For a long time the Lord was preparing an answer to the sin and death that man had introduced into his perfect creation. Now, in Abraham, he was ready to start unfolding it into human history. The covenant with Abraham is the beginning of the answer that we have all been looking for.

The Lord promised to do four things for Abraham and his descendants:

To give him a son: Abraham and Sarah had no children when they moved to Canaan in obedience to the Lord's command. They were advanced in years at the time, and had basically given up hope that they would ever have a natural-born son. But the Lord promised them that they would, in fact, have their own son — clearly an impossible thing.

> But Abram said, "O Sovereign LORD, what can you give me since I remain childless and the one who will inherit my estate is Eliezer of Damascus?" And Abram said, "You have given me no children; so a servant in my household will be my heir." Then the word of the LORD came to him: "This man will not be your heir, but a son coming from your own body will be your heir." (Genesis 15:2-4)

He was too old to have a son, and his wife was long past the child-bearing age for women. God was promising them the impossible — a miracle, which happens to be the very method he uses to build his kingdom in any age. At one point they both laughed at the idea of having a son in their old age; when the boy was born, then, they named him "Isaac" which means "he laughs" (perhaps because the Lord had the last laugh in this!).

The promise was fulfilled in Genesis 21:

> Now the LORD was gracious to Sarah as he had said, and the LORD did for Sarah what he had promised. Sarah became pregnant and bore a son to Abraham in his old age, at the very time God had promised him. (Genesis 21:1-2)

To give him the land: When the Lord brought Abraham to Canaan, it wasn't just for a sight-seeing tour! He had Abraham look around at this new place and promised him that one day, both he and his descendants would own this land.

> Lift up your eyes from where you are and look north and south, east and west. All the land that you see I will give to you and your offspring forever. (Genesis 13:14)

The problem was that this would have to be as much of a miracle as the first promise! The Canaanites who already lived there wouldn't take kindly to an alien with strange ways and accents settling down among them, taking their valuable pasture and resources — they especially wouldn't appreciate his notions of owning the whole place someday! So they no doubt kept their eye on him at all times and encouraged him to move on, not settle down. (You can see this very thing happen in the story of Isaac — Genesis 26:12-31.)

The fulfillment of this promise came about in a strange way, certainly not in the way that Abraham would have wanted. Sarah his wife eventually died, and after Abraham mourned over her he looked around for a place to bury her. Since he had no land of his own, he went to the Hittites (a Canaanite tribe living near

The Covenant

Hebron) and asked to buy from them a field with a cave in it so that he could bury her. They agreed on a price and the deed was made out in Abraham's name; he became the legal owner of a piece of Canaanite property for the first time.

> So Ephron's field in Machpelah near Mamre — both the field and the cave in it, and all the trees within the borders of the field — was deeded to Abraham as his property in the presence of all the Hittites who had come to the gate of the city . . . So the field and the cave in it were deeded to Abraham by the Hittites as a burial site. (Genesis 23:17-18, 20)

The remarkable thing about this transaction was that it was the beginning of the fulfillment of the second promise that God made with Abraham. He was to become owner of the entire land, in spite of the Canaanites already living there. This was the first step to that ownership. It happened in the midst of trial; certainly Abraham didn't want his wife to die. Nevertheless that trial was the means that the Lord used to bring about what otherwise would have never happened. That was the first down payment on the Lord's promise. The deed stayed in the family as part of the inheritance from Abraham for hundreds of years – till the Israelites came back from Egypt to claim the rest of the land!

To make a great nation from him: The Lord promised Abraham that not only would he get a son, but his descendants would become so numerous that they would be a great nation that nobody could count.

> I will make you into a great nation. (Genesis 12:2)

> He took him outside and said, "Look up at the Heavens and count the stars — if indeed you can count them." Then he said to him, "So shall your offspring be." (Genesis 15:5)

Now Abraham couldn't become a nation all by himself. And his son couldn't become a nation without getting married. So they had a problem on their hands: where to find a wife for Isaac? Abraham absolutely refused to get one of the local Canaanite girls for Isaac's wife; they were pagans, worshippers of idols and would lead his son into wickedness and away from the Lord. So Abraham had his servant go back home to Haran where his extended family still lived and find a wife there.

Most people use this story as an example of how to find a suitable marriage partner. But we miss the main point of the story if we limit ourselves to just that. Genesis 24 is really showing us the beginning of the fulfillment of the third promise — the making of a nation. He provided a wife (Rebekah) to be the mother of Jacob, who was the father of twelve sons, who were the fathers of the twelve tribes of Israel. The story is full of miracles, the hand of God guiding the family along his eternal plans. The promise had begun to unfold!

> And they blessed Rebekah and said to her, "Our sister, may you increase to thousands upon thousands; may your offspring possess the gates of their enemies." (Genesis 24:60)

To bless the nations through him: When man first sinned in the Garden of Eden, he brought upon himself and the entire world a tremendous curse of misery and death. As far as God was concerned, this was the worst thing that could have happened to his beautiful creation. He didn't curse us because he liked to, but because he

The Covenant

had to. He had to confront sin with the severity of the Law because justice is important to him.

But the Lord never did like that answer for the entire world. From the very beginning he set about putting together a new answer for the problem of sin and death. He hinted at what it might be in Genesis 3:15, but he didn't really say yet what he had in mind.

Now in Abraham's life he was ready to start putting the plan into action. The first step was to promise Abraham that he would be a blessing to the nations:

> And all peoples on earth will be blessed through you. (Genesis 12:3)

> And through your offspring all nations on earth will be blessed. (Genesis 22:18)

This *blessing* would overturn the original *curse* that fell on mankind. But what would it look like? Again, Abraham got a "foretaste", a glimpse of what that would look like, in his own experience. The Lord told him one time to take his only son Isaac and sacrifice him to the Lord "on one of the mountains I will tell you about." (Genesis 22:2) So Abraham took Isaac there and started to draw the sacrificial knife across his son's throat. Immediately the Lord stopped him and commended him for his faith.

What went through Abraham's mind during this crisis? He was about to lose his only hope! Upon Isaac rested the future of the entire covenant; it didn't make sense to put him to death, even if it *was* in obedience to the Lord. But the Lord showed Abraham a truth there that strengthened him to go on with the act:

The Covenant

Abraham reasoned that God could raise the dead, and figuratively speaking, he did receive Isaac back from death. (Hebrews 11:19)

Abraham learned about *resurrection* that day; he got the first sample himself when the Lord gave Isaac back to him. This was in fulfillment of the fourth promise — the blessing that God had in mind, eventually, for people all around the world: life from the dead, eternal life.

So in Abraham's own lifetime he saw the beginning of all four of the promises that God had made to him in the covenant. They weren't complete fulfillments; his descendants would see much more as God kept these promises of the covenant. But they were foretastes, glimpses, the first experiences of the reality that God had for him and his children.

What Abraham hoped for

We must move on, however. The Lord had much bigger things in mind for Abraham and his children. Not only was the first taste of the promises insufficient, but all the blessings that the Israelites experienced for many centuries failed to exhaust what God had in mind for Abraham's family. "These were all commended for their faith, yet *none* of them received what had been promised. God had planned something better for us so that only together with us would they be made perfect." (Hebrews 11:39-40)

Imagine a huge mansion, and the front door leads into a small room. From there you can go on into the rest of the mansion and see the richness and vastness of the place, or you can stay there in the little front room and miss out on the rest. Abraham's taste of what God had in mind in the covenant was like that little first room. The covenant that God promised him was actually referring to the huge spiritual realities that lay beyond the limitations of time and space; it speaks of the Kingdom of God, Heaven, the vast treasuries that lay in God's eternal vaults. The front room is part of the mansion, but it hardly begins to show us what lies beyond its doors.

Abraham himself knew that he was only tasting the first fruits of the Kingdom of God. We have proof of this from the inspired writers of the Bible, who knew for certain (through the Spirit who knows the thoughts and hearts of all men) what went through Abraham's mind during his life. In fact, without this testimony we would never know for sure what Abraham knew! But we *can* know with confidence what Abraham really believed about these things.

Let's go through each of the four promises in the covenant and see what Abraham knew in his day about the spiritual covenant:

The promise of the son: Abraham knew that his son Isaac wasn't the full promise that God had in mind, when the Lord promised to give him a son. We have proof of this from Jesus himself:

> Your father Abraham rejoiced at the thought of seeing *my day*; he saw it and was glad. (John 8:56)

There were several things about the birth of Isaac that taught Abraham what Jesus himself would be like. *First*, Isaac was a miracle baby — his birth was biologically impossible. Sarah was long past her age of bearing children. So was Jesus a miracle baby: he was born with no earthly father, by the action of the Holy Spirit on his mother Mary. *Second*, the covenant that the Lord gave Abraham was to be passed on to Isaac, not to the other son Ishmael (who was born of the slave woman). Isaac was the rightful heir of all that Abraham owned, including the special promises of the Lord. In the same way, Jesus is the rightful heir of all the promises of God, since he is the only natural Son of God (who first made the promises to Abraham). *Third*, as we shall see in a minute, Isaac's life was all but lost by God's decree, and yet Abraham received him "back from the dead." Jesus actually went through that death (a sacrifice, by the way, like Isaac was supposed to be) and still came back from the dead.

So Abraham knew, in several important ways, what God had in mind for the Son who was to come in the future. How much more he knew about Jesus, we don't know; but we do know, on the testimony of Jesus himself, that he understood the basics of the Christ child and looked forward to the Messiah's coming.

The promise of the land: Abraham also knew that the dusty piece of real estate called Canaan wasn't all that God had in mind when he promised him and his seed the land. Again, we don't have to guess what was in his mind; we have testimony from someone who was certain about how much Abraham knew about this matter:

> By faith he made his home in the promised land like a stranger in a foreign country; he lived in tents, as did Isaac and Jacob, who were heirs with him of the same promise. For he was looking forward to the city with foundations, whose architect and builder is God. (Hebrews 11:9-10)

This is another amazing statement, something that we couldn't be sure of unless we had this testimony. Abraham was glad enough to see that his immediate posterity would have a place to live, but the Lord showed him that Canaan itself wasn't good enough for *all* the people of God who would end up coming into the Kingdom. In fact, he himself looked forward to a far better place to live than Palestine, as these verses assure us.

The city that this refers to is the New Jerusalem that the New Testament describes, especially in the book of Revelation. (See Revelation 21-22) Christians don't lay claim to the old Jerusalem like the Jews do; we know that God's Temple is in Heaven, that he lives among his people — the Church — and we are to set our eyes on things above, where Jesus is now, not on things below. (Colossians 3:1-3) This world will one day disappear in judgment, and all of God's faithful servants, including Abraham himself, will live with God in Heaven forever.

In fact, Abraham got there ahead of us! Jesus himself assures us that Abraham has gone to his reward — not to the land of Canaan that his earthly descendants inherited from him, but the land of spiritual glory that God originally planned to give him. You can see this testimony in the story about Lazarus and the rich man. (Luke 16:19-31)

The promise of the nation: Abraham saw the beginning of the promise of a great nation when he got his son Isaac a wife and they started their family. Whether he knew at the time what would come of this marriage, we don't know; we do know that Abraham knows *now* what came of it! Obviously, as we see in the story of Lazarus (Luke 16), after Abraham died he evidently went into the presence of God. Shortly after arriving, he started receiving visitors — his own "children", in fact! As each new generation of Jews came and went in Canaan, some of them at least went on to glory to join Abraham there in Heaven. But don't miss the significance of who these people are: they are heirs of the promise of Heaven, just as Abraham was, because they are *children* of Abraham.

We don't know how many people there are in Heaven now, but we do know that the number is growing. Lazarus obviously is one of them. But look again at the testimony of Jesus, who came from Heaven and is an eyewitness of what is going on there right now:

I say to you that many will come from the east and the west, and will take their places at the feast with Abraham, Isaac and Jacob in the kingdom of Heaven. (Matthew 8:11)

The family of Abraham is getting larger, and they are gathering in Heaven for the great feast that God has planned for them. Perhaps Abraham was surprised to see *so many* Gentiles there, and *so few* of the Jews there! "But the subjects of the kingdom will be thrown outside, into the darkness, where there will be weeping and gnashing of teeth." (Matthew 8:12) At any rate he knows *now* exactly what God had in mind when he promised that he would become the father of a great nation.

The nation, of course, is the Church of God — the body of Christ, which consists of all believers whether they are Jew or Gentile. There used to be strict regulations about letting Gentiles around holy things, especially the Temple. But in Christ the barrier was broken down and the two parties were made one body, one believing Church, one with Christ. (Ephesians 2:11-22) Not everyone who was born a Jew became part of the Church, which shows that God never had only the physical family of Abraham in mind when he made that promise at the beginning. Only those who had the faith of Abraham would be a part of the family of God.

The promise of the blessing: When Abraham came so close to sacrificing his son Isaac, he thought that death was certain. Legally the boy was dead; when God declares his will, the thing is as good as done. But Abraham also knew that God wouldn't leave it that way. We already saw the testimony of Hebrews about this:

Abraham reasoned that God could raise the dead, and figuratively speaking, he did receive Isaac back from death. (Hebrews 11:19)

In other words, he learned something about God and his ways: the Lord intends to raise his promised children from the dead. Death will not be the end of us; we will live again, never to die again, to serve the Lord forever.

How much Abraham really knew about the resurrection that God has in mind for the Church of Christ, we don't know. Perhaps he didn't know the many details that we have now in the Scriptures — like the teachings of Thessalonians and 1 Corinthians 15. But he did understand the concept, and he knew the mind of the Lord about the matter. As far as God is concerned, death is *not* the last word over us: Abraham knew this for certain about his own son. There was just too much hanging in the balance, too much to happen in the coming kingdom, to let death be the end.

The resurrection is the great hope of the Church, and it's a hope that the unbelievers don't have. Nobody but Abraham and his children have the right to expect that God will raise them out of the grave into newness of life and give them eternity in Heaven. It's a special promise to the family of Abraham; it is going to overturn everything that sin and death has done to ruin us. The resurrection will be much more than just a physical reversal, however; it will be a new kind of life — as Paul carefully explains in 1 Corinthians 15. This life will defeat death forever; it will be a life open to God, never again open to sin or death.

Now these promises are things that every Christian knows about and hopes for. What we may not have known, however, is that they were originally given to Abraham long ago! They aren't our property but his property. We have them only by inheritance; he had them given to him directly by God. Abraham has the signed covenant in his hand, so to speak; that's his hope. We, however, have to prove that we are actually his children if we want to share in his property.

Let's look at this another way. What could you possibly be hoping to get from God except these four things? Isn't **Christ** the very one you love the most, your only Friend and Savior, your "all in all?" Isn't **Heaven** your hope, the place that Jesus went to prepare for your coming, your only home? Isn't the **Church** the place where God meets with you through others and their ministry and good works for you, your real family when your earthly family is long gone, the place where the Holy Spirit works to grow and strengthen the people of God? Isn't the **resurrection** going to be the end of all that is bad in this world and the start of an eternity of bliss and joy and holiness? Isn't the sacrifice of the Son of God effective for your salvation from sin and death? What more could you want but these things? What else did you hear about in the Gospel and put your hope in?

My point is that this covenant *is* your faith; there isn't anything else important that you could want from God but these promises. So if these are what you want and expect because of your faith, you are wanting the *covenant promises* that the Lord gave Abraham long ago! These spiritual realities, as fully as you know them now, were what Abraham received from God's hand. And if you want Abraham's property, you must prove your relationship to him in order to legally get it. Only Abraham's heirs will get the promises of God.

Christ and the Covenant

You can be sure that Jesus and the Father work together very closely on everything they do. What the Father wills, Jesus also wills. And they aren't careless or haphazard about what they do; they are the ultimate project planners. They worked on this thing about salvation from the beginning, mapped it all out ahead of time, planned every detail, laid the foundation for it all to make sure it would work, and followed the steps of the project as planned. They know that it will succeed in the end, and things will be right where they want them to be when time is no more and all come to the Judgment Seat of Christ for the final sentence.

The Covenant

When God first made the covenant with Abraham, therefore, Jesus was there too as part of the Godhead, making that covenant with the Father. We don't see the two of them separately at that point; but from some clues that we find in the New Testament (which we will look at in a minute) we know that the covenant with Abraham and his descendants was as much Jesus' business as it was the Father's.

If this is true, it throws a whole new light on the ministry of Christ recorded in the Gospels. We tend to view what he did as an aberration of history, just something that he decided to do once. As if he just showed up, taught and did miracles, and then left — with no rhyme or reason for why he came! But if we look at his ministry as the fulfillment of the covenant to Abraham then tremendous spiritual truths open up before us. It gives meaning to the things he said and did, and brings the story of the covenant to a finished polish.

Remember that in the covenant with Abraham, the Lord promised that he would do four things for him and his descendants. He sealed that promise with blood: if he would fail to do these things that he promised, Abraham (or his descendants) would have the right to split him in two just as the animals were. Ever since then we have been anxiously waiting to see if God really would keep his promises.

Now in the person of Christ we see that God has come back to keep his Word. He isn't going to break his promise to Abraham! Jesus came to fulfill those four things that the children of Abraham were heirs to. We have already seen much of how Jesus fits into the covenant with Abraham, because we just can't talk of one without the other. But we need to focus on Christ in particular so that we don't miss the point.

> **The promised Seed:** In Galatians, Paul refers to the covenant made with Abraham. The problem that the Galatians were grappling with was that they thought the Law was all-important; they thought they had to obey the Law if they wanted to please God. But Paul took them back to the covenant and showed them the thing that God was really interested in:

> The promises were spoken to Abraham and to his seed. The Scripture does not say 'and to seeds,' meaning many people, but 'and to your seed,' meaning one person, who is Christ. What I mean is this: The law, introduced 430 years later, does not set aside the covenant previously established by God and thus do away with the promise. (Galatians 3:16-17)

The *only* thing that we can do that will please God is trust in *what* he has given us (the spiritual object of the covenant, in other words) — and *where* we must look for those promises. In Abraham's day, the spiritual dimension of the covenant was not so clear to see for the average Israelite (though Abraham, through faith, saw that there was a spiritual dimension to it — "Your father Abraham rejoiced at the thought of seeing my day; he saw it and was glad." John 8:56). Now, however, we have heard the Gospel which says — *look to Jesus and you will be saved.* "For no matter how many promises God has made, they are 'Yes' in Christ." (2 Corinthians 1:20) He is the promised Child, the one through whom we will get our inheritance.

Paul refers to the way that Isaac was born — by miracle — as opposed to the natural means of Ishmael's birth. This has two fulfillments in Christ: first, his own birth was a miracle and therefore the work of God. Second, those who believe in him are also miracle babies:

> I tell you the truth, no one can see the kingdom of God unless he is born again ... I tell you the truth, no one can enter the kingdom of God unless he is born of water and the Spirit. Flesh gives birth to flesh, but the Spirit gives birth to spirit. You should not be surprised at my saying, 'You must be born again.' (John 3:3-7)

We are born into Christ, into life, by the Spirit of God — a completely unaccountable thing, but real nevertheless. Once we were dead to God, now we are alive to him and fully aware of him. Once we were rebels with hearts of stone; now we have hearts of flesh and love to serve him.

Anybody who has been born again, who is one with Christ, is now heir of the covenant with Abraham. "If you belong to Christ, then you are Abraham's seed, and heirs according to the promise." (Galatians 3:29) You can see from this how crucial Jesus is to the fulfillment of that covenant. You can also see, hopefully, how important it is to be one with Christ. Outside of him, the heir, there is no blessing, no inheritance, no life — only death with those who aren't of the Seed of Abraham.

The Land: Again in Christ we have the answer to the perplexing question of what the people of God will inherit. The Jews looked forward to ruling themselves, living in Palestine without any outside interference — especially from the Romans. But Jesus never promised that to them; in fact, when prompted even by his own disciples to restore the land to the Jews, he changed the subject and spoke of more important things. (Acts 1:6-8)

What does God have in mind, then? Jesus told us what he was going to do when his work on earth was done: not to set up a throne in Jerusalem and claim Palestine back from the enemy, but to go *somewhere else* to prepare the Land that God had promised his people:

> In my Father's house are many rooms; if it were not so, I would have told you. I am going there to prepare a place for you. And if I go and prepare a place for you, I will come back and take you to be with me that you also may be

where I am. You know the way to the place where I am going. (John 14:2-4)

Jesus said once that "my kingdom is not of this world. If it were, my servants would fight to prevent my arrest by the Jews. But now my kingdom is from another place." (John 18:36) He was interested in a new kingdom, a land where there would be no more sin or death. This world that we live in now will never qualify; it has been ruined by man and must be remade. Besides, the things that Jesus has in mind for his new world must last forever, without giving way to time or strain — and there isn't anything in this world that he can use to build a kingdom like that.

Jesus has in mind to give his people a place where they won't need created things to survive, but they will live directly from the hand of God himself. Instead of treasures that rot or rust or can be stolen, he counseled his followers to look forward to treasures that last forever. (Matthew 6:19-21) We don't understand much of what Heaven is like, but we do know that the Lord made it in such a way as to satisfy our souls — truly "a land flowing with milk and honey", if it is anything like the Lord Jesus, who is the fullness of the Godhead.

The Nation: In Jesus there is a new nation, a new people of God. This is the mysticism of the Church. We can't understand how a collection of individuals, scattered all over the world and across thousands of years, can be one unified body of people. And we certainly can't understand how people can be one when they argue over every single thing in the Bible! It seems to the observer that this is a bunch of lonely individuals instead of one group.

But, in spite of appearances, in Christ all believers are brought together to share one life. Just as Israel was one nation over against the rest of the nations of the world, Christians are one nation too — "There is *one body* and one Spirit — just as you were called to one hope when you were called." (Ephesians 4:3) And the Lord didn't just ditch the old system and do a new thing with the Gentiles. He *fulfilled* the old system by updating it, lifting it up to the level he intended for it. Then he brought the spiritual remnant of the Israelites together with the Gentiles (who had no rights to the original covenant, physically) and made them one people, calling the whole thing *Israel*.

> For he himself is our peace, who has made the two one and has destroyed the barrier, the dividing wall of hostility, by abolishing in his flesh the law with its commandments and regulations. His purpose was to create in himself one new man out of the two, thus making peace, and in this one body to reconcile both of them to God through the cross, by which he put to death their hostility. He came and preached peace to you who were far away and peace to those who were near. For through him we both have access to the Father by one Spirit. Consequently, you are no longer foreigners and aliens, but fellow citizens with God's people and members of God's household. (Galatians 2:14-19)

Now he is the Head of the new body: he leads, he counsels, he decides, he directs, he feeds and cares for, he gets all the glory from, and he expects the services of, the rest of the body. "And he is the head of the body, the church; he is the beginning and the firstborn from among the dead, so that in everything he might have the supremacy." (Colossians 1:18) "Now you are the body of Christ, and each one of you is a part of it." (1 Corinthians 12:27) There's life in this body; the Holy Spirit works through each of us, for the benefit of each of us, so that we can grow into a fuller relationship with the Father in Heaven.

The Blessing: We saw that, through the covenant, the Lord intended to overturn the effect of sin — which is death. After all, sin is what got us into the mess we are in, and unless God reverses the effects of death, we can't say that we have much going for us — even if we do call ourselves Christians! "If only for this life we have hope in Christ, we are to be pitied more than all men." (1 Corinthians 15:19)

The resurrection of Christ from the dead was the staggering news that the apostles had for the world. They could talk about "God with us", the teachings of the Messiah, the miracles, and the crucifixion — but the listening world would be no more impressed with that than with other wonders that have happened in history. But when Jesus rose from the dead, that gets the attention of everyone. When Paul preached to Festus about the Gospel, the Roman was interested but unimpressed; when he got to the point of the resurrection, however, he got an immediate reaction:

> "But I have had God's help to this very day, and so I stand here and testify to small and great alike. I am saying nothing beyond what the prophets and Moses said would happen — that the Christ would suffer and, as *the first to rise from the dead*, would proclaim light to his own people and to the Gentiles." At this point Festus interrupted Paul's defense. "You are out of your mind, Paul!" he shouted. "Your great learning is driving you insane." (Acts 26:22-24)

You see, if the resurrection is true, then that means that eternal life is true. It means that there is a judgment, there is righteousness, there is holiness, there is another world than this one — and there is a God who justifies sinners. And Jesus himself made it all possible by becoming the sacrifice that takes away our sin-guilt — the one barrier between us and eternal life.

Jesus rose from the dead a *new man* — not physical, but spiritual. You can study the exact nature of the resurrection body in 1 Corinthians 15, the great chapter on the subject of the resurrection. What he rose *to* is eternal life at the right hand of God, "far above all rule and authority, power and dominion, and every title that can be given, not only in the present age but also in the one to come." (Ephesians 1:21) The resurrection of Christ opens up all kinds of new realities that are not in this world — the new spiritual kingdom, the new life and world that God has planned for his people.

Whoever is one with Christ is also one with his resurrection, and *there* is the fulfillment of the covenant for Abraham's descendants. "If we have been united with him like this in his death, we will certainly also be united with him in his resurrection . . . Now if we died with Christ, we believe that we will also live with him." (Romans 6:5,8) Whoever is one with him has no fear of death: "Blessed and holy are those who have part in the first resurrection. The second death has no power over them." (Revelation 20:6)

This aspect of the covenant was only hinted at in the Old Testament, and it's an astonishing revelation of what God has in store for his people. It certainly makes sense for us to see if we are in Christ if we want to be justified and live forever.

There is an important "therefore" to all this. If Jesus is the fulfillment of the covenant with Abraham, if God put what he promised in Jesus and called us to come to Christ to get what we need — then *there is no other place that you can find blessings from God.* You can't expect God to save you or even do you *any* spiritual good unless you become one with Christ. You won't get what God promised Abraham by being children of believers, you won't get it just because you are a

Jew, you won't get it by leading a good life, you won't get it by being religious or being baptized. The only way you can lay claim to the treasures of Heaven is if you have become united to Christ, through faith.

> For you did not receive a spirit that makes you a slave again to fear, but *you received the Spirit of sonship*. And by him we cry, "Abba, Father." The Spirit himself testifies with our spirit that we are God's children. Now if we are children, *then we are heirs* — heirs of God and co-heirs with Christ, if indeed we share in his sufferings in order that we may also share in his glory. (Romans 8:15-17)

> If you belong to Christ, then you are Abraham's seed, and heirs according to the promise. (Galatians 3:29)

Anyone who is in Christ is heir to the covenant; anybody who isn't in Christ is outside the covenant. And you can be sure that, since the Lord made a binding oath in that covenant, he *will* stick to the terms of the covenant. We won't be able to talk him out of it.

The faith of Abraham

Abraham learned a certain kind of faith from God. Not any faith will do – people have all sorts of notions about what faith is, but God is only going to be pleased with a particular faith. Genesis 12-17 and Romans 4 show us the steps that "Abraham discovered" about true faith:

Hear God's Word – True faith always starts with the Word of God. We can't base our actions on our emotions, or opinions, or traditions, or philosophies. God reveals what we need to know and do, and our duty is to center on what he says to us.

Set your heart on it – Abraham turned his back on his family and land and went out to claim what God had promised him. That was no easy task for a 75-year-old man! But what God promises in his Word is not only better than what this world has to offer, it has nothing of this world in it. We have to make a decision about which God, and what treasures, we are going to spend our lives working for.

Face the impossibility of it – God's promises are impossible. Abraham's wife Sarah was too old to have a son. But God does the impossible – and true faith will look past the veil of this physical world and get hold of a God who can and will do everything he promises. That step of looking the impossibility square in the eye is necessary, because otherwise we would tend to turn to the world to give us what we need. But if it's impossible, then God is the only place we will ever get it.

Don't try it yourself – Abraham failed on this one point. After years of waiting for a son, he decided that maybe the promise was a little bit *too* impossible! So he let his wife talk him into having a son by her handmaid Hagar. The Lord, however, overruled and told Abraham that he meant what he said – the boy would be born to Sarah, through a miracle. We have our jobs that God expects of us, but he never expects us to do his work for him. Only he can do miracles – only he can make good on his promises and give us what we need spiritually. There are certain things in our salvation that we cannot do.

Wait on the Lord – The last point leads to this one. Finally after 25 years of waiting, Abraham got his "miracle baby." He learned the lesson that if it's really true that only God can do the miracle, then the only option that we have is to wait on him. Waiting honors God because it shows that, first, we believe him; second, that we know only he can do this; and third, it's worth waiting for. And for these reasons, God will often test our faith by making us wait for his promises.

Based on this kind of faith, God "credited it to him as righteousness." (Genesis 15:6) *This* faith is the family characteristic of all of Abraham's descendants. Now anybody who wants anything from God in the way of mercy and grace, forgiveness of sin and the Holy Spirit, a hope for Heaven and a new nature in Christ, must also show evidence of this faith. See Matthew 15:22-28 for a wonderful example of Jesus holding out on the covenantal blessing until he saw positive proof of Abraham's faith.

The Law

Christians have always had trouble deciding what to do with the Law. The Law is in our Bible, but we don't know whether we have to obey it or ignore it. Even if we are supposed to take it seriously, *how much* of it do we have to do? To make matters worse, each denomination has a different interpretation on the subject, and respectable Bible teachers will disagree on the Law even if they agree on other basics of the faith.

I believe that there are at least three reasons that the Law causes so many problems for Christians:

- *The Law is in our Bibles.* It's hard to argue against something when it's in the Bible. We have been taught to take all the Scriptures seriously; we know that we ignore God's Word at our peril. And the Law isn't just a problem verse or two but an entire section of the Old Testament. Not only that, the rest of the Bible takes the Law very seriously — Jesus as well as the apostles deal with the Law in some form or another. The Law, whether we like it or not, is a foundation in God's Kingdom and we simply can't ignore it unless we have a really good reason — preferably only if God himself tells us to!

- *The Old Testament and the New Testament overlap.* During the ministry of Christ and the apostles, the Old Testament system was still in full force. Jesus as well as the disciples went to worship at the Temple; the beginning of the Church included Jews as well as Gentiles. It was a time when the Old Testament realities were still in place, and at the same time the New Testament realities were beginning to take shape. There

The Law

are some confusing statements about the Law in the Gospels — and it's because of this overlap period. We Gentiles look at this period and wonder if anything changed when the last of the apostles died — or whether nothing changed, and the Old Testament system is still in force for us today in the same way it was for Christ and his followers. Or did the ways of the Old Testament officially end with the coming of the new?

- ***The Law appeals to human nature.*** This might sound strange, since the Law condemns sinners. But the root idea of the Law is for *us* to *do* something: do *this*, it tells us, and you will be pleasing and acceptable to God. And we *love* to do things; we are natural-born workers, and idleness doesn't suit us well. The Law very clearly outlines things we can do, and we eagerly set about working on those things. So when the New Testament tells us to quit working and *rest*, that doesn't appeal to us nearly as much as the Law's demands. We feel much better about things when we're in control, and not so completely at someone else's mercy.

Because of these facts, it's going to be difficult to understand the true relationship between the Christian and the Law. The Law has always been a major part of the works of the Lord, and since we're sensitive about pleasing the Lord in all that we do, it's not going to be easy to find out our responsibilities when it appears that the foundations in the Bible are shifting. But we have to dig into the Bible and understand this subject. In spite of the surface arguments in favor of taking the Law at face value, there are many Scriptures that teach a new approach to the Law — the approach that every Christian must take in order to please God.

The Law is a huge reality in the Bible. It rules from its beginning at Creation, to the full statement of the Law at Mt. Sinai; it guided the Israelites and their kings through their entire history; Jesus' ministry was designed specially to fulfill the Law; and the Apostles did their best to instruct and guide Christians on how to deal with it. One can't go anywhere in Scripture without having to grapple with the Law

The Law

in some way. When this life is over, and we enter into Heaven to live with God forever, we will find the Law there too – because it's the description of how God rules his Kingdom.

It's a mistake to roll over and let the legalists tell us what to believe about the Law. If it's wrong to obey the Law in the same way that the Old Testament saints did, then we must find out what is the right way. And if it's wrong to ignore the Law, then we must find out how to deal with it. We have to avoid both extremes and discover the truth about this.

It's also a mistake to argue over particular details in the Law and overlook the broader principles. The Law is God's work, and it reflects his limitless wisdom; and I doubt that anybody will understand it so well that he will know how every law relates to a Christian. Our duty is to obey what is plainly taught about it, not fight over obscure details. Paul warns us about fighting about the Law:

> Some have wandered away from these [*that is, the more important things of our faith*] and turned to meaningless talk. They want to be teachers of the Law, but they do not know what they are talking about or what they so confidently affirm. (1 Timothy 1:6-7)

Our approach here will be this: we want to back up, like the apostle Paul did in Galatians and other passages, and see the forest for the trees. We want to learn the basics of the subject first, before tackling particular issues. Get the principles down, and we will be able to deal with the less important issues correctly. As I said, Paul took the same approach: though he did some things in regard to the Law that positively baffles modern Christians, he laid down the fundamentals of our relationship with the Law in Romans and Galatians that we should study first before we try to untangle some of the stickier issues.

Definitions

Let's define some terms first. By the ***Law*** we mean this: the commands that God gave Israel through Moses. It's often called by its Hebrew name Torah (תּוֹרָה). Moses was the one who brought the Law from God and gave it to the Israelites. "For the Law was given through Moses." (John 1:17) "Has not Moses given you the Law?" (John 7:19) And the Law isn't just the Ten Commandments, but the entire five books that record the commands of God: Genesis, Exodus, Leviticus, Numbers, and Deuteronomy. For proof of this, see the passages in the Gospels that refer to the Law that Moses gave — they quote verses found all through these five books.

Teachers of the Bible have found it convenient to split the Law into three types: moral, ceremonial, and civil. The problem with this is that the Bible itself makes no such division of the Law. One *might* argue that the Temple laws focused on ceremony, and the relationships that a man had with his neighbor dealt with civil matters; but the fact is that *all* of it was called the Law of Moses. For example, a *ceremony* was called the Law of Moses (Luke 2:22), a *prophecy* of Christ was called the Law of Moses (Luke 24:44), and a *civil and moral* issue comes from the Law that Moses gave (John 8:5). Furthermore, almost all the laws had multiple levels: one law would have both moral and civil aspects to it. The Jews have always understood this. For example, in the introduction to a modern translation of the Talmud, the Jewish author explains:

> The Torah makes no essential distinction between "matters between a man and his Creator," and those "between man and his fellowman," because the structure of relationships between human beings is intimately connected to the relationship between man and his Creator ... the various laws are interrelated and intermingled. Ritual matters are connected with civil disputes; moral instruction is interwoven with laws of ritual purity and impurity, etc.[1]

The main reason that the Bible doesn't make a hard distinction between the three types is because it's *all* the Law of God; the Jews were responsible to keep them all – none of the laws were less important than the others. It's not fair to separate the laws into more and less important parts; when someone does that, they are just

---

[1] **Adin Steinsaltz, <u>The Talmud: The Steinsaltz Edition</u>; Vol. 1: Tractate Bava Metzia; Random house: 1989; Part 1; pp.1-2.**

conveniently explaining away large parts of the Law that they *don't* want to be responsible for. For example, many people agree that we should keep the Ten Commandments, some people think that we need to follow only the dietary laws and civil laws, and almost nobody thinks that the sacrificial laws apply to us today.

A **Christian** is someone who trusts in Christ alone for his or her salvation. Christ is, for them, their "all in all" — meaning that in him they have everything they need spiritually. They are forgiven and delivered from their sins in him, they are delivered from death and Hell in him, they are adopted as sons of God in him, they are made holy and righteous and justified in God's sight in him, they have a future hope of glory in him, and they have his Spirit. What more could they want? If they did not have Christ, they would not have anything.

You see, of course, what we are getting at here. If Christ is everything that a believer needs, this casts a doubt over whether a Christian needs anything more from the Law. If he can please God and gain a hope of Heaven by having Christ alone, what need is there of dealing with the Law about anything? The Law has nothing more to say to someone like this – and certainly nothing to offer him!

The purpose of the Law

One great purpose of the Law is this: to condemn mankind. Paul tells us in Romans what the Law does to us:

> Therefore no one will be declared righteous in his sight by observing the Law; rather, through the law we become conscious of sin. (Romans 3:20)

> Indeed I would not have known what sin was except through the Law. For I would not have known what coveting really was if the Law had not said, "Do not covet." (Romans 7:7)

The Law tells us exactly what sin is. We need that, because until the Law came, people didn't exactly know what offended God about human behavior. They made up their own definitions of what is right and wrong, and as a result there were as many systems of morality and ethics as there were men and nations! What was "right" in one culture was "wrong" in another. People were confused about the true nature of sin.

So, God gave the Law in order to clear up the confusion. "Here is what sin is," he told us. And with that definition of sin, he condemned every human being who has ever lived, because nobody has ever kept *this* Law perfectly. We are all guilty of breaking God's Law in some way, during some time in our lives. Even such a simple summary of the Law as the Ten Commandments is enough to prove every one of us a sinner. The Law isn't trying to make us friends with God; it is proving, without a shadow of a doubt, that we are already his enemies.

Keep in mind that the Law has a double edge. Not only does it define what sin is, it also demands a penalty for anybody who commits sin: punishment. The Law is no friend! If we fulfill the Law in every way, it will leave us alone. But if we offend God in even one matter, it rises up in wrath and condemns us.

> So then, the Law is holy, and the commandment is holy, righteous and good. Did that which is good, then, become death to me? By no means! But in order that sin might be recognized as sin, it produced death in me through what was good, so that through the commandment sin might become utterly sinful. (Romans 7:12-13)

Why some people feel so comfortable living in the shadow of the Law, I will never understand. They don't know that they live under the shadow of *death*. The Law means trouble for sinners; going to the Law for help or comfort is like reaching out to pet a guard dog that is trained to kill strangers.

The Law hurts. The only way that it wouldn't hurt anybody is if that person kept the whole Law, perfectly, all his life. With such a person the Law has no argument or problem. But if it finds the least blemish in him, the smallest offense, then the Law becomes a fierce enemy. That sin has challenged the glory of God, and the Law will not

The Law

rest until there is blood shed. "In fact, the Law requires that nearly everything be cleansed with blood, and without the shedding of blood there is no forgiveness." (Hebrews 9:22)

The whole Law

When God gave his Law to his people, he expected them to follow the entire Law. This was his way of ruling over them. It's the same as in an earthly government. It won't help things if we keep most of the laws and yet break a few of them for our convenience. The country runs best when we obey all of the laws. This is why Moses told the Israelites:

> And if we are careful to obey *all this law* before the LORD our God, as he has commanded us, that will be our righteousness. (Deuteronomy 6:25)

As far as God is concerned, this Law is the sum total of what it means to be righteous. If someone should keep all the laws and not break a single one, he would indeed be a righteous man.

According to one count (Maimonides – a Jewish scholar in the eleventh century), there are 613 separate laws in the Law of Moses. This means that a person has to keep all 613 laws if he wants to be perfect in God's eyes. There's just two problems with that, however:

First, nobody can keep all those laws now. Even the Jews can't keep them all! Many of the commands in the Torah have to do with the Temple and its sacrificial system. That, of course, is completely gone now; there's no way that they can observe those laws. And we Gentiles who don't have the benefit of synagogue services, Torah scrolls, priests, the Holy Land – we're in an even more awkward position when it comes to the Law's demands. We don't even know what most of those laws were!

Second, once you've broken just one of the laws, you're out of the picture. Now you are a law breaker and you no longer have the chance to be righteous. And that's understandable, once you think about it: if we sin just once, that means that we have the tendency to sin. There's nothing guaranteeing that we won't sin again. In fact, the very fact that we sinned in the first place proves that we weren't righteous! The Law just brought that out of us, when it told us that we couldn't do something and our hearts reacted in rebellion.

The Law is very picky about how we must observe it. For example, let's say that you managed to keep all of the Laws but one. Out of those 613 laws, you broke one of them – or failed to observe one of them. This means that you are now guilty of breaking the Law:

> For whoever keeps the whole law and yet stumbles at just one point is guilty of breaking all of it. For he who said, "Do not commit adultery," also said, "Do not murder." If you do not commit adultery but do commit murder, you have become a lawbreaker. (James 2:10-11)

Now that you are a law breaker, God isn't interested in any of your attempts at keeping the Law. All he is concerned about now is what to do with you. There is only punishment and rejection for those who break the Law. As you can see, this matter of keeping the Law to satisfy God is extremely difficult. One slip up, and you're out. No more second chances.

Even when we boil the Law down to a more manageable size, we still can't keep it. The Ten Commandments are really a summary of the whole Law: the first four describe our relationship to God, and the last six describe our relationship to other people. Can we keep these ten laws? Many people think that they can, yet Jesus had no trouble at all exposing the sin in the heart of the rich young ruler, who claimed to have kept the whole Law! He neither had love for God (he didn't want to follow the Lord), nor did he love his fellow man (he certainly didn't want to sell all he had and give it to the poor). The same thing holds true when we boil the Ten down to the Two:

> Love the Lord your God with all your heart and with all your soul and with all your mind. This is the first

and greatest commandment. And the second is like it: Love your neighbor as yourself. All the Law and the Prophets hang on these two commandments. (Matthew 22:37)

If there has been just one time when you haven't loved God with your whole heart and mind, or just one time that you haven't loved your neighbor over yourself, then you are a law breaker. You are now in another category – a sinner – and no long have the opportunity to stay in the race to get perfect righteousness by following the Law.

And just in case someone is still thinking that they have in fact kept the Law as it is stated in the books of Moses, we can eliminate them too by learning something about the Law from Jesus and Paul – the Law is spiritual as well as physical. It isn't good enough to keep the Law by means of outward ceremonies and actions; the Law must also be kept on deeper spiritual levels. For instance, the law against adultery includes simple lust, those thoughts of desire for someone you don't have the right to. The Law plumbs the depths of God's Kingdom, both in this world and the next; it searches out the thoughts and attitudes of the heart for the least infraction. It has to, because God will not tolerate another fiasco in Heaven like the one in the Garden of Eden – where the whole world, and the entire human race, was plunged into sin and death for a single rebellious act.

Another example. The Ten Commandments tell us to "honor your father and mother." The simple way to interpret this is to show them your respect when you're around them – "Yes, sir" and "No, ma'am." But even if someone does this and then goes out and lives in sin, he is dishonoring his parents in front of the community and embarrassing the family name!

A **wise son** brings joy to his father, but a foolish **son** grief to his mother. (Proverbs 10:1)

He who gathers crops in summer is a **wise son**, but he who sleeps during harvest is a disgraceful **son**. (Proverbs 10:5)

The Law

Picking and Choosing

A *legalist* is someone who finds it necessary to obey the letter of the Law. This means that they read the Law in the Old Testament and feel that they must obey exactly what it says. They also try to make others feel that same obligation.

Legalists tell us that all of us must obey the Law in some way; we may not have to obey *all* of the Law, they tell us, but at least the more important parts of it. They teach that the Ten Commandments are essential for every Christian. Some of the more extreme legalists even pick out other parts of the Law and try to obligate Christians to live by those too — for example, the Sabbath laws, and the laws concerning food, and the "clean and unclean" laws. Some legalists pick out the "ceremonial" laws that they feel we should use in church, and the "civil" laws that modern societies should use.

The biggest problem about legalists is this: they pick and choose the laws that they say we must obey. The reason that they are so choosy (which they usually won't be honest enough to tell you!) is that, when you read the Law of Moses, it becomes obvious to you that *nobody* can keep all those laws. Even if we wanted to, it would be impossible in our modern society to obey everything that the Old Testament Law demands. Even the legalists will admit this!

For example, in Exodus 20:2-17 the Lord gave the Ten Commandments to the Israelites. Then in verse 23 he repeats Commandments one and two; so far the legalists are staying right with the text. Then in verse 24 he commands them to make an altar and sacrifice animals to him; the altar must be formed without tools, and it must not have steps. Now the legalists are in trouble! What are they going to tell us about *this* command? If they say that Christ has offered all the necessary sacrifices for us and now we don't have to obey this additional command of sacrifice, then how is that different than the first part of the Law given here in the same text? If they say that we must keep this sacrifice *spiritually* and the other commands *literally*, they must show why they think one is literal and the other spiritual — they must give the principle that guides them into interpreting the text this way so that we can use that principle later on with other commands. Any way they go, they are in trouble.

Another example: one law that the legalists are fond of enforcing is the command about tithing. There are several passages that make tithing a necessary obligation on the Israelites; they didn't have any choice about the matter. The Law is never a matter of choice: it's a binding obligation which the legalist *must* do or else he is in instant trouble as a law breaker. The tithing laws, since they are also part of the Mosaic Law, were binding on the Israelites; they had to do it or be guilty of breaking the Law.

But there were other laws in the Old Testament that were just as binding; why aren't the legalists pressing us about those as well? For example, all the males twenty years old and older were obligated to pay the half-shekel tax to support the tent of meeting. (Exodus 30:11-16) They weren't to pay any more than this, nor any less than this. Also, each family was supposed to pay, under penalty of the Law, a five-shekel tax for each firstborn son in Israel. (Numbers 18:15-16) Now these laws were just as binding as the tithe law; why then aren't the legalists demanding those taxes from us as well? There is nothing in the Scripture that says the tithe law is still binding and these are not. If they answer that those had to do with specific "ceremonies" that we don't have to worry about now, then how is that different from the tithing law which also paid for those *same kinds* of ceremonies in the Temple?

If you look carefully into the tithing law, you will notice what the tithe was supposed to consist of: not money, but *food*. The tithe was used for a specific purpose. When all Israel collected in Jerusalem three times a year for the yearly feasts, they had a logistics problem on their hands. There was no way that the merchants of Jerusalem could support millions of pilgrims! The tithe was designed to address that problem. The priests were to collect the tithe from everyone in Israel *as food*, not money (it makes a special point about that — Deuteronomy 14:24-26 — people can't eat money!), and store the food in Jerusalem. Then when the people showed up for the yearly feasts, they would have enough to eat during their stay there. (Deuteronomy 12:17-19; Deuteronomy 14:22-29) Now if we are obligated to keep this law, why is it that we aren't doing exactly what the Law says to do? Why are we twisting it into exactly what the Law says *not* to do, and ignoring its most important elements? Are we free to twist God's Law around to suit our own tastes like this?

The best-known passage about the law of tithing is Malachi 3:8-10. It is a powerful incentive to take tithing seriously, and many a preacher has used it against his congregation to get them to start giving more to the church. However, first notice the context: the Israelites were supposed to bring the tithe *into the storehouse.* (Malachi 3:10) This means food, into the storehouses of the Temple, so that the people who gather in Jerusalem for the feasts will have something to eat – exactly what Deuteronomy was referring to. But another problem is that this isn't the *only* sin that Malachi accuses the Israelites of breaking! Again, legalists pick and choose what they want out of the text and conveniently ignore other things that are there. Malachi accuses ① the Israelites of bringing crippled animals to the sacrifice (Malachi 1:8); ② the priests of violating the covenant with Levi (Malachi 2:8); and ③ Judah of desecrating the sanctuary in the Temple. (Malachi 2:11) Why is only one of the scathing denunciations of Malachi picked out and the rest of them ignored? If someone answers that these other issues are spiritual for us Christians, then why isn't the tithing law spiritual for us too? What goes for one must apply to them all!

You can't pick and choose the laws that you want to obey. They are all one body of Law; it was God's Word given through Moses, all of it, and as the Scripture says, "Whoever keeps the whole Law and yet stumbles at just one point is guilty of breaking all of it." (James 2:10) When once you have set your hand to keeping the Law, you are obligated to keep *all* of it. "Cursed is everyone who does not continue to do *everything* written in the Book of the Law." (Galatians 3:10) The Lord will not be impressed with your arguments that you thought you only had to keep part of it; that's not what *he* said to do with it!

There are important reasons why you can't pick and choose the laws that you want to obey and ignore the rest. ***First***, there is the fact that these laws are all part of the great body of Law that the Lord gave the Israelites through Moses. It was all given to Israel, as the rules of the Kingdom of God, and none of them were given to other nations. It was the way the nation was to operate, the government over God's people. The Israelites were bound to keep the *whole* Law, not just the parts that they liked best. Now if any of those laws are still binding today, then they all are, since it's all the Law of God. There is nothing in Scripture which says that parts of the Law are still in effect while others are no longer in effect. And you certainly don't have the freedom to decide how you are going to obey the Law. If Congress passes a law that says you owe them a certain percentage of your income in taxes, you are not free to send them a truckload of apples in payment of the tax! If you don't do exactly what the law says, you are considered a law breaker, no matter what your intentions are. The same is true of God's Law.

Second, the laws are tied together inextricably. If you decide that you want to follow a particular law, you will have to decide what you are going to do about some of the other laws as well, because they tie into the one that you are looking at. For example, some modern groups teach that we must follow the food regulations that are given in the Law. Some foods were "unclean" to the Israelites and they weren't allowed to eat them. The problem was that this wasn't only a health issue, it was a ceremonial issue as well. Anybody who even touched one of these forbidden animals was unclean and had to undergo ceremonial washings and stay away from other people for an appointed time. Any pots that touched this food had to be destroyed. And this wasn't a small matter to God:

> Do not defile yourselves by any of these creatures. Do not make yourselves unclean by means of them or be made unclean by them. I am the LORD your God; consecrate yourselves and be holy, because I am holy. Do not make yourselves unclean by any creature that moves about on the ground. I am the LORD who brought you up out of Egypt to be your God; therefore be holy, because I am holy. (Leviticus 11:43-45)

When the Lord said something like this, you can be sure that he meant what he said — all of it — and you had better do *exactly* what he said. The problem is that if we were to take this seriously today, we may as well resign ourselves to being perpetual lawbreakers because none of us can do all that this law requires. Not only are we not capable of doing *our* part, but the society we live in isn't going to do its part either — which means that we are being polluted against our will! The point here is that once you decide to follow any particular law, you are immediately going to run into trouble with other laws that are tied into it. And you can't get out of the dilemma by saying, "Well, I must do the right thing even if others don't." According to the Law, what others do will make *you* unclean and affect *your* relationship with God.

Third, the Law not only consists of commands about how to live life, it also makes provision for enforcing those laws — the priesthood and the Temple. The priests were the enforcers of the Law, much as policemen are enforcers of the laws of our society. They didn't perform the Law for the people; the people themselves had to follow the Law's commands and report to the priests with the results. And many of the laws had to do with the daily and special functions that went on in the Temple. None of that is in operation today; even if we wanted to follow some of the laws, there is no way we can follow through with them and complete the requirements of satisfying the priest and offering sacrifices in the Temple. All that is gone now. Even the Jews understand this problem. Their system right now is almost useless to them; they are waiting for the day when they can rebuild the Temple and put the whole system back in place. Then keeping one particular law will be meaningful because all the other related laws will be there to support it.

If someone argues that we live in a time when most of the Law is spiritualized — that is, there is a spiritual way that we obey those laws, through Christ — I would answer that you must be very careful at this point. It's true that the Law is still in effect in a spiritual sense; but it's wrong to say that we are in the same relation to the Law as the Israelites were. They were obligated to keep the Law themselves; we Christians are only to enjoy the results of what Christ did to keep the Law. When the Law entered the spiritual dimension, and the Church came into being, a new thing developed — a new way of approaching the demands of the Law. More on this later.

Israel and the Law

Go back to Exodus 20 and look carefully at what it says.

> I am the LORD *your* God, who brought *you* out of Egypt, out of the land of slavery. *You* shall have no other gods before me ... (Exodus 20:2-3)

Notice that this Law is addressed to the Israelites. This is a very important point to get. When the Lord brought them out of Egypt, the first place he led them was to Mt. Sinai in order to receive this Law. What he was doing was forming a new nation out of these former slaves; he was placing himself at their head as their God, their King, who intended to rule over them and take care of all their needs. Israel got everything they needed here at Mt. Sinai to be a full-fledged nation complete with government.

The Lord didn't do this with any other nation. In fact, the Israelites knew how special they were, that they were the only ones who received this Law. "He has revealed his word to Jacob, his laws and decrees to Israel. He has done this for no other nation; they do not know his laws." (Psalm 147:19-20) As far as the other nations were concerned, they knew almost nothing about the true God, and they certainly didn't have the benefit of the Law to get themselves out of the moral disaster they were wallowing in.

The Law provided some precious advantages for the Israelites. **First,** we already mentioned the fact that it carefully defined what sin is. The Law not only condemns all men (because all men have sinned against God's Law) but it's the first step of salvation for those who know its doctrine. Until you know exactly what sin is, you don't know what you have done wrong — and therefore you don't know what you can do to make it right. If you don't know that you owe a particular tax, of course you are going to get caught when you don't pay it! And if you don't know what you are doing that makes God so offended with you, you have no hope of ever making it right. You will continue doing the very thing that will result in your eventual condemnation without even knowing it. So the Law informs us about what is going on in God's Kingdom.

Second, the Law carefully described how to make restitution for their sins. These are the laws concerning the sacrifices and everything that went on in the Temple. In this respect, the Law was the salvation of the Israelites. If they carefully kept the rules for sacrifice, the Lord promised to forgive their sins and not punish them. It was only a temporary measure, to be sure, since eternal, spiritual forgiveness of sins is only in Christ. But it *was* the Lord's promise, and it *did* keep the avenging angel away. The rest of the world had no advantage, no opportunity to come before God and get forgiveness. They were locked out of the Temple, so to speak, and only had the wrath of God to look forward to.

Paul confirms the fact that the Law was given only to the Israelites. In Romans 2 he says this:

All who sin apart from the Law will also perish apart from the Law, and all who sin under the Law will be judged by the Law ... (Indeed, when Gentiles, who do not have the Law, do by nature things required by the Law, they are a law for themselves, even though they do not have the Law) ... (Romans 2:12,14)

Notice he says here that the Gentiles *did not* have the Law. Here is the situation: the Lord has a certain way of doing things, and his Kingdom (which includes all of Heaven and earth, of course) must follow his rules. He created all things to please him, including the peoples on earth. The world that he created was supposed to abide by what *he* calls righteousness. That's what is meant by "the *requirements* of the Law" – all creatures are supposed to obey the Creator; this obligation, this sense of duty, is built into our beings.

But the *giving* of the Law – the written Word given to Israel through Moses – happened when he revealed those requirements of his Kingdom to Israel. He revealed the rules of righteousness, and the procedures that deal with forgiveness of sin, only to his own people.

So the Gentiles had in their hearts the stamp of their Creator — the evidence that they are not their own, that they belong to Someone

The Law

Else, that immorality doesn't fit into God's world — but they didn't have the benefit that the Israelites had of knowing the whole story of sin and salvation. Gentiles were obligated to please God; but when they didn't, there was no explanation, no merciful warning, that something was wrong, or what they could do to fix the problem.

The Israelites were supposed to take advantage of this special knowledge, but they didn't. They wasted the opportunity over and over throughout their history. And when Jesus came they missed the point again: though their own Law predicted the coming of the Perfect Man, they failed to recognize him; in fact, they hated him and killed him as if *he* were the law breaker!

They missed the biggest blessing of the Law. There is no life in the Law, of course, only the knowledge of our sin. But that knowledge is the first step in the salvation from sin! The second step is the description of the Perfect Man, someone who *could* keep the Law in all its complexity. The Law predicted the coming of Jesus Christ when it showed us the Perfect Man. "So the Law was put in charge to lead us to Christ that we might be justified by faith." (Galatians 3:24) The Law was given so that the Israelites would long for the things that *only* Christ, the Perfect Man, can do for them. After 1500 years of struggling with a system that they could not keep, Jesus should have been a welcome sight to them! Here is someone who can solve our problem with sin and get the Law off our backs. Peter recognized this crucial truth when he said to his fellow Jewish-Christians:

> Now then, why do you try to test God by putting on the necks of the disciples a yoke that neither we nor our fathers have been able to bear? No! We believe it is through the grace of our Lord Jesus that we are saved, just as they are. (Acts 15:10-11)

Notice that he was talking about Gentiles who were already believers, and the question was whether they should be made to "obey the Law of Moses" (Acts 15:5) in one particular point only. That's exactly what modern legalists are trying to do.

Christ and the Law

Christ stands in a unique position in regard to the Law of God. He alone was able to fulfill the Law perfectly; the Law has no complaint about the character and actions of Jesus Christ. This is an amazing record, in light of how complex and demanding the Law is. But it's also understandable, since Jesus is the Son of God and could do no other than keep his own Law to the letter!

Christ related to the Law on several levels; in order to understand our own relationship with the Law, we have to distinguish each of the things that Jesus did for us:

- ***What he did with the Law:*** Christ came to earth to do more than keep the Law for his own sake. He came to solve man's problem of sin, which is *lawlessness*. The Law's complaint is with us, not with him. So here is what Jesus did: he became a man, like us except for our sin, so that he could be "under the Law" and accomplish his goal. Then *as a man* he fulfilled the Law completely and perfectly. When he was done, the Law was forced to admit that *a man* had kept the Law to God's satisfaction! This was the first time that such a thing had happened. Even though the Israelites had the Law for almost 1500 years, nobody had ever kept it perfectly until Jesus came.

- ***What he did for us:*** Now for the final step in God's plan of salvation. Jesus sent his Spirit and made us *one with him* — we are in him, united to him in all ways, so that whatever happens to him will also happen to us. This means several things: ***first***, since the Law is satisfied with him, it is also satisfied with us. There is nothing more to be done! This is what Hebrews means when it says that we *rest* in Christ; he rested from his labors (remember his last words on the cross? "It is finished." John 19:30) and now we rest in him. "Take my yoke upon you and learn from me, for I am gentle and humble in heart, and you will find rest for your souls." (Matthew 11:29) The work of satisfying the Law is over now, for him *and* for us. If there were any more to do on this score then salvation wouldn't be done yet!

Second, whatever rewards are in store for Christ as the perfect man, we also can expect to receive. If he was lifted on high, we will be too. (Colossians 3:1) If he sits at God's right hand, so will we. (Colossians 3:3) If he will rule over the universe, so will we. (Colossians 3:4) Since we are one with him, we will share in his glory and receive the inheritance that Jesus bought for us.

Everything that happens *to us* must go *through him* first; he put himself between us and the Law for this reason. And since he did this, we never deal with the Law directly. There is no salvation in that! Our only hope is in what Christ, as the firstborn of many brethren, achieved for us and passes on to us.

Since Christ fulfilled the Law for us, what is left for us to do? Can we sin now and not have to worry about punishment since Christ took that burden upon himself? Paul tells us that such a thing is unthinkable! "By no means! We died to sin; how can we live in it any longer?" (Romans 6:2) Remember why Jesus came: he came to save us *from* our sin, not leave us in it. "You are to give him the name Jesus, because *he will save his people from their sins*." (Matthew 1:21)

- **_What he does in us:_** He died to save us from condemnation, but that's only one thing he wanted to do. The other was to get us out of the moral mess that resulted in our condemnation in the first place.

So, right now the Lord Jesus is busy with our sanctification — the process of making us holy and set apart for the Lord's use. He is applying *his* righteousness to *our* souls so that we look more and more like him. "And so he condemned sin in sinful man, in order that *the righteous requirements of the Law might be fully met in us*, who do not live according to the sinful nature but according to the Spirit." (Romans 8:3-4) Did you catch that phrase about the Law? The Law of God hasn't gone away; it wasn't put away permanently when Jesus fulfilled it. The Law isn't going away because the God whom it describes isn't going away. Jesus is *making* us conform to what the Law says is a righteous man; only he can do that, of course, since only he lived that righteous life. But the fact remains that the Law is still in full force; the only difference now is *who* has to keep the Law. If we do it, the outcome is in serious question; if Christ does it, it is certain to succeed.

There is a prophecy in Ezekiel that shows us what God had in mind long before Jesus came to earth, but is exactly in line with what the New Testament teaches about our present relationship with the Law.

> I will give you a new heart and put a new spirit in you; I will remove from you your heart of stone and give you a heart of flesh. And I will put my Spirit in you and *move you* to follow my decrees and be careful to keep my laws. (Ezekiel 36:26-27)

This agrees with what Paul says about the subject. The Lord will put his Spirit into us, and *the Spirit* will make us conform to the requirements of the Law; it's not something that we can do alone. Before this time the Israelites were doing their best to obey the Law — and failing at it. It just couldn't be done by sinners. God finally got tired of fooling with them and predicted the time when *he* would make them righteous; instead of waiting on them to do what is right, he would change their hearts himself. (Remember the Covenant with Abraham? He promised to keep both sides of the agreement by walking down the middle of the animal halves and not requiring Abraham to.) When this happens, of course, he will get the credit for the job, because if the Spirit is making you conform to the requirements of the Law then *you* can't claim any credit for doing it! But that's what being part of the Church is all about; it's an entirely different thing from what the Israelites were living under.

- ***What he's doing right now:*** Christ is also doing something *right now* in respect to the Law. He fulfilled its requirements as far as living a righteous life; but he is also in the Heavenly Temple right now fulfilling his duties as our High Priest. The earthly Temple was a picture of the one in Heaven: if you want to know what it's like in God's eternal Temple, read the description in the Law of the Israelite Temple. You must realize, however, that none of that has disappeared from Heaven as the earthly one has. Though the Jews lost their Temple, God still lives in his! And there must still be a sacrifice on the altar to atone for the people's sins — but now it's Jesus' eternal sacrifice that was made "once for all" for our sake. (Hebrews 12:24) There must still be incense burning day and night — though in God's Temple that's the "prayers of the saints" that always go up to him. (Revelation 5:8) There must still be a Holy of Holies, because that's where God sits and rules over his people and gives them what they come to him and ask for. Now, however, the veil that used to separate us from God is torn away and the way into the Holy of Holies is open to "whosoever will." (Hebrews 10:19-22) And the High Priest still lives to intercede for the people: Christ is always presenting our requests to the Father and getting answers for us. (Romans 8:34)

So the Law hasn't gone anywhere. It's still in full force, because that's still the way that God wants to run his kingdom. The difference now is that Jesus is doing all these legal requirements for us and sending us the benefits.

The sin of legalism

Legalism ignores one thing: that only Jesus can keep the Law in a way that satisfies God. A legalist thinks that he can do what the Law commands, and usually he is satisfied in keeping only a few laws since even he knows he can't keep them all.

But the problem with that is that no man except Christ can do what the Law expects of him. The depth of the Law is like an ocean; a sinner will quickly drown in it trying to make his way through it. Our sin is so deep-rooted, even when we are supposedly believers and have the Spirit of God in us, that any Law that we try to keep will be our undoing. Jesus gave us a small sampling of the depth of the Law in Matthew 5 when he took a few examples and showed us what the Law was really after: the heart, the spiritual dimension of our lives.

A legalist won't let go and admit that only Christ can keep every law. He doesn't want God's free grace; he doesn't want Christ to do all things for him. But the Spirit is the only one who can take the righteousness of Christ and mold our hearts with it. If we follow the Spirit, he will make us conform to Christ's image (2 Corinthians 3:18); if we do the Law on our own, however, we are veering away from the Spirit's leading and going on our own. *No man can succeed in righteousness without the Spirit of God.* This is what Paul meant when he rebuked the Galatians: "Are you so foolish? After beginning with the Spirit, are you now trying to attain your goal by human effort?" (Galatians 3:3)

This legalistic attitude is *a rejection of the Gospel.* The Gospel plainly states that Christ alone is our righteousness, that only he is perfect, that we get all our righteousness from him as a gift — not as a reward for our efforts at keeping the Law.

The legalist will immediately reply this way: "But I admit that we can't be considered righteous by following the Law! I believe that my only hope is in Christ's righteousness, that God accepts me on the basis of what Christ did and not my own works. All that I'm saying is

The Law

that we are not therefore free from the obligations of the Law; we must still do what the Law says."

The Scripture's answer to that is this: we are, indeed, not free from the Law's requirements. The Law still exists, because God exists. But Christ alone will see to it that the Law's requirements are met in me. He has a fail-safe way of making sure that I conform to the Law's expectations of a righteous man: through the Spirit. It's not up to me to keep the Law; rather, he will work his righteousness into my heart as I follow the Spirit.

There is *a lot* of difference between following the Spirit and keeping the Law! For one thing, if I set out to keep the Law, I will put the list of requirements in front of me and consciously watch all my actions and thoughts to make sure that I conform to its standards. One slip, however, and I'm dead — literally! The Law allows no mistakes. But if I follow the Spirit, I will open up my heart to the Lord and wait on him to do for me what I can't do. The Spirit takes from what is Christ's and puts it in me. More specifically, the Spirit does two things: he reveals the things of God so that I can see spiritual realities in Christ, and he empowers me to live in the Kingdom of God which is a spiritual kingdom. But more on the Spirit later.

Some people argue that once Christ saves our souls, he makes us *able* to keep the Law. At first glance this looks fine, but it falls apart when we remember some of the hard lessons of the Law. *First*, we're already out of the picture as far as impressing God with obeying the Law. Christ found us as sinners. He has to put us back together himself; he certainly isn't going to trust so great a charge to someone who has such a bad track record! *Second*, we're going to fail again, there's no doubt about it. Though a person might be saved from the power of sin, he hasn't yet been delivered from the presence of sin. We still have the "old man" in us that's going to fight us every step of the way. Paul says that there's going to be war between the Spirit in us and our flesh – Galatians 5:17. *Third*, this idea doesn't match what Paul says in Galatians about starting *and finishing* with the Spirit:

> Are you so foolish? After beginning with the Spirit, are you now trying to attain your goal by human effort? (Galatians 3:3)

To Paul, there's no hope for anybody in keeping the Law. We must not turn back to it, not even in the first flush of spiritual victory that comes in conversion. Our only hope is in this new way of righteousness that Christ gives us in the Spirit.

The legalist insists that *we* must do what the Law says; there is his sin. But there must be no more insisting about the Law for the Christian. Since it is Christ alone who works out the requirements of the Law in us, he alone decides when and what will happen in my heart as concerning righteousness. This is his work now, not mine, this business of making me holy. I can't think of anybody I would rather have watching over me!

The sin of antinomianism

Antinomianism comes from two words: **anti,** which means *against*; and **nomos,** which means *law*. So you see that an antinomian is someone who is against the Law. This is just as much of a sin as legalism.

An antinomian teaches that we don't have to obey the Law. In fact, the Law has nothing to do with us now — Christ was "the end of the Law." The Law is our enemy; Christ put it away from us, and now we only have to deal with him. To a Christian there is only love and mercy, not Law and punishment.

This, however, is a gross misunderstanding of the purpose of the Law and what Christ came to do. When Christ came to fulfill the Law for us, he didn't do away with the Law completely. He said, "Do not think that I have come to abolish the Law or the Prophets; I have not come to abolish them but to fulfill them." (Matthew 5:17) Whoever thinks that Christ did away with the Law doesn't understand what the Law is: it's a description of the Perfect Man, and the perfect kingdom that God wants to rule. Those standards are still as much true today as when the Law was first given.

What Christ did was to fulfill the Law *in our place*. Man wasn't getting anywhere with God's exacting standards. All that the Law was doing for man was showing him how guilty and rebellious he really was. None of us had any hope of satisfying the Law's requirements. But when Christ fulfilled that Law perfectly, he became the first man to do so; when he made us one with him, he made us share in his victory.

Now, you see, since Christ is accounted perfect by the Law's own declaration, we are also accounted perfect as long as we are one with him. We also live the way the Law says to live. Or at least we will someday; the deed was done in Christ, and now he is finishing the job through the Spirit. Remember, he intends to make us conform to the Law's standards: "in order that the righteous requirements of the Law might be fully met in us." (Romans 8:4)

The point isn't that there's no more Law, but that someone else is satisfying the Law in our place. We *will*, by God's decree, conform to the Law! He will see to it, since he cannot allow any sinner to live with him in glory. We *must* look more and more like Jesus or the Father will cut us off as unfruitful branches. (John 15:2) The Law will be the eternal standard of Heaven, much to the dismay of the rebellious at heart. But the mercy of God consists in this: Christ will see to it that our hearts *change* and we please God in everything that we do. Then the Law will be describing us, as well as Christ, when it talks about a Perfect Man.

The antinomians sin against God on several counts: **first,** they are saying that God isn't holy as the Law describes (since they claim that the Law has been "set aside" and is no longer in effect). But the Law is no more and no less than a description of God's holy nature; to say that it no longer applies is to deny the glory of God's holiness. Believe me, he is still holy! And so is the Kingdom that he rules over in Heaven. **Second,** they claim that Christ "set aside" the Law so that it no longer has anything to do with us. That dishonors Christ, as if he would willingly do away with something that glorifies his Father. Christ *honored* the Law; he *fulfilled* the Law. He didn't destroy the very thing that defines what sin is, and what describes the Perfect Man. That would be destroying the standards!

Third, they claim that the Law has nothing to do with us now. By saying this they are opening up the way for people to sin against God even while claiming to be his children. The Law is the definition of sin. By saving us from sin, Jesus upholds and honors the demands of the Law. If he would do away with the Law itself, he would be like a criminal who wanted to do away with rule and order so that he could live in his sin unmolested. This is the same as what Jesus referred to when he accused the Pharisees of leading God's children astray. For such a sin, he warned, it would be better to be thrown into the depths of the ocean with a millstone around your neck! (Matthew 18:6) Never, ever tell someone that they are free from God's righteous requirements! We are not free from them; Christ is changing his people right now so that they will conform to those standards. He will not have a kingdom full of sinners! The only thing that we are free from is the burden of earning that righteousness by our own efforts. That, in fact, is what the phrase "set aside" (Hebrews 7:18) refers to – only the requirement that we have to fulfill the Law *on our own*, as the Israelites did.

That quote about Christ being "the end of the Law" comes from Romans: "Christ is the end of the Law so that there may be righteousness for everyone who believes." (Romans 10:4) If people are going to quote a verse from the Bible then they need to quote the whole thing! It isn't hard to see here what the word "end" means: it's something that Christ does in relation to the Law which results in *us* being righteous, without our having to obey the Law ourselves. There is only one thing in God's Kingdom that defines what righteousness is — that's his Law. "End" doesn't mean "it's gone now." It means that the final judgment has been issued, the Law is satisfied with us now, and it has nothing more to say against us. We are righteous in the eyes of the Law, something that will only happen when someone obeys the Law completely *to the end*. Of course, Christ did this impossible thing for us.

Paul's argument in Galatians

The book of Galatians was written for one purpose: it was an argument against legalists in Paul's day. I cannot understand how legalists today can read his letter and miss his point. The only way I can account for such a thing is that their minds are darkened against the truth and the Spirit is not leading them into truth.

Paul starts out by saying that the Gospel of Christ is the supreme truth of the Church. Anybody who messes with that Gospel should be "eternally condemned!" (Galatians 1:8-9) In other words, we *must* get this thing right; we can't afford to have the least bit of doubt about it.

He then tells us why he is qualified to teach about this: he used to be an expert in the Law. In fact, for a long time he fought against the root idea of the Gospel, because *there is something in the Law that cannot exist side by side with the Gospel*. Either you live by one or by the other; you cannot have both. When he was finally enlightened about the Gospel of Christ, the rest of the Church recognized that Paul now knew the truth of the Gospel and was on their side, not on the side of the Jews. So what he says about this subject is the *last word*.

Then an occasion came up where Peter himself, one of the original disciples of Christ, had a problem about observing the Law. Paul immediately challenged him. Notice that the first thing that Paul jumped on was the fact that Peter was picking and choosing what laws to follow!

> You are a Jew, yet you live like a Gentile and not like a Jew. How is it, then, that you force Gentiles to follow Jewish customs? (Galatians 2:14)

Here is Peter, a Jew, doing away with most of the Law and living like a Gentile, not under the obligation of the Law's requirements. How, then, can he *force* the Gentiles to obey one or two laws when he himself doesn't feel the need to obey *all* of them? He just can't do that.

The Law

Now Paul hits at the root problem behind Christians obeying the Law.

> We who are Jews by birth and not 'Gentile sinners' know that a man is not justified by observing the Law, but by faith in Jesus Christ. So we, too, have put our faith in Christ Jesus that we may be justified by faith in Christ and not by observing the Law, because by observing the Law no one will be justified. (Galatians 2:15-16)

All Christians agree with this statement, but few know how to apply it. Paul is saying that Peter is wrong in making the Gentiles obey only one or two points in the Law. He is therefore saying that *making them obey any particular law is trying to be **justified by the Law** instead of by faith in Christ.* He is definitely not in the mood to hear such foolishness as some people come up with, namely that once we are justified by faith in Christ then we are free to obey the Law. Dealing directly with the Law is the same thing as *turning away* from Christ, whether you do it as an unbeliever or as a believer. He calls this "setting aside the grace of God." (Galatians 2:21) Going back to the Law is "rebuilding" the Law. (Galatians 2:18) No, he says emphatically, "through the Law I died to the Law so that I might live for God." (Galatians 2:18)

He pushes this idea further on.

> I would like to learn just one thing from you: Did you receive the Spirit by observing the Law, or by believing what you heard? Are you so foolish? After beginning with the Spirit, are you now trying to attain your goal by human effort? Have you suffered so much for nothing — if it really was for nothing? Does God give you his Spirit and work miracles among you because you observe the Law, or because you believe what you heard? (Galatians 3:2-5)

Notice carefully what he says here. "After beginning with the Spirit, are you now trying to attain your goal by human effort?" In other words, a Christian is *forbidden* to return to the Law in any way! A believer should know that obeying the Law is not how we receive the grace of God; it can do nothing for us except confuse us and lead us in the wrong direction.

Paul has much more to say about the Law and what it can't do for Christians. But someone may wonder if the "new way" that Christ introduced is really good enough to make us holy. How can we be good unless we obey the Law? How can we please God if we don't know and follow his commands? Paul is ready for this argument too.

> So I say, *live by the Spirit*, and you will not gratify the desires of the sinful nature. For the sinful nature desires what is contrary to the Spirit, and the Spirit what is contrary to the sinful nature. They are in conflict with each other, so that you do not do what you want. *But if you are led by the Spirit, you are not under Law.* (Galatians 5:16-18)

He is assuring doubtful Christians that the Spirit is fully capable of making us holy without resorting to the Law. Of course the Spirit will not introduce a righteousness into our souls that the Law doesn't recognize; remember that Paul said Christ would make sure *"the righteous requirements of the Law* would be fully met in us, who do not live according to the sinful nature but according to the Spirit." (Romans 8:4) But at no point will the Lord tell us to go back to the Law and keep it! Instead, he always tells Christians to "be led by the Spirit." There is life in that; there is only death waiting for the one who wants to do it the old way.

Our only Christian duty is this: "Since we live by the Spirit, let us *keep in step* with the Spirit." (Galatians 5:25) Doing that will keep you busy enough, without going back to the Law and trying to decide what you must do there. The Spirit of God will see to it that, as you follow him, the righteousness of Christ will show up in your heart and life. If you don't know what it means to "keep in step" with the Spirit, search the Gospels and the promises that Jesus made for his followers; study the letters of Paul and see how he unfolds the life of faith. But we are never, ever told to go back and keep the Law!

One more thing about Paul and the letter to the Galatians. This is such a strong statement about a Christian's relationship with the Law that only a blind man — spiritually blind, that is — can miss the point. He makes no bones about it: hands off the Law! We *must* get this right; we must believe this if we don't understand anything else. And, unfortunately, we *will* be confused by other issues — even in Paul's life! He continued worshipping in the Temple; he had his head shaved according to the Law; he was a Jew when among Jews, so that he wouldn't offend them. How does one explain these apparent contradictions when he came out so strongly in Galatians against us having anything to do with the Law? Well, this is what separates the good Bible students from the bad ones: we get the principles down first, *then* we deal with the exceptions. The exceptions *never* prove the rules wrong! Whatever we end up believing about Paul's personal behavior (and there are reasonable explanations for them), we must never let go of what is very clear in the Gospel.

The Christian and the Law

If you really want to do what the Law says — if you feel obligated to keep the Law in any way at all — there is nothing wrong with that. Christ did that very thing! If it was wrong to even try, then he would have been wrong for doing it. The problem is that *you would be a fool to try to keep the Law in any way at all*. The Law condemns sinners; that is its purpose. If you try to obey the Law and fail in any way at all, you are condemned as a law breaker and must be punished. When you start down that direction, you must do everything perfectly and not make a single slip or you have failed. And a sinner doesn't have the liberty to try again; there is only punishment in store for him, not mercy, when it comes to the Law.

One reason we get confused about our relationship with the Law is because we are continually enjoying the benefits of God's grace even while we struggle unsuccessfully with the Law. What I mean is this: we decide to solve our problem of sin by obeying the Law; then we fail, since sinful flesh can't keep the Law to God's strict requirements; then we go to God for forgiveness in Christ (a transaction of grace, not Law!) and are restored to fellowship with him; then we try the Law again. We often misinterpret the spiritual success that comes by walking in faith, thinking that our success came as a result of our attempts at walking according to the Law. We need to get it straight in our minds that any spiritual success we may have comes from the mercy of God in Christ, not by our pitiful efforts at keeping the Law.

Don't underestimate the power of the Law. It looks simple enough, as if you could successfully keep it if you tried hard enough. But better men than you have tried it and failed. Remember the rich young ruler who boasted that, as concerns the Law, "all these I have kept." (Matthew 19:20) Yet he did not have eternal life because his best efforts at Law-keeping weren't good enough for Christ. There is a spiritual depth to the Law that is truly frightening, and an honest soul knows better than to take on such work alone. It's far better to let Christ do it for us.

The question often arises – what about the Ten Commandments? Aren't even Christians obligated to follow that great Law? But if you've been following the argument so far, you will know two things already: ***first***, you can't obey the Ten Commandments either, not to the extent that God expects of you. Don't make the mistake that the rich young ruler made, thinking that a superficial obedience to this simple list will make you pleasing to God. Read about the true, spiritual depth of this Law in the Sermon on the Mount (Matthew 5-7) and then honestly answer whether you can do that (or, what might be more revealing, *have* you done that in your past without failure?) without anybody's help!

Second, Jesus fulfilled these commands for you, and by means of his Spirit he intends to change your heart so that you will look like what the Ten Commandments expect. But the *way* to that righteousness is unexpected: it's not by tackling the Commandments directly! Jesus gave us a clue on this:

> 'Love the Lord your God with all your heart and with all your soul and with all your mind.' This is the first and greatest commandment. And the second is like it: 'Love your neighbor as yourself.' All the Law and the Prophets hang on these two commandments. (Matthew 22:37-40)

Now we reach our goal of righteousness not by obeying the Law, but by walking in the Spirit of God – the Spirit that Jesus sent us from Heaven to make us one with him. Remember that love is one of the fruit of the Spirit. *There* is our salvation; and there is God's solution for our problem of sin.

Should we even study the Law then? By all means, *yes!* The Law has a lot to do with you. ***First***, the Law describes what is wrong with you, the reasons that God sent a Savior to save you. The Law proves to us that we are guilty before God, that we're in trouble for rebelling against him – every one of us. If something isn't done soon, and done well, we will suffer eternal punishment. So if we didn't have the Law we wouldn't understand the true nature of sin and would never know our real need for a Savior.

Second, the Law perfectly describes Christ. Jesus is what you were never able to become on your own. If for no other reason, you need to know the Law so that you can praise your Lord for being so perfect. ***Third***, Jesus kept the Law for your sake. These requirements are still in full force, even today. God still will not accept anybody into his Kingdom who doesn't conform to the strict requirements of the Law. We shouldn't be little children in our thinking. We should know what Christ has done for us, we should know our new standing with God and how it was possible. We should also know what Christ is doing on our behalf now — he is still fulfilling the Law's requirements before the Throne of Grace in the Temple in Heaven. All this, which is described completely in the Law, has a lot to do with our faith in Christ.

Finally, the end result is the same. The man who perfectly fulfills the Law is considered a "righteous man" in the sight of God. Only Christ has done this, however. And for the man who has faith in Christ, the Spirit will put Christ's righteousness into his life too, so that through his walk of faith, hope and love he will fulfill the righteous requirements of the Law. "Therefore love is the fulfillment of the Law." (Romans 13:10) In other words, as we follow the Lord in the Spirit, the Law is satisfied. This is a mystery, but the end result – righteousness – is the same. The difference is in *how* you go about it.

David

David is a key figure in the Bible. He was hinted at in the Law (in Deuteronomy 17 it spoke of what the king of Israel should do, should they ever have a king in their future). During the time of the Judges the nation desperately needed a single person to pull the warring, ignorant tribes together into a political whole and back to the Law of God. The entire book of Ruth is dedicated to explaining where David's family roots were. All of 1-2 Samuel, the beginning of 1 Kings, and all of 1 Chronicles record different aspects of his kingdom. The book of Psalms is a magnificent record of his times of worship. Most of the books in the Old Testament after the record of David's reign mention him in some way – usually looking back to the "good old days" under his rule when Israel prospered, and wishing that times were like that once again. Jesus was the Son of David, determined to reinstate his forefather's throne on a yet more glorious level.

In light of this wide coverage that David gets in the Bible, his actual reign was remarkably short compared to the entire history of Israel. He ruled only 40 years; his son Solomon extended that rule another 40 years. David didn't come onto the scene until about 1010 BC – about 500 years after the formation of Israel! It's as if we here in the United States had waited until the year 2300 AD (500 years after the nation was formed) before electing a president!

Though his time in Israel's history was short, his influence was disproportionately important to its life. The idea behind the Law of Moses was that God is King, and his people owed their lives and service to him alone. They should have been able to trust in him and obey him in all things. But after centuries of trying to do that, they only had failure after failure to show for their efforts. God needed a man on his side for a change, a man who would bring his people back to his Law and life in God's Kingdom. David was that man.

A man after God's own heart

The Israelites had only one King – God himself. They were different from other nations in that respect. While other nations could boast of a king on a throne, in all his pomp and glory and power of the sword, Israel struggled with an invisible God from the distant past. It was difficult for them to rally around an idea – which is what God had become to most of them. They had heard about God from their forefathers, they supposedly learned his laws and learned the traditions of the nation, but it was just too easy to ignore the book that described him and long for a king like other nations. And their personal lives reflected their inability to come to terms with a spiritual God. It became easier and easier to turn to the sins and wickedness of their pagan neighbors, especially when the priesthood of Israel failed to rebuke the people for that sin – in fact, the priests themselves often wallowed in those same sins. When lightning doesn't strike a person who commits a sin, he becomes bold enough to continue in it. So, how real is this God when he doesn't show himself?

Yet, things were bad enough politically and economically that the Israelites became desperate for a leader who would pull the nation together. They came to the prophet Samuel and demanded a king.

> So all the elders of Israel gathered together and came to Samuel at Ramah. They said to him, "You are old, and your sons do not walk in your ways; now appoint a king to lead us, such as all the other nations have." But when they said, "Give us a king to lead us," this displeased Samuel; so he prayed to the LORD. And the LORD told him: "Listen to all that the people are saying to you; it is not you they have rejected, but they have rejected me as their king. As they have done from the day I brought them up out of Egypt until this day, forsaking me and serving other gods, so they are doing to you. Now listen to them; but warn them solemnly and let them know what the king who will reign over them will do." (1 Samuel 8:4-9)

David

The Lord sent them Saul as their first king. Under Saul's leadership, Israel fell to her lowest point since some of the disastrous days of the Judges. For centuries, the Israelites had been used to doing whatever they thought was right, without any one person leading the people back to the Law to see what God wanted them to do.

> In those days Israel had no king; everyone did as he saw fit. (Judges 21:25)

When Saul was king, Israel had hopes that for once the people would be drawn into a single nation under one head, and they would be able to defeat their enemies and prosper for a change. And at first it seemed that this would happen: Saul won victories over the Philistines. But it wasn't long before Saul showed the true nature of his heart. He began to disobey the Lord's commands and do things his own way. For example, when Samuel passed on the Lord's command to put every living creature in the Amalekite camp to death, Saul evidently thought that this was an unnecessary waste – so he saved the livestock, and even spared the life of the Amalekite king. When Samuel found out that Saul hadn't carried out his orders, he was furious. The Lord's commands were clear about this! Saul made the excuse that –

> The soldiers brought them from the Amalekites; they spared the best of the sheep and cattle to sacrifice to the LORD your God, but we totally destroyed the rest. (1 Samuel 15:15)

But God isn't interested in our opinions; when he gives us a command to carry out, he expects strict obedience:

> Does the LORD delight in burnt offerings and sacrifices as much as in obeying the voice of the LORD? To obey is better than sacrifice, and to heed is better than the fat of rams. For rebellion is like the sin of divination, and arrogance like the evil of idolatry. (1 Samuel 15:22-23)

Obviously Saul wasn't going to work out as the king over God's people. The Lord needs someone for the job who will be careful about the Law of Moses, someone who is filled with the Spirit and knows the mind of God, someone who is primarily interested in God's glory and not his own.

So the Lord sent Samuel out to find a replacement, which he found in the shepherd boy David, the eighth son of Jesse. At the time not even his own family – not even the prophet Samuel himself! – thought that this young boy would measure up to the exacting requirements of this job. But the Lord saw something promising in David:

> The LORD does not look at the things man looks at.
> Man looks at the outward appearance, but the LORD
> looks at the heart. (1 Samuel 16:7)

David, the Lord could see, was "a man after his own heart" (1 Samuel 13:14) who would work to build God's Kingdom, not his own, over the Lord's people.

Five requirements for God's kingdom

David inherited a mess from King Saul. There was moral and physical disaster everywhere in the nation. He had to do something to meet the needs of the people, to restore God's glory and Kingdom, and to lay the foundation for a solid kingdom that would last long into the future. Unless he would make a bold move now, Israel would probably cease to be a nation in the world, given her tremendous problems. With the wisdom that God gave him, David took a new approach to rebuilding Israel.

When he took over as king (you can read about the ceremony in 2 Samuel 5:1-5) he immediately set about working on five critical areas:

- **First, he established a capital city.** The Jebusites were Canaanites who had remained unconquered from Joshua's day. They held the fortified hilltop called Jerusalem and dared David to conquer them. Unfortunately for them, they seriously underestimated him. He took it from them and made it his official residence. The story is in 2 Samuel 5:6-10.

The king needed a capital for a central location for his realm. Up until this time, even in Saul's day, the center of government was wherever the judge or king happened to live – and that changed frequently. The Israelites from Dan to Beersheba had no one place to bring their problems or concerns to.

David, however, made his kingdom much easier to manage and deal with by setting up his throne in Jerusalem. His subjects brought him tribute there, came there for his judgments, and gathered there for the religious festivals. He himself sat on the throne in Jerusalem and sent out his officers from there over the entire nation to carry out his commands. In fact, the city of Jerusalem became identified with the King (for example 1 Kings 2:10 calls it the "City of David") – it was known as the "holy" city because it was the seat of the King and the place where God also lived in the Temple.

Setting up Jerusalem as the capital was probably the single most important factor in bringing stability to the nation. Up until this time Israel was just a collection of confused, warring tribes who couldn't pull themselves together to work on anything. But now in one stroke David had turned Israel into a nation in her own right with a king to be reckoned with – with the resources of a nation behind him, both for war and for peace.

By creating a capital, David made it easy for his people to find him and God. The head of state would no longer be wandering around from tribe to tribe; nor would the throne of God be subject to wanderings and (it happened on occasion!) capture by the enemy. Everyone would know where to go when they needed help. It gave God's people pride and loyalty, it symbolized the nation before other nations, it was the home of the glory of God itself.

- **Second, David finally crushed the enemies of Israel.** For too long the Israelites had been persecuted, harassed and defeated by her pagan neighbors. The book of Judges is a graphic example of her history: because she hadn't exterminated all the Canaanites living in the land, Israel repeatedly suffered at their hands. The Lord would raise up judges to save the Israelites from their oppressors, but in a short time they would go back to worshipping the false gods of their neighbors, and God would again punish them with wars and persecution.

At first it seemed that King Saul was going to break the cycle of war and oppression – he did win a few victories over their enemies in the beginning. But when he himself fell into sin and rebellion the Lord again allowed the Israelites to suffer defeat, especially at the hands of the Philistines.

When David ascended the throne, the time had come to put this issue to rest – permanently. As you can see in 2 Samuel 5, he promptly went to battle against the Philistines and the Moabites and defeated them conclusively. What he did to the Moabites shows us how determined he was to settle the issue for good: he put to death two thirds of the men of the nation, in a harsh way! That act alone no doubt impressed the Israelites that they finally had a leader who could deal summarily with the enemy – their foreign policy problems were over.

Enemies are a thorn in the side for the people of God. They have to be dealt with; in fact, they have to be destroyed, because they take up a lot of resources and time that could better be used in more productive matters in the Kingdom. Someone has to take the initiative and get rid of the trouble that threatens God's people. Then in freedom they are able to serve God without fear, without harassment.

- **Third, he led the people back to God.** Another problem in Israel is that the pure worship that Moses laid down to them in the Law was almost a thing of the past. Several stories in Judges show us that the people of God had seemingly forgotten how to worship the Lord – false priests, altars to foreign gods, immorality, no justice. The ark traveled around the country side – it was at Bethel, or at Shiloh, or carried into battle with the army. The religion of the Lord God of Israel seemed to be of little importance to the people. Even the priests – for example, Eli and his notorious sons – treated the service of the Lord as an opportunity for personal gain.

It was time to bring the Israelites back to their God. In 2 Samuel 6 we read of David bringing the ark from the house of Abinadab into the city of Jerusalem. After the little problem about Uzzah touching it without authority (and getting put to death for his trouble!) David and the people entered Jerusalem and set up the ark in the tent on Mt. Zion. It was a magnificent ceremony – dancing, singing, worship, food and drink – and it was purposely designed to impress the people with how central the Lord and his worship was to the nation. Whatever the other nations might do, Israel must come together around her God in praise and worship, obeying his Law, offering the stated sacrifices for sin and atonement. David made the worship of the Lord a fixed institution of his new Kingdom. The book of Psalms alone is an invaluable aid to worship.

The important thing to grasp is that David *had* to step in and restore the worship of the Lord, because being the head of the state he had the authority as well as the responsibility to provide an example of what the Israelites must do to please God. The nation will do as the King does; so if David goes back to the Lord, so will his people.

And he went on to lead the people to the Lord again and again in worship, as we can see from his many psalms.

The point is that God's people exist to worship him. They can't live without him. If the ties between them and God are broken, they will suffer and die as a result. The Lord set up his Kingdom in such a way that they depend on him for everything in life. He is our life, our victory, our joy, our redemption, our sole reason for living. We exist as his people, and we have rich treasures, because God gave us life and an inheritance. Our strength is in him alone. So when David led his people back to God, he was plugging them back into the power that first created them and making sure that they would prosper and grow under his love.

- **Fourth, he established a government.** David was only one man. Though he set up Jerusalem as his capital and sat on the throne of Israel, he couldn't go out himself and execute the laws of his Kingdom from Dan to Beersheba. He needed a system of government, administrators and officials to carry out his orders.

He made his sons government officials, because he could exert the necessary influence over them to carry out his will. He also had many trusted friends and army comrades whom he made government officials – see the list of some of them in 2 Samuel 8:15-18. These were men who came out to David when he was an outlaw in the wilderness, hiding from Saul's unjust wrath. Men like these needed to be rewarded for their loyalty. And because of their loyalty, he could depend on them doing the work he sent them out to do faithfully and well.

Of course he wouldn't have picked fools for important government posts. He knew the skills of each man and put them in the places where they would do the most good for the nation. David's goal, remember, is to build up Israel in the fear and knowledge of the Lord. So he is going to make sure that whoever he puts in authority over the various aspects of Israel's life will help build the kind of Kingdom that God requires.

And the rule of his government must be the Law of God. David once wrote the following lines –

> The law of the LORD is perfect, reviving the soul. The statutes of the LORD are trustworthy, making wise the simple.
>
> The precepts of the LORD are right, giving joy to the heart. The commands of the LORD are radiant, giving light to the eyes.
>
> The fear of the LORD is pure, enduring forever. The ordinances of the LORD are sure and altogether righteous.
>
> They are more precious than gold, than much pure gold; they are sweeter than honey, than honey from the comb.
>
> By them is your servant warned; in keeping them there is great reward.
>
> Who can discern his errors? Forgive my hidden faults.
>
> Keep your servant also from willful sins; may they not rule over me. Then will I be blameless, innocent of great transgression.
>
> May the words of my mouth and the meditation of my heart be pleasing in your sight, O LORD, my Rock and my Redeemer. (Psalm 19:7-14)

David knew how important it would be for the nation to live by God's Law, just as it's important also for the individual. To David it would never be a problem of deciding what was the right or just thing to do, or what

David

justice would be – it's all written in God's Word. There's simply no better way to run a country in righteousness.

God remains King over his people. David knew enough to keep from getting in the middle of that relationship! He simply brought the two together: he consulted the Lord about what he should do for God's people, and he made available the resources of God's Kingdom for every subject in the realm. The children of God all have the right and privilege to hear from their God, to enjoy blessings from his hand, and to serve him in whatever way they have the opportunity. What David did was to put the people in touch with their God – God wasn't a tradition or mythical idea that hid in the dark places of the Temple, but a living God who touched the lives of all of his subjects throughout the land.

- **Fifth, he prepared the plans and materials for the Temple.** Many people think that Solomon, since he built the Temple, must have drawn up the plans for the Temple. They are mistaken. It was David who drew up those plans. Not only that, he also gathered the materials for the Temple. When he was about to die, he handed over the entire project to his son Solomon – so that all that Solomon had to do was follow the instructions that his father had left him!

    > Then David gave his son Solomon the plans for the portico of the temple, its buildings, its storerooms, its upper parts, its inner rooms and the place of atonement. He gave him the plans of all that the Spirit had put in his mind for the courts of the temple of the LORD and all the surrounding rooms, for the treasuries of the temple of God and for the treasuries for the dedicated things. (1 Chronicles 28:11-12)

David

David, at one point in his career, had wanted to build a Temple for the Lord; he felt bad that he had a fine palace to live in while the ark of the Lord was still sitting in the old, original tent that Moses had made hundreds of years ago. But the Lord had someone else in mind as the builder of the Temple. David, the Lord told him, was a man of blood:

> You have shed much blood and have fought many wars. You are not to build a house for my Name, because you have shed much blood on the earth in my sight. (1 Chronicles 22:8)

It's not that David had done wrong (after all, it was God who sent him out and gave him victory over his enemies), but that the hands which built this special House must be those of a man of peace.

> But you will have a son who will be a man of peace and rest, and I will give him rest from all his enemies on every side. His name will be Solomon, and I will grant Israel peace and quiet during his reign. He is the one who will build a house for my Name. He will be my son, and I will be his father. And I will establish the throne of his kingdom over Israel forever. (2 Chronicles 22:9-10)

In fact, the name Solomon comes from שלם – Shalom – which means "peace." The Temple is where God will dwell among his people in peace – peace between God and man, and between man and man.

But David was going to play an important role in the Temple. The Lord showed him what the Temple must look like, what it must be made of, and even the required personnel to work in the Temple and their duties.

> "All this," David said, "I have in writing from the hand of the LORD upon me, and he gave me understanding in all the details of the plan." (1 Chronicles 28:19)

This was appropriate for two reasons: *first*, because David had a special relationship with the Lord and knew the heart of God. God shared his thoughts and plans with David so that he could rule over the Israelites in truth, according to God's Law. So he had an insight into God's ways and works that would result in the kind of Temple that would be acceptable to God.

Second, he is the model king for Israel, and what he's doing through his realm would be the pattern for all the kings to follow – especially for the Messiah, the Son of David who would sit on David's eternal throne. For this reason the Lord appointed David as the architect of the Temple – for the sake of the spiritual Temple that Jesus would later build, as the Son of David. This is the final step to ensuring that Israel would get back on track and be restored to the Kingdom that God first set up through Moses. The Temple was the center of Israelite life; here their God could be found, here their true King reigned, here was forgiveness and life. They needed these things badly.

The Temple is where we can find God and see what he is really like. Here God sits in glory. He invites sinners to his throne to be cleansed and forgiven. We have access to God at this throne of his, and we are encouraged to present our requests to him to get answers from Heaven. Our deepest problems are solved here. Nowhere else in the world will we find such a satisfying relationship with someone who can help us and fill us with life and light.

David had his share of problems in life, some of them caused by his own sin and foolishness (for example, his adultery with Bathsheba and cover-up murder of her husband). And the Lord certainly punished

David for his sins; not even the King of Israel is above the Law. But even when he sinned, he showed that he had the kind of heart that God wants to see in his servants. The restoration of Israel that David worked so hard on worked in his own life as well. For example, Psalm 51 shows us a sinner in the agony of guilt and repentance for his sin. The Lord showed himself a merciful God in how he handled the great sins of David. David surely saw the wisdom of God in all his works when God was there for him too, so freely available, when he needed him.

The point, however, about David is that he successfully accomplished the five tasks that made Israel a great nation under God. Here was a people who lived by God's Law, who treated each other with justice and righteousness, who trusted in God to take care of them, and who regularly came to God's throne for worship and submitting themselves to his will. What more could God want out of a people than this? This is the nation that God created at Mt. Sinai. They were in a perfect position for him to bless them and lead them – and David got them there when generations of leaders and kings before him failed to do so. Or more correctly, the Lord got them there – he just wanted a man to open the doors for him to work in power.

As their father David had done

David ruled over Israel for forty years. Being mortal, the time came to turn over the kingdom to his son Solomon before he died. But as it says in Ecclesiastes, we can work hard all of our lives and then turn over our estates to someone who just may mess everything up!

> I hated all the things I had toiled for under the sun, because I must leave them to the one who comes after me. And who knows whether he will be a wise man or a fool? Yet he will have control over all the work into which I have poured my effort and skill under the sun. This too is meaningless. So my heart began to despair over all my toilsome labor under the sun. For a man may do his work with wisdom, knowledge and skill, and then he must leave all he owns to someone who has not

worked for it. This too is meaningless and a great misfortune. (Ecclesiastes 2:18-21)

Fortunately Solomon was the wisest man of his age – so he managed to preserve the Kingdom that his father left him. In fact, he made Israel the richest nation in that area, certainly richer than she had ever been or ever will be, and there was peace along all of her borders during his reign. David's hard work made the job a lot easier for Solomon. It was Israel's height of glory. But even Solomon had his faults that laid the seeds for future problems:

> As Solomon grew old, his wives turned his heart after other gods, and his heart was not fully devoted to the LORD his God, as the heart of David his father had been. (1 Kings 11:4)

There are two important things to notice in this passage. *First*, David is used as the pattern, the model king of Israel, with whom all his descendants were compared. In other words, David's works were fundamental to the life of Israel and the glory of God. The work that he did is the method that God expects of any king over Israel; he ran the country in the exact way that pleases God. The kingdom of God works best when it's run according to the principles laid down by David. So, any king who succeeded him must do as his father David had done in order to get God's approval.

And that's the *second* thing to notice here – all the descendants of David who sat on the throne of Israel *were* compared to their ancestor David. Here even Solomon strayed from the royal program that God expected his kings to follow: whereas David led the people back to God, Solomon began leading them away from God to worship false gods. "His heart was *not* fully devoted ... as the heart of David his father had been." You see? The Scripture judges a king by whether he followed the five-point plan of David, the model king.

Other kings in Israel's history were judged in the same way:

> He committed all the sins his father had done before him; his heart was not fully devoted to the LORD his

David

God, *as the heart of David his forefather had been.* (1 Kings 15:3)

He did what was right in the eyes of the LORD, but *not as his father David had done.* (2 Kings 14:3)

He did what was right in the eyes of the LORD, *just as his father David had done.* (2 Kings 18:3)

The last example was from the record of Hezekiah's reign. He was one of the few kings of Judah who got a 100% approval rating from the Lord. And as you can see here, the Lord approved of him because he "did as his father David had done."

The Son of David

The Scriptures also call Jesus the Son of David. For example, these passages use that name when referring to him:

A record of the genealogy of Jesus Christ the son of David, the son of Abraham. (Matthew 1:1)

As Jesus went on from there, two blind men followed him, calling out, "Have mercy on us, Son of David!" (Matthew 9:27)

All the people were astonished and said, "Could this be the Son of David?" (Matthew 12:23)

The crowds that went ahead of him and those that followed shouted, "Hosanna to the Son of David!" (Matthew 21:9)

While the Pharisees were gathered together, Jesus asked them, "What do you think about the Christ? Whose son is he?" "The son of David," they replied. (Matthew 22:41-42)

It was a popular concept – one which these and other passages emphasize – that the Messiah would be not only a descendent of David but would sit on David's throne, ruling over David's kingdom. There's a good reason for that. Many people could claim to be descendants of David; even Joseph, Jesus' so-called "step-father," was a "son of David." But the Messiah would actually rule over the kingdom that was given to David – *and do the same things that his father David had done*. This is the key to understanding the ministry of Christ as he set up his kingdom.

Let's go back through the five-point plan of David and see if Jesus followed it in his own ministry.

- **First, he established a capital city.** Jesus also needs a central location for his government, and a place to set up his throne from which he will rule his kingdom. His disciples, in fact most of the Jews of his time, thought that the Messiah would march into downtown Jerusalem and set it up there. But they misunderstood what kind of Kingdom that Jesus came to set up – it would be a *spiritual* kingdom, not an earthly one.

    > Jesus said, "My kingdom is not of this world. If it were, my servants would fight to prevent my arrest by the Jews. But now my kingdom is from another place." (John 18:36)

    So he wasn't interested in downtown Jerusalem. He left this world and ascended the throne in Heaven, at God's right hand. From there he rules over his kingdom, which extends beyond the borders of the land of Canaan to include people and nations all around the globe, all through time. His position there in Heaven gives him the vantage point of power, authority, glory and majesty. His coronation story is recorded in Psalm 2.

    Now whoever wants to see the King must ascend the steps of the Heavenly Mt. Zion and approach the throne that sits above all earthly thrones. It's a spiritual world that Jesus reigns over; the location was chosen specifically so that Jesus could accomplish all that he had in mind. In this world he set aside his glory, and limited his works to individuals and places close at hand. But in the Jerusalem in Heaven he is free to extend his Kingdom to whatever places he chooses, which includes the human heart.

The beauty about making Heaven his base of operations is so that it is accessible to all who wish to approach him. If he would have set up his base on earth, it wouldn't be easy – in fact, for many it would be impossible – to get to it whenever they need something from him. But in Heaven, anybody who wants to can find him on his throne, day or night, whatever the circumstances. And from his throne there he can easily draw from the resources of Heaven and send them to anybody who needs them.

- **Second, he crushed the enemy.** The time had come to deal conclusively with the enemy. So Jesus confronted the primary enemy – Satan – head-on, as soon as he was anointed from on high:

> Then Jesus was led by the Spirit into the desert to be tempted by the devil. (Matthew 4:1)

And just as David confronted Goliath, the champion of the Philistines, with a surprising weapon which in God's power proved the undoing of the enemy, Jesus confronted Satan with the Word of God and sent him reeling back. From that point on, it will only be a matter of time until all the dominions that lay under the hand of Satan and his followers will be either destroyed or taken away from them by this new King:

> The reason the Son of God appeared was to destroy the devil's work. (1 John 3:8)

This has to be done, because God's people need some relief from the enemy of their souls. It's impossible to get about the business of repentance, salvation, and holy living as long as we have a persistent foe constantly tripping us up and destroying everything we do. We need some protection from him, and some peace from the battle, so that we can get ready for Heaven. So Christ battles with the enemy for us so that we can be free to tend to the matters of our souls.

Sin is a persistent enemy. It was the downfall of the human race at the beginning, and it is still part of our very makeup. No power on earth can clean the stain of rebellion from the heart of man. We need a greater power than anything in the world to effectively deal with it. Jesus, however, brings the power of Heaven to bear on the problem. His first job in a conversion is to break the power of sin from over the life of the sinner. Now we don't have to sin anymore. Once we were slaves to sin and couldn't help but follow its leading; now we are free to follow Christ into righteousness and holiness.

- **Third, he led the people back to God.** Sin is rebellion against God's Law. As it says in the Bible, "sin is lawlessness." (1 John 3:4) And everyone is guilty of sin. This means that the entire human race has turned its back on its Creator and is following its own feelings and opinions, instead of carrying out the orders that God gave us at Creation.

So another essential work of the Son of David is to turn us around and bring us back to the God we left. We must find God; we can't afford to live without him any longer. And Jesus takes several steps to do this: *first*, he reconciles God to us – he took our punishment upon himself so that God won't hold anything against us any more. Because of what Christ did for us on the cross, the Lord now looks upon us with favor – if we come under the shadow of that cross and let the blood from that death cleanse our souls.

Second, he fills us with his Spirit who turns our path toward Heaven. We are now God's children, destined to live and rule with him in Heaven forever. But before we assume such a high role in the universe, we have to be made fit for the job. So the Spirit is going to lead us into holiness, give us skill at kingdom-building, put our minds on the matters of Heaven, reveal the new world to us to motivate us, and so on. The Spirit is Christ's Spirit (see Romans 8:9; Philippians 1:19; 1 Peter 1:11). So when Jesus said to "follow me," (Matthew 16:24), he meant to follow the leading of his Spirit within you as he prepares you for life in Heaven. (Galatians 5:18,25) He himself, through his Spirit, will lead you into Heaven where God is –

> I am the way and the truth and the life. No one comes to the Father except through me. (John 14:6)

God is light, he is love, he is life. He is the source of all good things. We were designed to depend completely on him for everything. Ever since the fall of mankind, we have been doing our best to do without God – and dying as a result. Man simply can't live without his Creator supporting him, leading him, training and teaching him, and making his life worth living. What Christ does when he brings us back to God is restore that original fellowship that we had with our God in the beginning. Now that the two are back together, the Lord has great plans for us in eternity.

- **Fourth, he established a government.** Being the Son of God, I'm sure that Jesus could very easily administer his entire Kingdom without our help. In this way he differs from his father David – who literally couldn't do the entire thing himself.

But one of the ways that God likes to do things is to use people to do kingdom work, even though he wouldn't have to. Paul says that we who work with the King are "fellow workers" (1 Corinthians 3:9) through whom he rules his kingdom.

Jesus made promises to his disciples that they would be part of his government administration. It wasn't going to be exactly what they expected, however – they thought they would rule as the Gentiles do, in power and impressive majesty. Instead, Jesus' administrators would be servants living for the benefit of others:

> You know that the rulers of the Gentiles lord it over them, and their high officials exercise authority over them. Not so with you. Instead, whoever wants to become great among you must be your servant, and whoever wants to be first must be your slave – just as the Son of Man did not come to be served, but to serve, and to give his life as a ransom for many. (Matthew 20:25-28)

But he will have a government complete with officials carrying out his orders and administering his grace to the people. The entire system of spiritual gifts in the Church is the government of Heaven at work:

> But to each one of us grace has been given as Christ apportioned it. This is why it says: "When he ascended on high, he led captives in his train and gave gifts to men." (What does "he ascended" mean except that he also descended to the lower, earthly regions? He who descended is the very one who ascended higher than all the Heavens, in order to fill the

whole universe.) It was he who gave some to be apostles, some to be prophets, some to be evangelists, and some to be pastors and teachers, to prepare God's people for works of service, so that the body of Christ may be built up until we all reach unity in the faith and in the knowledge of the Son of God and become mature, attaining to the whole measure of the fullness of Christ. (Ephesians 4:7-13)

We can see in this passage the kingdom of Christ at work: the King ascends his throne, and assigns administrators over his Kingdom. Each of his officials, the people with spiritual gifts in the Church, carry out his will for the benefit, well-being and growth of the Kingdom.

And we can be sure, since Christ rules over his kingdom by sending out his Spirit, that everything will be done according to God's holy standard of righteousness. As Paul tells us in Romans,

… in order that *the righteous requirements of the Law* might be fully met in us, who do not live according to the sinful nature but according to the Spirit. (Romans 8:4)

The administration of Christ's Kingdom – that is, the Church – is no small matter. The tasks at hand are huge. He has to take former rebels and so change their hearts that they not only love the God they used to hate, but are so filled with love for him that they will willingly serve him for eternity. He has to clean their hearts of the smallest trace of sin, so that it will never show itself again. He has to teach them the language and customs of Heaven so that they will fit right in on their arrival there, ready to assume their new responsibilities. He has to protect them from their enemies while in this world, and make them skilled at resisting any who would want to hurt or destroy them. He has to make them skilled also at testifying about God to a world that needs to hear about him. The job would be overwhelming to mere mortals. It's a mercy that Jesus the Son of God has taken upon himself the government of his Church! And through his servants, the ministers of the Spirit in the Church, he unerringly and methodically builds up the body of believers to reach these amazing goals.

- **Fifth, he laid the foundation for the Temple.** If Jesus' kingdom is ruled from Heaven, if the capital city of Jerusalem is in Heaven, we can therefore expect that the Temple itself would also be in Heaven.

When Moses first made the Tabernacle, he was instructed to make it like the Temple that was in Heaven:

> Make this tabernacle and all its furnishings exactly like the pattern I will show you. (Exodus 25:9)

> They serve at a sanctuary that is a copy and shadow of what is in Heaven. This is why Moses was warned when he was about to build the tabernacle: "See to it that you make everything according to the pattern shown you on the mountain." (Hebrews 8:5)

And that's why we are told, whenever we pray, that we are in reality coming into the Temple in Heaven – into God's very presence as he sits on his throne in the Temple in Heaven (just as the Israelites did in the Old Testament):

> But you have come to Mount Zion, to the Heavenly Jerusalem, the city of the living God. You have come to thousands upon

thousands of angels in joyful assembly, to the church of the firstborn, whose names are written in Heaven. You have come to God, the judge of all men, to the spirits of righteous men made perfect, to Jesus the mediator of a new covenant, and to the sprinkled blood that speaks a better word than the blood of Abel. (Hebrews 12:22-24)

So while Jesus was on earth, his goal was to build the Temple of Heaven. The plans for it were constantly in his mind, and he gathered materials for that Temple. We know this by some hints that he dropped about it along the way. For example, he called his disciples to follow him so that he could make them "fishers of men." (Matthew 4:19) The role that the disciples would play in the Kingdom of God was going to be crucial: it was *their* testimony of what they saw in Christ that we now have in our Bibles. Their writings became, quite literally, the foundation of the Church of Christ.

> Consequently, you are no longer foreigners and aliens, but fellow citizens with God's people and members of God's household, *built on the foundation of the apostles and prophets*, with Christ Jesus himself as the chief cornerstone. In him the whole building is joined together and rises to become a holy temple in the Lord. And in him you too are being built together to become a dwelling in which God lives by his Spirit. (Ephesians 2:19-22)

This passage, in fact, graphically illustrates what Jesus had in mind when he chose the apostles to carry the message to the world. Everyone who believes that message becomes part of the House of God, the Temple where God lives among his people. Jesus had them in mind too, during his ministry:

> I have other sheep that are not of this sheep pen. I must bring them also. They too will listen to my voice, and there shall be one flock and one shepherd. (John 10:16)

His intention is to draw all of his people together, from all parts of the globe and across all of time, into one Temple where God will live with them. The people of God are the building materials, the stones, out of which the Temple will be built:

> As you come to him, the living Stone – rejected by men but chosen by God and precious to him – you also, like living stones, are being built into a spiritual house to be a holy priesthood, offering spiritual sacrifices acceptable to God through Jesus Christ. (1 Peter 2:5)

So you see that Jesus was planning and collecting for the Temple during his entire ministry, just as his father David had done.

Keep in mind that since the Old Testament Scriptures judged the descendants of David by comparing their works with the works of their father David, we must also look at the works of Christ in the same light. He can justifiably lay claim to the title "Son of David" *only if* he did the same things as David had done.

I think that this is easy to see now. David pulled God's people out of a mess and led them to greatness – by leading them back to God and his power and wisdom. Jesus Christ is doing the same thing today, but on a much higher level. David's kingdom was only to last through the days of the Israelites; but Jesus' kingdom will last forever. The principles, however, hold true to both. Only by making room for God himself to rule over his people will you have a righteous, prosperous kingdom.

The Prophets

One of the things that causes the bitterest fights in the Church today is the subject of prophecy. That's really unfortunate, because the prophecies were given to us so that we might have hope (2 Peter 1:19), not discouraging fights! If people can only fight about it and separate from each other about it, that only shows that they aren't getting the *point* even though they might know the *facts*.

Rather than starting with the many issues involved, let's start at the beginning. If we lay a good groundwork for our study of prophecy, by looking carefully at Scriptural principles, we can be more certain that what we end up believing about prophecy will be true. If the foundation is good, the rest of the building has a better chance of being good.

What prophecy is not

When we think about prophecy, what usually comes to mind? Predicting the future! Almost all the prophets in the Bible predicted the future in some way. But that's not the only thing there is to Biblical prophecy. If it were, then astrologists are prophets — and the Bible condemns them. (Deuteronomy 17:2-5; 18:9-13) If prophecy were just predicting the future, then "woolly worms" are prophets, because many people think that their color predicts the kind of winter coming. We know that's not what the Bible means by a prophet.

Another definition of a prophet that many people use is this: he is someone who confronts people with God's Word. He gets in our faces, so to speak, and forces us to listen to what God has to say. The Old Testament prophets certainly did that. But preachers bring God's Word to us too, though we can't consider them prophets. A prophet, however, *knew* what was in the hearts of his hearers, because the Lord showed him. Preachers can't know; they can only (if they are doing their job right, that is!) announce the truth and let the Spirit of God convict hearts. There is a lot of difference between Old Testament prophets and modern preachers, in this respect.

So prophecy has in it these two elements — predicting the future, and confronting man with God's Word — but it isn't limited to just that. There is more to Biblical prophecy that we must discover.

The problem

Perhaps we can get closer to an understanding of what a prophet is if we first look at man's problem. Paul tells us that every one of us are (or have been) subjects of the powers of darkness; we have willingly "followed the ways of this world and of the ruler of the kingdom of the air, the spirit who is now at work in those who are disobedient." (Ephesians 2:2) Rather than knowing God, as we were created to do, we know nothing about God; in fact, our abysmal ignorance of God is the very reason we live in such wickedness and fall into suffering and death so easily.

Physically speaking, man has lived under the rule of many types of governments and kingdoms. Some have been good, some bad. But none of them have been able to address the problem of man's sinful heart. No matter how much law we impose on the outside, the heart of man rebels at righteousness and prefers to do things his own way, *not* God's way. "This only have I found: God made mankind upright, but men have gone in search of many schemes." (Ecclesiastes 7:29) Of course this has brought people to their many miseries: "The wages of sin is death." (Romans 6:23) Death comes in many forms: physical, spiritual, psychological, economical, intellectual, and so on — but all of them share the same devastation and pointlessness.

All this and more happens because man refuses to live under the rule of God.

> The kings of the earth take their stand and the rulers gather together against the LORD and against his Anointed One. 'Let us break their chains,' they say, 'and throw off their fetters.' (Psalm 2:2-3)

And if God doesn't rule this earth, then what will? The passions of men, of course, and ignorance, and rebellion, and whatever dark powers over us that can take advantage of our confusion. When God isn't running things, the result is "sexual immorality, impurity and debauchery; idolatry and witchcraft; hatred, discord, jealousy, fits of rage, selfish ambition, dissensions, factions and envy; drunkenness, orgies, and the like." (Galatians 5:19-21) The result is this: what once used to be a peaceful, serene kingdom with happy subjects (we're describing the original Creation, of course) is now a ruined battleground with struggling opponents fighting over what isn't worth having anymore.

The solution: A new kingdom

The Lord God Almighty isn't going to look down on a rebellious earth for long. He made this place, it belongs to him, and he is determined to rule over it. He gave man a chance to obey him and we wouldn't; now he is going to get what he wants through another method.

In Isaiah 9 we read a prophecy that tells us what God is going to do:

> For to us a child is born, to us a son is given, and *the government will be on his shoulders*. And he will be called Wonderful Counselor, Mighty God, Everlasting Father, Prince of Peace. Of the increase of his *government* and peace there will be no end. He will *reign* on David's throne and over his kingdom, establishing and upholding it with justice and righteousness from that time on and forever. The zeal of the LORD Almighty will accomplish this. (Isaiah 9:6-7)

This prophecy is about Christ, of course. Don't miss the point, however! It isn't simply predicting that Jesus would come; it is telling us *what will happen* when Jesus comes: the Kingdom of God. He is coming to assume control; he will sit in the throne and rule over us. The times of men doing their own thing will come to an end, and from that point on he will *rule*.

When Jesus rules, things happen. For once there is justice, because he will make sure everyone gets their just reward and punishment. He can do that because he is the Judge, able to see into our hearts and discern what is really there; he isn't fooled by outward appearances as we are. He saves people from what is destroying them — their sin. He fills their hearts with the Spirit which will lead them in the way of life for a change, a way of holiness that pleases God. Jesus also defeats our enemies, as any good king should, so that we are free from the tyranny of the world, the flesh, and the devil and can settle down peaceably to live our lives for him. When Jesus reigns, peace settles over the people, they enjoy life, the wicked are thrown out, and God gets the glory that is his due.

That's the prophecy — but did it happen? Check out the stories in the Gospels to see if these things came true. You will find that this prophecy was completely fulfilled there: not among the Jews, nor the Gentiles, but among the believers, the followers of Christ. Not everyone had eyes to see this new kingdom: "The knowledge of the secrets of the kingdom of Heaven has been given to you, but not to them." (Matthew 13:11) "I tell you the truth, no one can see the kingdom of God unless he is born again." (John 3:3) Simeon saw it (Luke 2:30), the disciples saw it (Luke 10:23), but most of Jerusalem didn't see this new kingdom. (Luke 19:42) Nevertheless, the Kingdom of God finally arrived in the reign of Christ in the Church.

The Prophet

Notice *where* we got the description of the kind of kingdom that Jesus would set up: from the prophet Isaiah. In fact, if you read through the prophets of the Old Testament, you will begin to find a common theme running through them all: they not only *predict*, they not only *confront* us with God's Word, they also **reveal the coming kingdom of God.** Each prophet is showing us what God intends to do in the future. The Lord is going to tear down the kingdoms of this world, destroy the works of the devil, and shake out what he didn't create. Then when he has thoroughly destroyed all competition, he is going to set up his kingdom in their place. All the prophets deal with this subject in one form or another.

Just about everything we know about what the Kingdom of God will be like was first described — predicted — in the prophets. For example, what is the best known passage that we use to describe the Spirit's working on the sinner's heart? This one:

> I will give you a new heart and put a new spirit in you; I will remove from you your heart of stone and give you a heart of flesh. And I will put my Spirit in you and move you to follow my decrees and be careful to keep my laws. (Ezekiel 36:26-27)

This is a prophecy that best describes how people would be changed so that they could be part of a spiritual kingdom.

What passage best describes what Christ's kingdom would do to the kingdoms of this world? This one:

> While you were watching, a rock was cut out, but not by human hands. It struck the statue on its feet of iron and clay and smashed them. Then the iron, the clay, the bronze, the silver and the gold were broken to pieces at the same time and became like chaff on a threshing floor in the summer. The wind swept them away without leaving a trace. But the rock that struck the statue became a huge mountain and filled the whole earth. (Daniel 2:31-45)

How about the passage that best describes the Suffering Messiah?

> Surely he took up our infirmities and carried our sorrows, yet we considered him stricken by God, smitten by him, and afflicted. But he was pierced for our transgressions, he was crushed for our iniquities; the punishment that brought us peace was upon him, and by his wounds we are healed. We all, like sheep, have gone astray, each of us has turned to his own way; and the

LORD has laid on him the iniquity of us all. (Isaiah 53:4-6)

And we could go on and on, quoting the prophets as they described this kingdom that God was going to set up. They predicted what it would be like when God runs things, both positively and negatively. Some long-standing problems are going to get solved for good! The wicked will be dealt with forever; the righteous will be able to breathe free again. The world is going to run like God wants it to run for a change.

How did the Prophets know what the kingdom would be like? God showed them. Through the Spirit, the Lord showed the prophets what would happen when the Lord came to rule over earth. The prophets didn't make any of this up, nor did they guess what the Lord would do. This is, in other words, the *Word of God* — that's why we are counseled to pay attention to what the prophets are saying: "And we have the word of the prophets made more certain, and you will do well to pay attention to it." (2 Peter 1:19)

The two greatest prophets

You may not have known this, but there were two prophets in Israel who were greater than any other prophets. Not just in how much they said, but in *what* they said; not greater in *quantity* but in *quality*.

The first one was Moses. We read this about him in Deuteronomy:

> Since then, no prophet has risen in Israel like Moses, whom the LORD knew face to face, who did all those miraculous signs and wonders the LORD sent him to do in Egypt — to Pharaoh and to all his officials and to his whole land. For no one has ever shown the mighty power or performed the awesome deeds that Moses did in the sight of all Israel. (Deuteronomy 34:10-12)

This is a high rating! When Moses' sister and brother tried to cut in on the act and get some glory for themselves, the Lord rebuked

The Prophets

them and told them that Moses was special among the prophets. "With him I speak face to face, clearly and not in riddles; he sees the form of the LORD." (Numbers 12:8) There was a reason for this, which we will look at in a minute.

The other great prophet of Israel was Jesus Christ. Moses told us (of course!) that he would be coming: "The LORD your God will raise up for you a prophet like me from among your own brothers. You must listen to him." (Deuteronomy 18:15) Peter confirmed that this was Jesus in Acts 3:22.

Now what did these two men do that made them prophets? Just this: *they revealed the kingdom of God.* Only they did it in a big way! Let's begin with Moses. When the Israelites left Egypt they headed straight for Mt. Sinai. At this point they were still only a mob, blindly following Moses wherever he led them. When they got to Mt. Sinai they met their God — and there they found out that *he* was their real leader, not Moses.

The next forty years was a crash course on the kingdom of God. They learned his laws, they learned how to please him, they learned his plans for the future, they were fed and watered by him, they watched the miracles he did for their benefit. The Lord was making a people, a nation, out of these Israelites. He set up his government over them, complete with laws and promises.

How did they learn all this? Remember that they were too afraid to get close enough to God to hear his voice! (Deuteronomy 5:23-27) Moses was the one chosen to take all the words of God to the people; as God built the nation Israel, he did it all through Moses. And the foundation that was laid during these forty years through Moses' ministry lasted for the next 1500 + years until the next prophet could take over — Jesus.

When Jesus came, he too announced the kingdom: "The time has come, the kingdom of God is near. Repent and believe the good news!" (Mark 1:15) Only this time the kingdom was to be completely spiritual; nothing on earth would adequately represent the things in the kingdom of Heaven. He, like Moses, set up a nation of God's people where the Lord would rule over them and they would enjoy his blessings. In this kingdom, however, people were really saved from their sins! They ate spiritual manna from Heaven; they drank from the spiritual rock in the desert; they felt the Law penetrate their hearts in severe conviction of every thought and act; they received the Spirit who enabled them to obey God; they were protected from spiritual enemies; and so on. It's easy to see, in the work of Christ, a new world in the making; he was forming a new nation out of Jew and Gentile and creating the circumstances necessary for a happy life with God the King.

Moses and Christ were actually working on the same project, the same house, the same kingdom. After all, this is the kingdom of God — and he doesn't have two kingdoms but one. In Hebrews we find this:

> He was faithful to the one who appointed him, just as Moses was faithful in all God's house. Jesus has been found worthy of greater honor than Moses, just as the builder of a house has greater honor than the house itself. For every house is built by someone, but God is the builder of everything. Moses was faithful as a servant in all God's house, testifying to what would be said in the future. But Christ is faithful as a son over God's house. (Hebrews 3:2-6)

This explains in a nutshell why these two prophets were so great — and what they were doing as "prophets." They were responsible for setting up the house, so to speak; through their ministry they revealed to the people the kind of world they were to live in. Through their words, the people saw God in his holiness, in his love, in his anger, in his government, in his redemption, in his promises.

Keep in mind that Moses didn't actually do the work himself; he only revealed the hand of God to the people as the Lord did the work. That's the role of the prophet: to reveal the kingdom of God. Jesus, however, did what he predicted, or the Father did it through him. He was still a prophet, however, in that he revealed this kingdom that God was setting up to his followers.

God sent all the prophets to his people for this reason: the Israelites were getting pretty comfortable in their wickedness, and they thought that God would never come to upset their little world. The prophets, however, brought disturbing news. The Lord *will* come; the wicked had better listen up and change their ways, and the righteous need to hang in there a while longer. They predicted the crashing down of the old world and a new world taking its place. To some it was a dreadful message; to others, their only hope.

The kingdom of the Spirit

> Above all, you must understand that no prophecy of Scripture came about by the prophet's own interpretation. For prophecy never had its origin in the will of man, but men spoke from God as they were carried along by the Holy Spirit. (2 Peter 1:20-21)

Every prophet of God was moved by the Spirit of God to say what he said. This means a couple of things: *first*, what he had to say was a message told him by the Spirit; he wouldn't have known the subject or the right words if the Spirit hadn't told him. *Second*, the situation he was facing — the need of the people he was speaking to — was something that only the Spirit of God understood. The Lord could see into the people's hearts and therefore knew the message to tell them. The prophet himself could never have figured out either of these things on his own.

You will find the Spirit of God involved in the message of every single prophet in the Bible:

> As he spoke, the Spirit came into me and raised me to my feet, and I heard him speaking to me. (Ezekiel 2:2)

> On the Lord's Day I was in the Spirit, and I heard behind me a loud voice like a trumpet. (Revelation 1:10)

> Belteshazzar, chief of the magicians, I know that the spirit of the holy gods is in you, and no mystery is too difficult for you. (Daniel 4:9)

> Then the LORD came down in the cloud and spoke with him, and he took of the Spirit that was on him and put the Spirit on the seventy elders. When the Spirit rested on them, they prophesied, but they did not do so again. (Numbers 11:25)

Why is the Spirit of God involved in every one of the prophets? If you understand the special work that the Spirit does, the mystery clears up: God's Spirit *reveals* the hidden things of God so that we can see what we didn't see or understand before. Paul describes this in Corinthians:

> We have not received the spirit of the world but the Spirit who is from God, that we may understand what God has freely given us. (1 Corinthians 2:12)

The Spirit opens our spiritual eyes so that we can see God's world. For example, Jesus told Pilate that he was a king, though his kingdom wasn't of *this* world — but Pilate couldn't see that or understand it at all. (John 18:36-38) But when the Spirit revealed the same truth to the Roman centurion, he saw Jesus as the Master, who is able to command disease with authority. (Matthew 8:5-13)

The Lord sent his Spirit upon the prophets for some very good reasons:

Dead-on accuracy — When any man thinks he has something to say to the hearts of his hearers, he can only hope that he gets it right; he doesn't really know what is in their hearts like God does. But when a prophet spoke to people, he *knew* what was in their hearts because the Spirit showed him. He was able to say exactly what they needed to hear from God; there wasn't any guessing about it. This means that the people *had* to listen to the words of the prophet because it was *straight from God*.

The Prophets

So do we. The Lord spoke through the prophets to us as well, and we have to take their message seriously. "And we have the word of the prophets made more certain, and you will do well to pay attention to it, as to a light shining in a dark place, until the day dawns and the morning star rises in your hearts." (2 Peter 1:19) This may sound surprising to "New Testament" Christians who never look in the Old Testament for much of anything. But it's true that the Lord has much to say to you through the message of the prophets.

A spiritual kingdom — The prophets spoke of the kingdom of God; that much we can see. But when you think about it, a kingdom where God rules has to be totally different from any kingdom that this world has seen. "God is Spirit, and his worshipers must worship in spirit and in truth." (John 4:24) If we want to see our King, we have to have spiritual eyes to see him; if we want to hear what he has to say, the Spirit has to give us the ability to hear with our spirits. God rules from Heaven, which is a spiritual place (not like this physical earth) and he is building, right now, a kingdom on earth (called the Church) where the Lord rules and takes care of his people. All of this is of a spiritual nature, not physical like the kingdoms of this world.

So when the prophets spoke about the kind of kingdom that God had in mind to set up among men, you will find them talking about very spiritual things happening: like righteousness, seeing God's glory, changing the heart, and so on. They never said that God would rule on a physical throne, covered with gems and gold like an earthly king, wielding a physical sword over his enemies! The Jews didn't appreciate the spiritual nature of God's kingdom when Jesus showed up and claimed to be a king. They thought that, if he were really a king, he should start acting like one! They didn't understand his "spiritual" approach to the kingdom.

Correct interpretation of events — The prophet "saw" circumstances differently than other people did. Most people think that circumstances in our lives, even strange circumstances, are just Mother Nature at work. The prophets, however, saw the hand of God, because the Spirit opened their eyes to be able to see God's work. So when they told the people what was really

The Prophets

going on and why, the people should have accepted their interpretation.

For example, when the Israelites were suffering under the military might of foreign empires like Egypt and Babylon and Assyria, they tended to see it as we would: they hated their enemies and longed for the day when they would get out from under their control. But the prophets who spoke the Word of God to them during those centuries had an entirely different interpretation of the events: this was the hand of God, using their enemies to punish them for their sins. "O LORD, you have appointed them to execute judgment; O Rock, you have ordained them to punish." (Habakkuk 1:12) Instead of hating their enemies, they should have been humbling themselves before God because of their sins that he was punishing them for. We need the message of the prophets to tell us the correct way to think about what happens to us in life.

Reveals the mind of God — A prophet, since he spoke what the Spirit showed him, is really telling us the very thoughts of God. And that is exactly what the Spirit does: "The Spirit searches all things, even the deep things of God. For who among men knows the thoughts of a man except the man's spirit within him? In the same way no one knows the thoughts of God except the Spirit of God." (1 Corinthians 1:10-11)

This is important because we need God to tell us what he is thinking; we can't continue to make up stories about what God is like. We have so many opinions about God and what his will is! Has nobody ever asked God himself to see what he thinks? Do you think he will sit around and let us make up ridiculous theories about him, without ever getting up and proclaiming the truth about himself and silencing all arguments forever? This is exactly what he has done through the prophets; these words, these messages are on God's heart, and these are the things that are important to him, the things he intends to do on earth. We do not need to guess or wonder about what he thinks anymore. And we ought not to ignore it either! Someday these things that the prophets spoke about will come true.

The role of the Prophet

We've seen the *definition* of a prophet, and the *qualifications* of the prophet. Now we're ready to look at his message and learn about the job he's been given to do. The prophets of the Lord had four parts to their message:

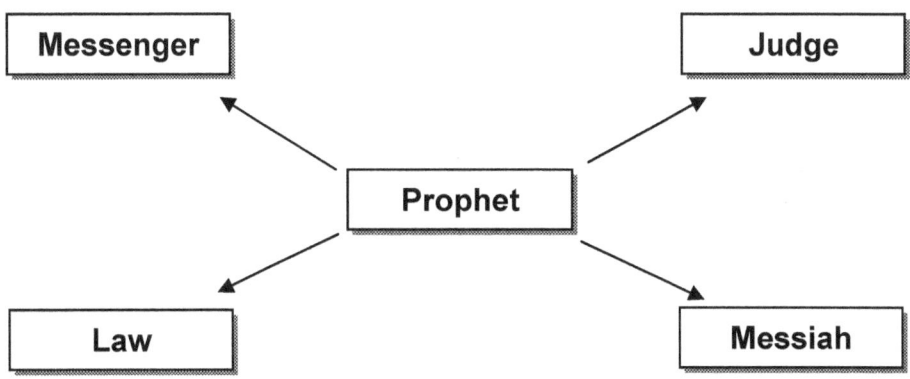

Prophecy: **A message of war**
Prophecy: **Upholding the Law**
Prophecy: **The Judge speaks**
Prophecy: **The need for a spiritual Kingdom**

Prophecy: A Message Of War

Perhaps you know how two armies would face each other in the field, in the old days when warriors came against each other to fight. First they would each send a spokesman ahead to parley: the two would deliver messages from their respective kings (usually insults!) and demands for a surrender. Only when that failed would they return to the lines and the battle would begin.

Most people don't know that this is exactly what the prophets of the Bible were doing. The King (God, in this instance) sent his prophets ahead to warn sinners of the coming conquest. Did you ever notice that the prophets almost always confronted the kings of Israel? The heads of state? This was obviously a showdown of kings! The King of kings demanded the surrender of Israel's rebellious leaders who were leading the people into sin and wickedness. He threatened them, through his prophets, with destruction — in fact, his Heavenly hosts were on the way even as the prophet spoke, to deal God's enemies a mortal blow in combat. In other words, the message of the prophets wasn't a game or an idle threat: it was the Lord's challenge to his enemies. War was on its way.

> Listen, a noise on the mountains, like that of a great multitude! Listen, an uproar among the kingdoms, like nations massing together! The LORD Almighty is mustering an army for war. (Isaiah 13:4)

> I myself will fight against you with an outstretched hand and a mighty arm in anger and fury and great wrath. (Jeremiah 21:5)

> I saw Heaven standing open and there before me was a white horse, whose rider is called Faithful and True. With justice he judges and makes war. His eyes are like blazing fire, and on his head are many crowns. He has a name written on him that no one knows but he himself. He is dressed in a robe dipped in blood, and his name is the Word of God. The armies of Heaven were following him, riding on white horses and dressed in fine linen, white and clean. Out of his mouth comes a sharp sword with which to strike down the nations. "He will rule them with an iron scepter." He treads the winepress of the fury of the wrath of God Almighty. On his robe and on his thigh he has this name written: KING OF KINGS AND LORD OF LORDS. And I saw an angel standing in the sun, who cried in a loud voice to all the birds flying in midair, "Come, gather together for the great supper of God, so that you may eat the flesh of kings, generals, and mighty men, of horses and their riders, and the flesh of all people,

free and slave, small and great." (Revelation 19:11-18)

The prophecies are full of warnings like these; we would have to be pretty dense to miss the point. God is declaring war against us rebels, and he is using the prophets to tell us what he intends to do to us if we do not lay down our arms against him. The prophet was given a vision of the Lord and his army – he saw the King assembling his hosts for battle in his spiritual Kingdom, and he saw them start out from Heaven to come to earth here to do battle. The prophet spoke of what he knew.

To God, our problem isn't just a matter of sin and death, destruction and misery, ignorance and materialism (although all that is bad enough!). Rather he sees us in this light: when we sin, *we are attacking him and his kingdom.* We are a threat to the state, an enemy, someone who wants to replace him with another king more to our liking. We have a deep-seated resentment against the King:

> The kings of the earth take their stand and the rulers gather together against the LORD and against his Anointed One. "Let us break their chains," they say, "and throw off their fetters." (Psalm 2:2-3)

We want to rule ourselves, or at least pick a king that we prefer more. So this is a direct insult against the glory of God the King. You may not have realized the true nature of sin — you may have thought that it was just a weakness of the flesh, an occasional lapse in self-discipline — nothing so serious as to warrant God's special attention. But you are wrong if you think this. Sin is *rebellion*: "Everyone who sins breaks the law; in fact, sin is lawlessness." (1 John 3:4)

Sin means to defy the King and his Law. And everyone knows what you have to do with a rebel and traitor: hang him! Governments usually do it with a lot of publicity, as a matter of fact, because of the serious nature of the crime. Rebellion tries to destroy the authority, the laws of the land, the peace of the citizens, and the values that the country holds precious. It is a political threat as well as a moral threat.

God considers sin in this light, and his response is to amass an army and come against us *in war!* Who would have thought that he would take our sin so seriously? But he does, and therefore the message of the prophets ought to scare the wits out of us. I don't know about you, but I would hate to be standing on the wrong side of the battlefield when the Almighty God himself comes to fight his enemies!

There is also a note of hope in this message that the prophet has been sent with. If you surrender now, the Lord will accept your surrender and draw you over on his side. He will change you, of course, because he can't let you continue in your rebellion in the middle of his ranks. But to think that he would willingly accept one of his former enemies and then make him part of the army of Christ is an amazing act of grace on the King's part! But you must act on this *now*. There was always a note of urgency in the prophet's offer. The King is coming soon; you don't want to be caught on the wrong side if he gets to the enemy camp and starts shooting soldiers wearing the enemy's colors! You must change sides now, with all your heart, and give yourself up to God. If you do that, you will find him to be a compassionate and gracious God, ready to make you his servant and (even more amazing!) a part of his family. If you don't surrender, your life is forfeit.

Prophecy: Upholding the Law

If the Israelites would have taken Moses seriously – and the Law that God gave through him – things would have worked out wonderfully for them. Life was good when God took care of them, and when they obeyed God. In his Kingdom they had everything they needed to be happy and prosperous. All they had to do was stay close to him and follow his Law. After all, how could they go wrong when they had the Creator himself for their King?

But sinners are sinners, even when they know they could lose all the good things in life if they turn their backs on God. The Israelites often strayed away from the Law of God, playing around with the sins of their neighbors and being tempted to worship false gods.

The Prophets

What the Prophets did was to confront the Israelites with their commitment to the Lord. They had agreed under Moses to serve the Lord only, to worship him alone, and to obey all of his Law. Now they were rebels against that same Law. It's time to remember our roots and go back to that original agreement.

> Now fear the LORD and serve him with all faithfulness. Throw away the gods your forefathers worshipped beyond the River and in Egypt, and serve the LORD. But if serving the LORD seems undesirable to you, then choose for yourselves this day whom you will serve, whether the gods your forefathers served beyond the River, or the gods of the Amorites, in whose land you are living. But as for me and my household, we will serve the LORD. (Joshua 24:14-15)

> To the Law and to the testimony! If they do not speak according to this word, they have no light of dawn. (Isaiah 8:20)

> Yet they rebelled and grieved his Holy Spirit. So he turned and became their enemy and he himself fought against them. Then his people recalled the days of old, the days of Moses and his people – where is he who brought them through the sea, with the shepherd of his flock? Where is he who set his Holy Spirit among them, who sent his glorious arm of power to be at Moses' right hand. (Isaiah 63:10-12)

> Remember the Law of my servant Moses, the decrees and laws I gave him at Horeb for all Israel. (Malachi 4:4)

Moses had a special relationship with God, as we've already seen. Through him the Lord set up his Kingdom on earth. God was the King of the Israelites, and naturally a king is going to have a government, a throne, laws to live by, defense against the enemy, and blessings for his people. In order to do this without any confusion, to such a complexity and careful detail, and do it in such a way that it would last for thousands of years – God needed to deal directly with Moses, face to face, not through visions and dreams. So we have this passage that describes how God spoke to Moses:

> Listen to my words: When a prophet of the LORD is among you, I reveal myself to him in visions, I speak to him in dreams. But this is not true of my servant Moses; he is faithful in all my house. With him I speak face to face, clearly and not in riddles; he sees the form of the LORD. (Numbers 12:6-8)

The point is that the system that God laid out through Moses was good enough for the Israelites no matter when or where they lived. The other prophets who followed Moses didn't need to add a thing to his system. All they were supposed to do was *bring the people back* to the Law of Moses; that was still their righteousness and glory, if they would only follow it. Of course life changes, cultures change, and even the Israelites changed over time. So we find the prophets interpreting the Law of Moses for their own day – applying the individual laws to particular cases. But at no point did they need to preach something new; indeed, they weren't supposed to stray from the same sermon outline, which is righteousness according to the Law.

In a way the Apostles of the New Testament play the same role as the Prophets of the Old. They too preach the Kingdom of Christ to the Church. They aren't supposed to come up with anything new either; they've been called to faithfully pass on the faith of the Gospel to each succeeding generation of Christians. Their role, too, is to bring the Church back to the spiritual Kingdom that Christ set up for us to prepare for and live in.

Prophecy: The Judge speaks

Another reality that the Israelites were faced with in the ministry of the Prophets was that of the Judge. Through their words they heard the voice of God himself, and felt the heat of his white-hot examination of their souls. They couldn't escape the penetrating judgment of God – the Prophet seemed to put his finger right on the problem every time. Even kings squirmed under the scrutiny, their own consciences testifying to the truth of the Prophet's words.

A judge is an important person in a society. His job is to find out what's really going on in a situation. Consider a courtroom: the prosecuting attorney brings a charge against the accused, and the accused tries to defend himself against the charge through his attorney. Both bring in witnesses and evidence to try to prove their point. We need someone to listen to both sides and come to a decision in the matter. That's what a judge does – he weighs the evidence, listens to the testimony, and comes to a final judgment in the case. This, in his opinion, is what really happened. Once he passes his judgment, the court goes with that and either frees the innocent defendant or punishes the convicted felon.

Many people confuse the function of judging with issuing punishments. If being a judge was simply a matter of handing out punishments, then the policeman who first arrested the suspect could have looked up the crime in a book and handed out the punishment right on the spot. But our system doesn't work that way. The suspect has the right to defend himself against the charge in a court of law, and the government's job is to listen to his argument and make its own decision. The judge, therefore, represents the government and has the power of upholding the charge or dismissing it. Once he does his job of finding out what really happened, *then* someone can look up the crime in a book and issue an appropriate punishment. The hard part is making a correct judgment.

An important reason we need a judge is, at bottom, because people don't usually tell the truth about themselves, especially when accused of a crime. If you don't believe this, spend a day in court sometime. Most people plead "innocent" before a judge – you would think by this that the police are arresting a lot of innocent people! Someone who has committed a crime doesn't want to get punished, so he will most likely add to his crimes and lie about what he did. We need a judge who will study the situation and decide whether this person really is innocent. Then, once he has issued his judgment, we don't really care what the person claims about himself; the state has spoken, and that's all we need now.

God is the Judge of all the earth. He has penetrating insight into all people's hearts and minds, and into all situations.

> "Far be it from you to do such a thing – to kill the righteous with the wicked, treating the righteous and the wicked alike. Far be it from you! Will not the Judge of all the earth do right?" The LORD said, "If I find fifty righteous people in the city of Sodom, I will spare the whole place for their sake." (Genesis 18:25-26)

> For the word of God is living and active. Sharper than any double-edged sword, it penetrates even to dividing soul and spirit, joints and marrow; it judges the thoughts and attitudes of the heart. Nothing in all creation is hidden from God's sight Everything is uncovered and laid bare before the eyes of him to whom we must give account. (Hebrews 4:12-13)

> I saw Heaven standing open and there before me was a white horse, whose rider is called Faithful and True. With justice he judges and makes war. His eyes are like blazing fire, and on his head are many crowns. (Revelation 19:12)

When you read the Prophets, you soon learn that nothing escapes God's scrutiny. He knew their hearts so well that he even knew what they were thinking! He knew when they were bringing sacrifices to him out of duty instead from heart-felt devotion. He knew their secret sins – the gods they worshipped, the crimes they committed against each other, the lusts and passions that were unbecoming to the people of God.

God uses a terrifying standard to judge people by: his Law. We've seen already that the Law is very precise about spelling out what is right and wrong. We have no freedom to reinterpret the Law. When it says that a certain activity is righteousness, and another activity is sin, then that's exactly what God thinks about it and we're not going to change his mind – no matter what age or culture we live in! And the

The Prophets

Law of God has many levels; we can't just keep the Law on a superficial physical level and satisfy its deep requirements. Jesus and Paul both proved to us, for example, that the Law is also very spiritual. We have an impossible job on our hands if we want to make the Law satisfied with our hearts and lives.

This is the standard that the Judge uses against us. As you can guess, God can make short work with all of us. We know down inside that God is absolutely right about us. Nobody else may know our secret sins, but God knows them and so do we. When he sends the prophet to confront us with our sin, all we can do is wither under his judgment. When David, for example, committed two sins that he probably thought he would get away with, God sent Nathan the prophet to him to expose his sin to public view:

> The LORD sent Nathan to David ... Then Nathan said to David, "You are the man! This is what the LORD, the God of Israel, says: 'I anointed you king over Israel, and I delivered you from the hand of Saul ...You did it in secret, but I will do this thing in broad daylight before all Israel.'" (2 Samuel 12:1,7,12)

And, perhaps from personal experience, David later said about the searching eyes of the Judge of all the earth –

> O LORD, you have searched me and you know me. You know when I sit and when I rise; you perceive my thoughts from afar. You discern my going out and my lying down; you are familiar with all my ways. Before a word is on my tongue you know it completely, O LORD. You hem me in – behind and before; you have laid your hand upon me. Such knowledge is too wonderful for me, too lofty for me to attain. Where can I go from your Spirit? Where can I flee from your presence? If I go up to the Heavens, you are there; if I make my bed in the depths, you are there. If I rise on the wings of the dawn, if I settle on the far side of the sea, even there your hand will guide me, your right hand will hold me fast. If I say, "Surely the darkness

will hide me and the light become night around me," even the darkness will not be dark to you; the night will shine like the day, for darkness is as light to you. (Psalm 139:1-12)

People lie so much about themselves, even in the face of the Law. How many times have you heard someone say that they think they're basically good (even if they've done a few things wrong in life) and they think that God will let them into Heaven on Judgment Day? Human memory is short; we tend to forget the bad times in life and remember the times that make us look good. God, however, is the perfect Judge. Unlike earthly judges who have to work hard at getting at the truth (at least we hope they will, though sometimes they get it wrong too), God knows the truth about us immediately. He doesn't even need our testimony, or the testimony of others – he's been keeping accurate records of our lives since the day we were born.

> His eyes are on the ways of men; he sees their every step. There is no dark place, no deep shadow, where evildoers can hide. *God has no need to examine men further*, that they should come before him for judgment. Without inquiry he shatters the mighty and sets up others in their place. Because he takes note of their deeds, he overthrows them in the night and they are crushed. (Job 34:23)

The Israelites didn't get away with anything while their God had them under such a careful scrutiny. Consider the following passage. The elders thought they were doing their sins in secret, but God sees through walls and brings their sins to light so that others can see.

> Then he brought me to the entrance to the court. I looked, and I saw a hole in the wall. He said to me, "Son of man, now dig into the wall." So I dug into the wall and saw a doorway there. And he said to me, "Go in and see the wicked and detestable things they are doing here." So I went in and looked, and I saw portrayed all over the walls all kinds of crawling things

and detestable animals and all the idols of the house of Israel. In front of them stood seventy elders of the house of Israel, and Jaazaniah son of Shaphan was standing among them. Each had a censer in his hand, and a fragrant cloud of incense was rising. He said to me, "Son of man, have you seen what the elders of the house of Israel are doing in the darkness, each at the shrine of his own idol? They say, 'The LORD does not see us; the LORD has forsaken the land.'" (Ezekiel 8:7-12)

God *has* to know everything we do and think; otherwise he couldn't judge the world according to justice. If he were as much in the dark about what's in our hearts as an earthly judge, Judgment Day would be a farce – the wicked would be able to get away with almost everything they've done. But there *will* be justice on that day. Everyone is going to know that the rewards that the righteous get, and the punishment that the wicked get, are fair and just. Everything about us and about our past will come out into the open for all to see, so that nobody will be able to accuse God of being unfair.

> There is nothing concealed that will not be disclosed, or hidden that will not be made known. What you have said in the dark will be heard in the daylight, and what you have whispered in the ear in the inner rooms will be proclaimed from the roofs. (Luke 12:2-3)

Which leads to one more point about the Judge that the Prophets showed us. Though the Israelites first came under the ministry of the Prophets, we need to understand that we too will come under this kind of scrutiny from God. On Judgment Day, he is going to look into our hearts with the same care for detail that we read in the Prophets. He's going to be upset with the same kinds of sins that he found in them, and he's looking for the same kind of righteousness that he called for in them. In other words, this is a preview of what to expect on Judgment Day when we stand before the throne of God to be judged.

The Prophets

Prophecy: The need for a spiritual Kingdom

The Israelites were a special people in history. It was through them that God first worked out the details of his Kingdom on earth, among men. This means that whatever they learned about God is solid doctrine for the rest of us. The Church now has the information that we need to relate to this God, due to the lessons first learned in the Old Testament.

The problem was that the Israelites were sinners as we are. It would have been a nice system if it would have worked; but even though God made demands of them to be righteous, and to be perfect as he is perfect, they just didn't measure up. It's not that God was making the standard too high, it was that the people didn't want to submit to God's rule over them.

There was another problem inherent in the system that made it difficult to meet God's high standard of purity. The following passage says it best:

> The Law is only a shadow of the good things that are coming – not the realities themselves. For this reason it can never, by the same sacrifices repeated endlessly year after year, make perfect those who draw near to worship. If it could, would they not have stopped being offered? For the worshipers would have been cleansed once for all, and would no longer have felt guilty for their sins. But those sacrifices are an annual reminder of sins, because it is impossible for the blood of bulls and goats to take away sins. (Hebrews 10:1-4)

Just about everything in the Old Testament system was on a physical level. Animal blood just can't take away the sin in one's heart. In order to take advantage of the sacrifices, therefore, as well as the many other promises that God gave the Israelites, they needed to approach them *in faith*. They had to be able to see that these physical aspects of their religion – the land, the Temple, the sacrifices, the throne of David – were only shadows of the real treasures that God has in the future for his people. They were dealing with patterns, symbols, clay models, so to speak, which can (if one has the faith to see it) show us the truth of the real items in Heaven.

Without true faith, however, one tends to trust in the shadow and miss the whole point. For example, the Israelites forgot that the Temple sacrifices pointed to the eternal, spiritual sacrifice of Christ. They brought their sacrifices to the Temple, offered them in blood, and then went home and right back to their sins. That sacrifice was designed to *wash away* the sin, not allow them to continue wallowing in it! The sight of the death of the animal, and its shed blood for our sake, should shake us into a fear of this holy God who demanded this payment. So when the Israelites went right back into their sin after worshipping God, the time was ripe for change.

> For when I brought your forefathers out of Egypt and spoke to them, I did not just give them commands about burnt offerings and sacrifices, but I gave them this command: Obey me, and I will be your God and you will be my people. Walk in all the ways I command you, that it may go well with you. But they did not listen or pay attention; instead, they followed the stubborn inclinations of their evil hearts. They went backward and not forward. From the time your forefathers left Egypt until now, day after day, again and again I sent you my servants the prophets. But they did not listen to me or pay attention. They were stiff-necked and did more evil than their forefathers. (Jeremiah 7:22-26)

Again, it's not as if the system itself was to blame – anybody who followed the Lord with his whole heart would have prospered spiritually, even under the Law. But people don't usually follow what they can't see. They think that this spiritual God (wherever he may be) will be satisfied with an outward show of religion, while they go back to living as they please after the service. The result was predictable: if we don't walk in faith, we will walk in rebellion and sin. The Israelites were notoriously wicked by the time that the Lord had to punish them in the Exile.

The Prophets

Something had to give. God would send prophet after prophet to warn the people about their sin, and they would go on ignoring the prophets, live in their sin, worship false gods, yet continue to worship the Lord in the Temple. Things were going from bad to worse. The only way to fix the problem was to fix the heart. So the Prophets promised the coming of the day when God would change sinners hearts and *make* them follow his decrees:

> I will give you a new heart and put a new spirit in you; I will remove from you your heart of stone and give you a heart of flesh. And I will put my Spirit in you and *move* you to follow my decrees and be careful to keep my laws. (Ezekiel 36:26)

There would be a Messiah for God's people. He will change their hearts with his Spirit; he will cleanse their hearts in a way that animal blood couldn't. He would bring them into an eternal Promised Land where there would be no more sin, crying or pain. He will destroy their enemies (sin, the world, and the devil) once for all; he will sit on David's throne, and set up an eternal Kingdom. He will not only restore the high standards of God's Kingdom according to the Law of Moses, but he will also lift it up to a new spiritual level where nothing can corrupt it. In fact, the promises of the Covenant will reach a new height by bringing the people of God before the very presence of God, to enjoy his treasures from his own hand. This will be a new kind of world where things can't go wrong anymore.

This is a constant theme in the prophets because they were constantly dealing with the shortcomings of the old physical system. Though the Israelites *were* guilty of breaking the Law even in the Old Testament system, one can understand that, in a way, since the system had its shortcomings. So let's put this Kingdom on a level where it can't fail anymore.

This is also the point where the Gentiles come into the picture. During the Old Testament the covenant was basically a Jewish matter. But the prophets all pointed to the day when God would expand the covenant to include any who come to God through the Messiah. The Messiah – this Son of David and Son of God – is the solution for turning a physical system into a spiritual one. The Temple is now in Heaven, where all of God's people must worship. And now that Jesus has opened up the veil of the Holy of Holies, anybody who becomes one with Christ through faith in him can also enter into the Temple, into the presence of God, and serve him. Anyone. Now we see that the Jewish race of the Old Testament was, again, just a picture of the entire Church. For a time only the Jews were the receivers of God's grace, the chosen people of God; now anybody who has the faith of Abraham is one of the chosen race. So David's Kingdom will extend around the globe and include all races of men and women in the hands of Christ.

Moses and the Prophets

The prophets were on an extraordinary mission. They saw God in his glory, received his Word from his own mouth, and were sent out by God to confront people with the Kingdom of God. The words of the Prophet were the very words of God himself. To turn one's back on a Prophet is to throw away your last chance at salvation – which the Israelites found out to their shame and hurt!

The Prophets also had an insight into the Messianic Kingdom that was the solution to sin and death in this world. Though they saw the misery that mankind lives in, they also saw the answer in Jesus and his spiritual Kingdom. What the Law could never do on its own, the Messiah would do on a spiritual level – and do it so well that it would forever cure the problems of sin and death. It was time to switch from a faith in earthly things to the sacrifice of the Son of God for forgiveness, and eternal riches in Heaven. No wonder, then, that Jesus pointed people to the Prophets for the message of salvation!

> "I have five brothers. Let him warn them, so that they will not also come to this place of torment." Abraham replied, "They have *Moses and the Prophets*; let them listen to them." "No, father Abraham," he said, "but if someone from the dead goes to them, they will repent." He said to him, "If they do not listen to *Moses and the Prophets*, they will not be convinced even if someone rises from the dead." (Luke 16:28-31)

The Prophets

The New Testament

What the New Testament is all about

We learned two things from the Old Testament. *First*, we learned what God is like. He is holy, and he expects all his servants to be perfectly righteous. The standard that we have to live up to is the Law, which is really a description of God's perfect Kingdom.

Second, we learned in the Old Testament that nobody can reach that high ideal of righteousness. Sin is deeply rooted in the hearts of even God's people. Try as they might, the Jews continually missed the mark of perfection. It's not as if there was a problem with the Law; if that was the case, then God himself would be to blame for our not reaching the goal. We could accuse him of setting the standards beyond our means! No, the problem is in our own hearts. We don't want to obey God. Even if we wanted to keep most of the Law, there would be something in his legal code that would irritate us and we would turn to our own opinions and our own way of doing things. We are *rebels*, pure and simple. We have been since the beginning of the world.

Now we are at an impasse. God simply won't repeat the fiasco of the Garden of Eden and let potential sinners into his Heaven. He wants a perfection in our hearts so complete that, even after millions of eons, we will still only have love for him and an undying devotion to his glory. *That's* going to take a miracle!

Since we can't achieve that kind of righteousness by tackling the Law directly, we need another option – one that will work perfectly. The answer that God came up with is in two steps.

The New Testament

Over the ages, people have had some strange notions about the Bible. One of the most destructive doctrines to ever arise is that the New Testament can exist – in fact, *must* exist – just fine without the Old Testament. It's as if they are two different books talking about two different Gods. The Old Testament God, we are told, was a God of blood and wrath. He was a product of ancient cultures who knew nothing of Christian grace. Our New Testament God, on the other hand, preaches forgiveness and love. The New Testament marks the beginning of a modern era, and the Church's business is to bring the brotherhood of man, all around the world, into reality.

But this notion totally ignores the actual text of the Old and New Testaments. We've seen that there are crossover ideas between the two. The same doctrines are in both, and what the Bible has to say about God and righteousness and salvation is the same no matter which half of the Bible you look for it in. If there appears to be any difference, it's only because you're missing some key explanatory passages in both.

The Old Testament preached the Gospel of Christ; we are told this plainly in such passages as Galatians 3:8. The lesson about the Law of Moses was designed not to force the Israelites into a perfection that they couldn't attain, but to a stark realization that they needed to find another option. There was no way they could reach that standard of holiness; their whole history proved that point. The Lord was bringing them to the point of enlightenment: God must have another way for man to become righteous, besides trying to follow the Law. They should have been ripe for the message of the New Testament.

When Jesus came, he found the Jews hopelessly mired in the Law and all their thousands of by-laws that they made to enhance the Law. They still weren't getting the idea. Like dealing with little children, he had to prove to them again that there was no way they could keep the Law, even on the simplest level. When the rich young ruler came to Jesus asking about the way to eternal life, Jesus told him (naturally, being a Jew he would start with this) that he had to measure up to the Law's standards. When the man claimed that he did just that his entire life, Jesus very easily proved that he had, in fact, been able to keep *none* of the Law! He neither had love for God nor love for man in his heart – which is the summary of the Mosaic Law. (Luke 18:18-24) Over and over again, Jesus exposed the superficial obedience of the Jews and proved to them that they weren't making any progress at all at being righteous, at least not to God's satisfaction.

So the basic problem that existed since the beginning of time, the very issues that the Old Testament grappled with, still remained in Jesus' day. What is God offended with? What does he want to see in us? How are we going to take care of the offenses against God that we're guilty of? What hope, if any, do we have for this life and the life after this one? These are the same questions that the Old Testament saints grappled with; we, too, grapple with them. The Old Testament showed us the answers to these questions, but it didn't exactly tell us how to get hold of the answers and start taking advantage of them. It only held them out at a distance as promises, not as dreams fulfilled.

In the New Testament we are going to learn how to reach those high goals. Everything that God promised in the Old Testament (and that's where we first learn what the promises are) are going to be given to us now. The process is going to be strange, especially to the Jews who were instructed in the ways of the Lord through physical means. No wonder that they showed so much resistance to the Lord's answer at the beginning! The new Kingdom didn't look at all like what they were used to. The trouble was that they didn't have eyes of faith to see through the superficial differences, and realize that it was the same God, using the same principles, as they had learned in the Old Testament system, but now it's on a spiritual plane where things actually work. The Old Testament system, though good (because it taught the truth) didn't change anything. The New Testament system is going to change the heart forever.

The revelation of Jesus Christ

The Jews should have been asking questions at the end of the Old Testament. The Lord presented them with a supposedly workable system of salvation from sin and death. There was a long stretch of centuries in which they tried but failed to make it work, but still the Lord himself acted as if it *was* a workable plan. Can someone become holy according to its doctrine? Is it possible to live with this God, with all his rules and regulations?

That's the question that the New Testament was designed to answer. Yes, it is possible – and here is how: Jesus Christ is our entry into the presence of God. It's through him that we can experience and enjoy the God of the Old Testament, on his terms.

There were many promises made in the Old Testament about what man *could* have from God if he so desired. Those promises are now available for the asking in Christ:

> For no matter how many promises God has made, they are "Yes" in Christ. (1 Corinthians 1:20)

> For in Christ all the fullness of the Deity lives in bodily form, and you have been given fullness in Christ, who is the head over every power and authority. (Colossians 2:9-10)

This is going to take some explaining, of course. To the Jew, the very idea of a man being our "interface" with God (in other words, he's both man and God and can serve the needs and requirements of both) is blasphemy. So the New Testament writers carefully lay out the truth about Christ so that, when we're finished reading about what he has done, we will know that he truly is the Son of God and the answer to our spiritual dilemma.

> But these are written that you may believe that Jesus is the Christ, the Son of God, and that by believing you may have life in his name. (John 20:31)

The New Testament is therefore a ***revelation*** of Jesus Christ. We're not only going to learn exactly who he is, but we're going to see the point about him being the fulfillment of the Old Testament system. God has been planning all along to make Christ the solution to our spiritual problems. If we pay attention, we're going to be able to make the connections between his story and the Old Testament lessons.

The New Testament reveals Christ in different ways. We can divide the books up like this, with each section coming at the point from a different angle:

The Gospels – These are, on the surface, the story of the life of Christ. But what's underneath the surface is the staggering revelation of *a man* achieving God's long-time goal of living a completely righteous life. From his birth to his death, the Lord is saying in effect that this is what a righteous man looks like, according to God's standards. In contrast, we see our true colors as the sinners we are. No matter – the promise is held out all through these four books that Jesus intends to make us look the same way he looks. But it's going to be by sharing his life, not by going back to the Law and once more attempting what is impossible for us to do. Once he's done with what he came here on earth to do, he's going to address our problem once for all by carrying us on his shoulders to our reward.

Acts – This is the story of the Church. At the beginning we find Jesus pouring out his Spirit on the disciples, transforming them and uniting them with himself. The mystery becomes plain now: Christians are made one with Jesus through his Spirit, and are enabled to live the same life that Jesus himself lived. And we find out that the same principle of attaining the new life holds for Jew and Gentile – the old promise of blessing the world is carried out through the missionary efforts of Paul as he takes the Gospel of life in Christ to those who had no hope otherwise.

The Epistles – Here we have the Apostles examining what it means to be one with Christ. They review the life of Christ, and we see that living by the Spirit of Christ is going to result in the same holiness, the same righteousness, the same Heavenly-mindedness that Christ had. The point isn't that you believe that there was a Jesus, and that he was holy. The goal is you might become one with Jesus so completely that he literally lives his life out through your life.

Revelation – This is a fascinating book, because it finishes the revelation of Christ that the other New

Testament books only hinted at. If we had only the rest of the New Testament and not Revelation, we very likely would get the wrong idea of Christ – that he was a gentle shepherd, a teacher, the humble servant, the crucified Savior. Revelation shows us the other side of the coin. He is the glory of God, the overwhelming King on God's throne, the Master who demands obedience and faith from his subjects or there will be war! We need to know about this side of him too. To the wicked, Jesus will be their Judge who will punish them for their sins. To the righteous, Jesus is their hope that, for everything he promised them, he has the power and authority to give them. And it's going to be glorious!

Jesus Christ – the New Man

To many Christians, Jesus is very simple to understand. They like Paul's statement which cuts right to the heart of the matter:

> For I resolved to know nothing while I was with you except Jesus Christ and him crucified. (1 Corinthians 2:2)

"I believe in Jesus." That's sounds simple enough, but actually with a little bit of thought, you will quickly see that this statement is anything but simple! Jesus is a profound reality; this is like saying, "I believe in the universe!" What is it about Jesus that people believe? Have they looked "beneath the cover" yet and seen "how wide and long and high and deep is the love of Christ, and to know this love that surpasses knowledge"? (Ephesians 3:18-19) Do they realize that Jesus is as mysterious and as complex as the God of the Bible – that he is the "radiance of God's glory and the exact representation of his being?" (Hebrews 1:3) Do they know *how much* God has put in Christ for us? "For no matter how many promises God has made, they are 'Yes' in Christ." (1 Corinthians 1:20) They say that we must have a simple faith in Jesus, but can they say (as Paul did), "I *know* whom I have believed, and am convinced that he is able to guard what I have entrusted to him for that day?" (2 Timothy 1:12) Did they know that

Jesus is the righteousness of God, the work of God, the ways of God, the names of God, the Prophet, Priest and King, and many more offices and functions?

Our "faith" needs to be more than just saying, "I believe in Jesus." We need to know who he is, and what he does. We need to know why believing in Jesus is the key to our faith. In fact, the more we know about him the more we will believe in him — faith and knowledge *must* go together when it comes to believing in Jesus. Paul said that our goal is that "we all reach unity in the faith *and* in the knowledge of the Son of God and become mature, attaining to the *whole measure* of the fullness of Christ." (Ephesians 4:13) What we need is a well-rounded, filled-out picture of who Jesus is — then our faith will be based on what we *know* about him. Then we will trust him for things that are true about him, not for things that we have made up.

However, we don't want to get lost in the details at this point. What we want to do is back up and see the bigger picture first. Jesus accomplished something that perfectly fulfills all the preparation work that God had been doing in the Old Testament. He did what no man before him had ever done, yet what every man should have done to satisfy God. The staggering accomplishment of Jesus Christ is that, *as a man, he did God's will perfectly.*

Mankind's problem has always been that, instead of doing what our Creator made us to do, we have chosen to rebel against his will and Law and do our own thing instead.

> This only have I found: God made mankind upright, but men have gone in search of many schemes. (Ecclesiastes 7:29)

Our rebellion has made God furious. This is the driving force behind his fierce wrath against the wicked. God is not one to be trifled with; he is a good God, he knows what he's doing, and when he made us to obey him and serve him with our whole lives, he expects just that. He will not be ignored!

So when we failed him miserably, God had two options. He could have just wiped out all of mankind and put the project aside. He had every right to do that. The option that he chose, however, was to redeem mankind and put him back on track. He is determined that we do what he created us to do – one way or another.

The route to redemption is fully explained in the Old Testament, but the actual work of changing our hearts and making us into new creatures doesn't happen until the New Testament. Jesus is the first step of that final process. He came as a man for the purpose of himself taking the first journey from sin and death to resurrection and life. He became the first son, the new Adam, the beginning of the new race of men. Instead of staying in Heaven and dictating to us what we should do, he came and did it himself to make sure it got done correctly.

Jesus fulfilled the Law completely, to the letter, not only on its physical level but on its deep spiritual levels as well. Jesus took our sin on his shoulders and fell under the just condemnation of God against sinners. This removed the threat of eternal damnation from God's children. Then Jesus rose from the dead, ascended into Heaven, and took his seat (remember, still as a man!) at God's right hand. This is the blazed trail that all of God's people will eventually take themselves. Jesus paved the way for man to achieve righteousness, exaltation, and living in the presence of God forever.

He also achieved many other things than the ones we've just mentioned. For example, he is now (as a man) in the image of God, as man was supposed to be at the beginning. (Genesis 1:26-27) He fulfilled the Abrahamic Covenant, so much so that he himself is the great Heir through whom we receive the covenant blessings, if we are part of him. He is the Son of God, and so he passes on to us the same privileges of family, since we are adopted sons of God.

No wonder, then, that Jesus is so crucial to *our* salvation! He bought and inherited everything that God wanted to give us, so that he could pass it all on to us without any danger of us missing out. He makes sure, in other words, that we enjoy the same life he now has. Remember the Covenant with Abraham? God swore to uphold both sides of the Covenant; he is determined to save us, and he isn't going to allow us to fail him. So Jesus is now our elder brother who is looking out for us; he's the new Man, the second Adam, the beginning of a new race of humanity, of which we are also a part when we believe in him.

> For as in Adam all die, so in Christ all will be made alive. But each in his own turn: Christ, the firstfruits; then, when he comes, those who belong to him. (1 Corinthians 15:22-23)

> So it is written: "The first man Adam became a living being"; the last Adam, a life-giving spirit. The spiritual did not come first, but the natural, and after that the spiritual. The first man was of the dust of the earth, the second man from Heaven. As was the earthly man, so are those who are of the earth; and as is the man from Heaven, so also are those who are of Heaven. And just as we have borne the likeness of the earthly man, so shall we bear the likeness of the man from Heaven. (1 Corinthians 15:45-49)

The Mystery of the Holy Spirit

The first step of the process of actually delivering us from sin and death was to have Jesus himself grapple with those forces and get the victory over them. But it would be of no use to us if God had left things at that point. Why did Jesus need to go through all that – for his *own* sake? He was already righteous! He was already the Son of God and heir of Heaven. There was no point for him to humiliate himself at the hands of his own rebellious subjects – unless there was another goal in mind. That goal was to save *us* from our enemies.

Step two now comes in. Jesus ascended to Heaven and sat down at God's right hand. From there, according to his promise, he sends his Holy Spirit to complete the process of our salvation. What Jesus couldn't do for the whole world in person, he now does efficiently through his Spirit.

> But I tell you the truth: It is for your good that I am going away. Unless I go away, the Counselor will not

come to you; but if I go, I will send him to you. (John 16:7)

He is called the Spirit of Christ. (Philippians 1:19; 1 Peter 1:11) He brings the words, the righteousness, the power, the mind, and the very life of Christ himself inside our hearts. In fact, Paul says that Christ lives in me, through his Spirit. What happens is that, through the Spirit, we now become one with Jesus Christ and live his life.

> But because of his great love for us, God, who is rich in mercy, made us alive with Christ even when we were dead in transgressions – it is by grace you have been saved. And God raised us up with Christ and seated us with him in the Heavenly realms in Christ Jesus, in order that in the coming ages he might show the incomparable riches of his grace, expressed in his kindness to us in Christ Jesus. (Ephesians 2:4-7)

The Spirit of God is the power behind the works of God. He was there at the beginning of the world. (Genesis 1:2) He gives power to the people of God, enabling them to do miraculous things. And he gives each Christian the very life of Christ, so that they can enter the throne room of God, see the reality of Heaven, arm themselves against the forces of wickedness in the world, and prepare for their time in eternity. The Spirit is our deposit, our "first payment" on our inheritance from Heaven, to enable us to know and get ready for life with God.

That's why the Apostles keep coming back to the subject of the Spirit. Pleasing God is no longer something beyond the reach of sinners. The perfection of Jesus is a high standard, but we can attain that goal easily if we keep in step with the Spirit, are led by the Spirit, pray in the Spirit, are filled with the Spirit, exercise the gifts of the Spirit, and are filled with the fruit of the Spirit.

The shift to the spiritual

One more point about the New Testament that we have to understand. Since mankind fell into sin and death, God has been interested in rebuilding Creation – but not in the same way he did the first one. What he wants is a spiritual Kingdom now, one that will last forever. Not only does he want his subjects to have eternal life themselves, he wants righteousness to last forever. No more of this business of falling away from his Law!

During the days of the Old Testament, God used the physical creation to both work out the solution to the problems of sin and death, and teach his chosen people the answers he was forming. In other words, though he wanted a spiritual Kingdom in the long run, he put up with the physical creation and all of its limitations and problems for the time being. It was never in his mind, however, to perpetuate this first world into eternity; it was doomed from the start.

When Jesus came to work out the key link in the process of salvation, he introduced the idea that (surprise, surprise!) this physical world was doomed for destruction and he was laying the foundation for a new, spiritual, eternal world. He predicted the destruction of the Temple. He predicted the day when the sun and moon would go awry, when war and destruction would precede the end, and the Judge would come and the world would then disappear. He predicted the day when God's people would no longer go to Jerusalem and the Temple to worship – they wouldn't need that anymore.

Jesus' goal was to get the Jews used to the idea of parting with the shadows and symbols of the Old Testament system. The new has come! Let go of the blood of animals; such things can't save you; they never were intended to save you. Now is the day to become mature and live by faith, not by sight. We're going to learn how to set our hearts and minds on things above, not on things below. The light has come into the world, and he is going to show us the real world of God that the Old Testament promised us.

So during Jesus' ministry the Kingdom of God went through a transitional phase, so to speak. He worked with the Jews through physical miracles, physical events and circumstances, physical religious symbols – but only to carry them *from* there *into a new world*. One of the most striking examples of this is the story of the ten lepers. Though all ten of them were healed of their deadly disease, only one came back to praise God for his healing. In other words, *only one was spiritually healed*. But it was the spiritual healing that Christ was after!

> Jesus asked, "Were not all ten cleansed? Where are the other nine? Was no one found to return and give praise to God except this foreigner?" Then he said to him, "Rise and go; your faith has made you well." (Luke 17:17-19)

Jesus himself was still working within the physical system of the Old Testament Law and Temple. So he was careful to fulfill the whole Law, on that level as well as on the spiritual level, so that at the very least no Jew would be able to accuse him of not obeying the Law. However, there were plain statements all through the Gospels that change was in the wind.

In the book of Acts, that change becomes plainer, as Paul takes the Gospel out to the Gentiles who have no interest in obeying the Jewish Old Testament laws. And, to the Jewish Christians' consternation, Paul says that the Gentiles don't have to obey the Law! The Kingdom now is spiritual, not physical. There are some miracles done by the Apostles, but not to the extent or type that Jesus himself did in his day. But, according to Jesus' prophecy, the Apostles are actually doing greater things than he did. (John 14:12) Now that Jesus has sent his Spirit from Heaven, thousands of people are being saved from their sin (not just from disease). Thousands are becoming children of God, with inheritance rights to the treasures of God (not just with rights to attend Temple ceremonies). The unimaginable is happening as Jesus builds his spiritual house through the Apostles and the Church.

So we shouldn't be surprised at such statements that Paul makes, that there are greater works to be done in the Church than physical healings and speaking in tongues. The physical manifestations of the Spirit's work convinced the Jews that their Creator God was at work; but the results of those miracles are soon gone. However, the spiritual work of the Church – teaching the Word, love and faith, etc. – actually lay the blocks of God's future home in Heaven. And that's where God's heart is.

So, we have come full circle. God originally made man to be in full communion with him, ruling in his Name over his Kingdom, enjoying the blessings of Heaven while being human. Though we did our best to destroy all that, Jesus succeeded in restoring us to full fellowship with God, the right to commune with God and live with him, and rule his realm in his Name. The beginning of the Bible reminds us of the height we fell from, and the end of the Bible promises us the unimaginable glory of gaining back what we've lost – and then some.

Jesus Christ the New Man

Jesus Christ is so much a part of modern culture that it's difficult to think of him without a lot of historical baggage. To boil down his message in simple terms, Jesus came to save sinners from their sin – that's the primary reason he came to earth. We've built up a lot of theology around him over the centuries, and he has affected all of human history around the globe, but the long and short of it is that he came to rescue us from this world of sin and death.

The way he did it is stunningly effective. Of course the problem was to remake us so that we aren't sinners anymore. If the goal is to live with God forever in Heaven, we have to be made ready for that experience first. We can't exist in Heaven with even the slightest inclination to sin. And the first step is to change our hearts so that we don't even want to sin anymore, as well as get rid of the stain of sin from our past. But instead of waving a magic wand over each of us as we pass through the gates of Heaven, he chose to become one of us and, so to speak, carry us to Heaven on his own shoulders. We learn the true meaning of love by the way Jesus came to save us.

We *are* going to be changed, to be remade, to be made new creatures fit to live with a perfect God in a holy Temple – but our path leads through the life of Christ who, as a man, first walked that path himself. Our salvation rests solidly in Jesus.

Made through Christ

The first step to fixing the world, believe it or not, was to make it a certain way. If an engineer wants to be able to quickly probe his machine when it breaks down and fix things, he is going to design it in a way that lets him into it easily and gives him the most freedom to repair what is broken. In the same way, God made the world through Christ, and he created it in a *certain way* – it is wide open to the hand of Christ to allow him the freedom to change, fix, dispose of, or correct anything in it. He has total control over the world because he *made* it to be under his control.

The world was actually made *through* Christ; it exists day by day because of his direct, constant action upon it. In other words, he himself made the world in the beginning; it's his special creation, the work of his hands. And he made it in such a way that it depends completely on his daily care for it. Without his constant attention to its affairs, the world would cease to exist.

From the very beginning, Christ has maintained a rigid hold on the universe that it can't escape. In fact, that explains why the universe is still running exactly according to God's original plans. Christ rules over the universe with intimate knowledge of every detail, with full responsibility for its progress, with full power to direct everything according to his will. Earthly kings can't possibly attend to every detail of their kingdom, nor can they directly affect every circumstance in the life of each subject in the kingdom. Christ, however, can and does work at that level throughout his kingdom. He determines when and where people will live (Acts 17:26), he gives them the food they eat every day, he leads them daily through circumstances of his own choosing. Through his wisdom and power he maintains complete control; the "command" aspect of Creation insures that.

Hebrews tells us the unique relationship that Christ has with the Father:

> In the past God spoke to our forefathers through the prophets at many times and in various ways, but in these last days he has spoken to us by his Son, whom he appointed heir of all things, and through whom he made the universe. The Son is the radiance of God's glory and the exact representation of his being, sustaining all things by his powerful Word. (Hebrews 1:1-3)

Jesus Christ represents his Father's interests on earth. God gave him a job at the beginning of Creation, a charge to accomplish by the end of time:

> *First*, the way that God makes himself known to his creatures is by means of Christ. Since none of us can see God directly, we instead look at Christ to learn about God. He is the manifestation of God, the fullness of God in the flesh, the way we learn about God. In him we learn the character of God. By his actions we understand the works of God. He's an accommodation to our limitations, so to speak, since unless God revealed himself in this way to us we would never know God.
>
> > ... God, the blessed and only Ruler, the King of kings and Lord of lords, who alone is immortal and who lives in unapproachable light, whom no one has seen or can see. (1 Timothy 6:15-16)
>
> So, since God himself is unapproachable, Christ is the special way that God has provided for us to know him: we *can* approach Jesus, hear him speak, touch him, and know through him that God exists:
>
> > That which was from the beginning, which we have heard, which we have seen with our eyes, which we have looked at and our hands have touched — this we proclaim concerning the Word of life. The life appeared; we have seen it and testify to it, and we proclaim to you the eternal life, which was with the Father and has appeared to us. We proclaim to you what we have seen and heard, so that you also may have fellowship with us. (1 John 1:1-3)
>
> *Second*, God made the universe *through Christ*. This was to be Christ's Kingdom, and *he* will be its absolute

ruler. We can better understand this if we think about a new market that a business wants to get into. The board of the company will assign a certain department head to lead the new project: it will be up to him to hire new employees, buy the supplies needed, set up the production line, set the schedule, take care of the finances, and make regular progress reports back to the board. In short, he's responsible to make a profit – using the resources of the company, with the board's blessing, acting in the name and authority of the board but doing the work himself.

In Psalm 2 we read about this same kind of business transaction when God turned over this new Kingdom of Creation to the Son, for him to manage and build up:

> I have installed my King
>   on Zion, my holy hill.
> I will proclaim the decree of the LORD:
> He said to me, "You are my Son;
>   today I have become your Father.
> Ask of me, and I will make the nations your inheritance,
>   the ends of the earth your possession.
> You will rule them with an iron scepter;
>   you will dash them to pieces like pottery." (Psalm 2:6-9)

Notice the degree of control that the Son has over his Kingdom: even rebellion by the kings of the earth is useless, because he intends to rule over all with an iron scepter – nobody can resist his will. This is *his* world now.

Third, God made Christ the heir of all things. It all belongs to him to do as he pleases. He especially proves his ownership in what he is *able* to do with it. Ownership isn't just a matter of possession for him, as it is for us; the entire world lays bare under his hand, under his scrutiny, and he uses it to serve his purposes. He speaks and it obeys, instantly, and does whatever he demands of it. For instance, a dog will obey its master but it will ignore a stranger. In the same way, the universe responds immediately to Christ's word of power. He wields *miraculous* power over his kingdom. Since every part of the universe lies open to his power, it's clear who is the Master and who is the subject; he proves his authority by his power.

Fourth, Christ sustains the universe through his Word. The same Word that created the universe supports it and keeps it going day by day. The power of that Word is illustrated in the fact that, unknown to them, and in spite of their disobedient hearts, people and nations nevertheless end up doing exactly what the Master wants from them all through history. "For he must reign until he has put all his enemies under his feet." (1 Corinthians 15:25) His Word is that of a King; he commands, and his subjects *must* obey. But what he is making out of all this is a well-balanced kingdom: in the end, when it's all over, he will be pleased with the results and he will then turn everything over to the Father.

The point in Hebrews 1:1-3 is that, from the very beginning, Christ has been the head of the universe; God relates to his Creation at all times and in every way *through* the powerful and effective administration of Christ.

Other Scriptural testimony teaches the same truth.

In the beginning was the Word, and the Word was with God, and the Word was God. He was with God in the beginning. *Through him* all things were made; without him nothing was made that has been made ... He was in the world, and though the world was made *through him*, the world did not recognize him. (John 1:1-3, 10)

> ... yet for us there is but one God, the Father, from whom all things came and for whom we live; and there is but one Lord, Jesus Christ, *through whom all things came* and *through whom we live*. (1 Corinthians 8:6)

> For *by him* all things were created: things in Heaven and on earth, visible and invisible, whether thrones or powers or rulers or authorities; all things were created *by him* and *for him*. He is before all things, and *in him* all things hold together. (Colossians 1:16-17)

But even the Old Testament only gave hints about this King, so that when Paul writes about him he calls Jesus the "mystery of God." It wasn't made plain that Jesus himself was the Master of the world until he came in the flesh "to his own" – when he came into his Kingdom in the same outward form as his subjects.

> He was in the world, and though the world was made through him, the world did not recognize him. He came to that which was his own, but his own did not receive him. (John 1:10-11)

Over time, especially after the resurrection when they finally understood the true nature of Christ, the Apostles saw *the Creator* in Jesus. They wrote their Gospels reminiscing about the *kind* of work that Christ did among them – a work that no one except the King could do.

- Only the **Creator** of the world could do miracles. The kinds of things that Jesus did reflected not only the same kind of work that happened at Creation, but in the same *way* that it was done. For example, he created enough bread and fish to feed thousands of people immediately – out of basically *nothing*. There just wasn't a natural explanation for how he did such a thing. And he brought the dead back to life with a *command* – remember the original Commands of Creation in which something that couldn't obey God found power in his Word to obey his wish? He *cursed* the fig tree, and *blessed* the food he used to feed the crowds, both acts in which his Word had power in itself to either kill or proliferate – again, the same kind of work that God did in the beginning.

- Only the **King**, through whom the world was made, could speak with such authority and wisdom. The people were astonished at his teaching, because he spoke with an authority that ordinary teachers didn't have:

> When Jesus had finished saying these things, the crowds were amazed at his teaching, because he taught as one who had authority, and not as their teachers of the law. (Matthew 7:28-29)

That authority had power and conviction to it; his words stab the conscience, so that we know we are in the presence of the One to whom we must give account of ourselves. We belong to him; that's why he has the right to challenge our actions, and why we know that we must do as *he* says, since he's the Lord of all.

- Only the **Lawgiver** could rightfully expect such complete obedience from men. Our obedience isn't allowed to be superficial because Christ's realm, and the depth to which he reaches in our hearts, isn't superficial. An ordinary ruler can only hope to make our outward actions conform to his laws; but Christ, who rules all of Creation with infinite precision, requires obedience from the heart. His Sermon on the Mount is an excellent analysis of how far-reaching his realm is over men. "Surely you desire truth in the inner parts; you teach me wisdom in the inmost place." (Psalm 51:6)

The Creator leads the way

There are two reasons that it's necessary that Christ be the Creator. **First**, he has to have such power and authority over the first

Creation that he can destroy sin and its effects. "The reason the Son of God appeared was to destroy the devil's work." (1 John 3:8) And that's exactly what we see in his ministry, as he tackled sin and its destruction head on. He has the authority to name sin and rebuke it; he undoes the effects of sin – misery, destruction and death; and he lays the ax at the root of sin so that it can't continue to destroy his people. For such work he needs absolute power and authority, as he claimed several times:

> All authority in Heaven and on earth has been given to me. (Matthew 28:18)

> But take heart! I have overcome the world. (John 16:33)

This is what we saw before about the Creator being able to fix his creation. He certainly wouldn't have made a universe that he had no control over, and no ability to repair. If that were true, he could only sit by the side helplessly as his beautiful world spun off in chaos and fell to pieces with no hope of redemption! But the Creator does all things in wisdom, including building in safeguards and openness so that the world will *never* slip out of his control. He's working right now to overcome man's ruin, step by step, doing his work with precision and perfection. On Judgment Day he will be finished bringing the world back into perfect alignment to his specifications.

Second, and this is the amazing part, *Jesus himself* will lead the first Creation through death and resurrection into the second Creation. The first Creation is doomed to destruction, because of the sin and death that entered the world at the beginning. We need a new model, a new world, and a new nature because the old nature is no good anymore. And we would have expected God to just wave his hand over the world and cure its ills miraculously. But our God is full of surprises, and his answers not only fix the problem but lift us up higher than we thought imaginable. God's solution was to make Jesus a man (that brings us into the picture) and then lift him up (along with us) above the first creation to sit at his right hand, to rule the universe.

We know what *we* will be in eternity by looking at what Jesus is *now,* after his resurrection from the dead and ascension into Heaven.

> Blessed and holy are those who have part in the first resurrection. The second death has no power over them, but they will be priests of God and of Christ and will reign with him for a thousand years. (Revelation 20:6)

The world itself, as well as the sons of God, wait for the day when the old Creation will be shaken out (Hebrews 12:26-27) and we will be made new – in the image of the Son of God who rose from the dead as a spiritual man:

> The creation waits in eager expectation for the sons of God to be revealed. For the creation was subjected to frustration, not by its own choice, but by the will of the one who subjected it, in hope that the creation itself will be liberated from its bondage to decay and brought into the glorious freedom of the children of God. We know that the whole creation has been groaning as in the pains of childbirth right up to the present time. Not only so, but we ourselves, who have the firstfruits of the Spirit, groan inwardly as we wait eagerly for our adoption as sons, the redemption of our bodies. For in this hope we were saved. (Romans 8:19-24)

> For since death came through a man, the resurrection of the dead comes also through a man. For as in Adam all die, so in Christ all will be made alive. But each in his own turn: Christ, the firstfruits; then, when he comes, those who belong to him. (1 Corinthians 15:21-23)

And in what Paul calls a mystery, Christ represents in his own body the passage of the first Creation to the second Creation. Rather than destroy the world and be done with the mess once for all, God wants to undo the damage by resurrection. But rather than entrust the job to someone else (least of all to us, who were responsible for the mess in the first place!) Christ himself will shoulder the world and carry it into judgment and death, and lift it up into life and eternity. God became man, and as man walked back into Heaven in victory. By himself carrying the old world into the new, he redeemed the world in a way that the process could not fail.

> Although he was a son, he learned obedience from what he suffered and, once made perfect, he became the source of eternal salvation for all who obey him. (Hebrews 5:8)

The first physical kingdom will change into a new spiritual kingdom; that new life is what we will be like, if we join ourselves to him. So, he became one with us physically so that we could become one with him spiritually.

> Since the children have flesh and blood, he too shared in their humanity so that by his death he might destroy him who holds the power of death — that is, the devil — and free those who all their lives were held in slavery by their fear of death.(Hebrews 2:14-15)

> So will it be with the resurrection of the dead. The body that is sown is perishable, it is raised imperishable; it is sown in dishonor, it is raised in glory; it is sown in weakness, it is raised in power; it is sown a natural body, it is raised a spiritual body. If there is a natural body, there is also a spiritual body. So it is written: "The first man Adam became a living being"; the last Adam, a life-giving spirit. The spiritual did not come first, but the natural, and after that the spiritual. The first man was of the dust of the earth, the second man from Heaven. As was the earthly man, so are those who are of the earth; and as is the man from Heaven, so also are those who are of Heaven. And just as we have borne the likeness of the earthly man, so shall we bear the likeness of the man from Heaven. (1 Corinthians 15:42-49)

The job that the Father assigned to Christ was to address the problems that we aren't able to solve. Matters like sin and death, righteousness, judgment, resurrection from the dead, our calling in life under God the King, our spiritual inheritance. We have been making a mess of things, going from bad to worse. Nobody has been able to cure the ills of man, nor have we been able to get anywhere with being reconciled with God or our rebellious hearts. Jesus had a lot to take care of when he came here! But he managed to succeed completely where we have failed. Now a man has addressed each of these issues and more, and secured our salvation so completely that God is ready, so to speak, to bargain about the rest of us. Jesus has cleansed the human soul, he has found the path of life, and he has made it possible for any who want to follow him to also end up in Heaven. Now the stage is set and all owe have to do is follow.

This great work of the Redeemer blazing a trail to Heaven for us wasn't a last-minute solution to sin, as if our rebellion caught God off-guard and he hurriedly put together a remedy for the damage we had done. God isn't caught off-guard by anything that we do. He knows from the beginning how things will end; he planned his works of salvation before even the world was created. Therefore Creation itself was the first step to an overall plan which included Christ's physical life, death, resurrection, and our union with him to form a Second Creation.

> He was chosen before the creation of the world, but was revealed in these last times for your sake. (1 Peter 1:20)

> ... the Lamb that was slain from the creation of the world. (Revelation 13:8)

To summarize, the world was made *through Christ* because, **first**, it must be totally under his control. **Second**, he intends to destroy it completely, because as it stands – under the effects of sin and death – it can't continue on into eternity in God's plans, nor can it contribute anything of value to a new, eternal, spiritual kingdom. **Third**, when the time is ripe (and in himself he already took the first step) he will do away with the physical creation that we are familiar with and replace it with a perfect spiritual Kingdom. The universe then is a kingdom in which Christ is working out his own agenda, from beginning to end.

Fulfillment of the Covenant

Remember that the Covenant was given to Abraham and his Seed. At the time, Abraham and the Israelites understood this to mean the physical descendants of Abraham. This was an critical issue to them, because in a legal situation in which one is trying to find the heirs of an inheritance, it's very important who the will actually spells out as the legal heirs. In this case, there's a lot of property and rights involved – the rights to eternal life!

Paul lets us in on a secret, however, about the legal heir that God had in mind. It's not the Israelites after all – but one Israelite in particular:

> Brothers, let me take an example from everyday life. Just as no one can set aside or add to a human covenant that has been duly established, so it is in this case. The promises were spoken to Abraham and to his seed. The Scripture does not say "and to seeds," meaning many people, but "and to your seed," meaning one person, who is Christ. (Galatians 3:15-16)

There's a good reason for this. We saw already that the Covenant actually deals with spiritual realities, not just the physical object lessons that the Israelites first enjoyed. We're dealing with matters of the soul here: a real cleansing of the heart through the blood of Christ; eternal life with God in Heaven, not just a good life in Canaan. Since the full inheritance deals with these things, Abraham needed an heir who could handle them – and only Jesus Christ qualifies. Not only is he legally a physical descendant of Abraham, but he is the Son of God as well – which puts him in touch with the resources and power of Heaven. He has the right and power to deal with the realities of God's spiritual world. He can do miracles here, pushing aside the limitations of this world to bring about God's eternal purposes in our lives. In other words, he can do the impossible.

Abraham himself knew that the Covenant consisted of more than just the Temple in Jerusalem, and land claims in Palestine. He knew that the sacrificial system of the Temple wouldn't cure the human heart of its sin and rebellion. The Israelites didn't always know this, but their forefather did!

> Your father Abraham rejoiced at the thought of seeing my day; he saw it and was glad. (John 8:56)

The Lord essentially promised Abraham that he would one day have an heir capable of handling the precious inheritance of the Covenant, in a way that all of the children of Abraham would be able to get the full benefit of that Covenant. This is going to take a capable "executor of the will."

If you know anything about wills and inheritance, one person is usually designated the executor of the will. He or she is responsible to see that the terms of the will are carried out. They are the legal representative of the deceased; if anybody has any questions about the will or its terms, they have to see the executor about it. And the executor (at least in Biblical days, because he was usually the first-born son in the family) would be charged with carrying on the deceased person's business and personal affairs. Often the well-being of the servants, family members, business and possessions were solely in the hands of the executor.

This is exactly the situation we have in Christ. He has been designated the executor of Abraham's inheritance (just as Isaac, the "miracle baby," was the executor of Abraham's physical estate). If anybody is interested in the Covenant with Abraham, they must first go through Jesus – Abraham's legal representative. Furthermore, Jesus is in charge of Abraham's family and is charged with their well-being.

> In bringing many sons to glory, it was fitting that God, for whom and through whom everything exists, should make the author of their salvation perfect through suffering. Both the one who makes men holy and those who are made holy are of the same family. So Jesus is not ashamed to call them brothers. He

says, "I will declare your name to my brothers; in the presence of the congregation I will sing your praises." And again, "I will put my trust in him." And again he says, "Here am I, and the children God has given me." Since the children have flesh and blood, he too shared in their humanity so that by his death he might destroy him who holds the power of death – that is, the devil – and free those who all their lives were held in slavery by their fear of death. For surely it is not angels he helps, but Abraham's descendants. For this reason he had to be made like his brothers in every way, in order that he might become a merciful and faithful high priest in service to God, and that he might make atonement for the sins of the people. Because he himself suffered when he was tempted, he is able to help those who are being tempted. (Hebrews 2:10-18)

And Jesus is certainly able to pick up the "family business" (the Covenant was given to Abraham in the first place as a way to *save sinners*) and see it through to the end, like no other descendant of Abraham could. Being the Son of God as well, he has the wisdom, authority, and power to completely fulfill every single term of the Covenant, to God's original purpose and satisfaction, for anybody who comes to be saved. There is no case too hard for him. And he faithfully carries out his responsibilities as Abraham's heir to the extent that nobody will be able to complain that he was not willing to do his job, or that he was unable to do his job:

I am the bread of life. He who comes to me will never go hungry, and he who believes in me will never be thirsty. But as I told you, you have seen me and still you do not believe. All that the Father gives me will come to me, and whoever comes to me I will never drive away. For I have come down from Heaven not to do my will but to do the will of him who sent me. And this is the will of him who sent me, that I shall lose none of all that he has given me, but raise them up at the last day. For my Father's will is that everyone who looks to the Son and believes in him shall have eternal life, and I will raise him up at the last day. (John 6:35-40)

Now that we know who the executor is, how do *we* get in on this Covenant? The executor is charged to make sure that the inheritance is given only to the rightful heirs. Now this is the tricky part. The Jews thought that physical circumcision bought them the right to be heirs of the Covenant, based on this passage:

> This is my covenant with you and your descendants after you, the covenant you are to keep: Every male among you shall be circumcised. You are to undergo circumcision, and it will be the sign of the covenant between me and you. (Genesis 17:10-11)

What they didn't understand was that this circumcision is a sign that they *were* heirs of the Covenant, not that circumcision *made* them heirs. Plus, the Israelites typically missed the point again about symbol and reality by confusing physical circumcision with what it symbolized:

> Circumcise your hearts, therefore, and do not be stiff-necked any longer. (Deuteronomy 10:16)

> The LORD your God will circumcise your hearts and the hearts of your descendants, so that you may love him with all your heart and with all your soul, and live. (Deuteronomy 30:6)

The lesson is this: *if* they qualified as heirs (that is, they were physically descended from Abraham) then they could take on the sign of that right (circumcision) and act like it (live in righteousness).

But, even the fact of being physically descended from Abraham was a symbol of a spiritual reality. If the Covenant was only intended for Jews, then no Gentile would ever have the rights of a descendant – which means non-Jews would never be saved! This was not God's intention; from the very beginning, he had plans to include Gentiles alongside Jews in the Church of Christ.

> All peoples on earth will be blessed through you. (Genesis 12:3)

> Abraham will surely become a great and powerful nation, and all nations on earth will be blessed through him. (Genesis 18:18)

You can usually tell when someone is a son or daughter of another person by certain family characteristics. The color of their hair, unique mannerisms or habits, the way they talk, and so on. In Abraham's family there's a family characteristic that is common among all the children, no matter what race they are a part of or where or when they live: they all have Abraham's faith:

> And he is also the father of the circumcised who not only are circumcised but who also walk in the footsteps of the faith that our father Abraham had before he was circumcised ... Therefore, the promise comes by faith, so that it may be by grace and may be guaranteed to all Abraham's offspring – not only to those who are of the law but also to those who are of the faith of Abraham. He is the father of us all. As it is written: "I have made you a father of many nations." He is our father in the sight of God, in whom he believed – the God who gives life to the dead and calls things that are not as though they were. Against all hope, Abraham in hope believed and so became the father of many nations, just as it had been said to him, "So shall your offspring be." (Romans 4:12, 16-18)

This is our hope in the Covenant. If we have the faith of Abraham (a certain kind of faith, not what most people think it is! See Romans 4 and Genesis 12-17 for a detailed explanation of this faith) then we prove that we are his spiritual children. And if we are his children, we have full rights to the inheritance. Or, to say it the same way that it applied to the Israelites, if we are heirs (one with Christ) then we take on the sign of that right (a circumcised heart) and we will live like it (in righteousness). Note, however, that the Israelites were bound to *make* it happen, whereas it naturally happens for us through the power of the Spirit working it in us.

That's a big "if." How do we get this faith that we need? We find out from Paul that it's a gift from God, given to us when we are first brought to Christ for salvation:

> For it is by grace you have been saved, through faith – and this not from yourselves, it is the gift of God. (Ephesians 2:8)

When we hear the Gospel of Christ, the Spirit opens our eyes and hearts and we see Jesus, our salvation from sin and death and our only hope for eternal life. We see our great need of him, and we reach out to take what God so freely offers us in Jesus. In that moment, in the enlightenment of the soul and the will and power to take what Jesus gives us, we become new-born into the family of God. We are now awake to God, to spiritual realities, to the inheritance of Heaven. We can hear God speaking to us now.

This is the same enlightenment that our father Abraham had when God first promised him the Covenant:

> Then the word of the LORD came to him: "This man will not be your heir, but a son coming from your own body will be your heir." He took him outside and said, "Look up at the Heavens and count the stars – if indeed you can count them." Then he said to him, "So shall your offspring be." Abram believed the LORD, and he credited it to him as righteousness. (Genesis 15:4-6)

And in a mystery that only God understands, but that we enjoy the benefits of, God makes us one with the great Heir of the Covenant through our faith in him:

> The body is a unit, though it is made up of many parts; and though all its parts are many, they form one body. So it is with Christ. For we were all baptized by

one Spirit into one body – whether Jews or Greeks, slave or free – and we were all given the one Spirit to drink. (1 Corinthians 12:12-13)

Now we're in. We become one with Christ, with the heir himself. This mystical union through his Spirit puts us in a unique position: whatever happens to Christ, happens to us also. This means that if he is the heir of the Covenant, then so are we.

You are all sons of God through faith in Christ Jesus, for all of you who were baptized into Christ have clothed yourselves with Christ. There is neither Jew nor Greek, slave nor free, male nor female, for you are all one in Christ Jesus. If you belong to Christ, then you are Abraham's seed, and heirs according to the promise. (Galatians 3:26-29)

There's a powerful example of the covenant and the legal requirements for claiming its blessings in an incident in Christ's ministry. When Jesus was done preaching in a certain area of Galilee, he left there and went to non-Jewish territory — the area of Tyre and Sidon. While there, a Canaanite woman (non-Jewish, in other words) came to him and pleaded with him to heal her demon-possessed daughter. Jesus refused to talk to her.

This is so out of character for him that it surprises us at first. Why didn't the one who loved sinners respond to her? The man who rescued the woman caught in adultery, who ate at the houses of tax collectors and sinners, who offered the water of life to a sinful Samaritan woman, wouldn't even talk to this Canaanite woman. Why not?

The woman wouldn't give up, however; she evidently made a pest of herself to the point that his disciples pleaded with him to at least send her away. His response was even harsher than his silence:

I was sent only to the lost sheep of Israel. (Matthew 15:24)

Finally the woman came to him and knelt before him, pleading with him for help. Then he says the most startling thing of all — an outright insult!

> It is not right to take the children's bread and toss it to their dogs. (Matthew 15:26)

Where is the famous love of Christ?! To unravel this mystery, we have to go back to the terms of the covenant that Abraham received from God. We have to keep in mind this one important fact: everything that Jesus is, everything he came to do, was *in fulfillment of the covenant to Abraham.* God had the gospel in mind, in other words, when he made those promises to Abraham. The promises weren't limited to physical fulfillments but all the spiritual richness that is in Jesus Christ.

Second, remember that the covenant was given to Abraham and his *legal descendants* — nobody else had any right to them. God bound himself with an oath, with the threat of death, to keep this covenant with Abraham's family.

So when this woman asked for something from Jesus, *he had to refuse her* on the basis of the legality of the thing. She was asking for one of the blessings in the covenant, something that she had no rights to, and he had no right to give her. If he had just given her what she wanted, he would have broken the terms of the covenant and every Jew in Palestine could have justly cried out for God's blood! But the covenant was a precious thing to God, and Jesus was not about to compromise any of God's promises. His refusal was no less than him giving honor to the promise that God made to Abraham and his seed.

And there's where the story starts to break open. *Who* are Abraham's heirs? Notice what the woman says next:

> "Yes, Lord," she said, "but even the dogs eat the crumbs that fall from the master's table." (Matthew 15:27)

That statement was like a brilliant spotlight out of Heaven that revealed the true nature of this woman's heart. Here was the *same faith* that moved Abraham to believe in the promises of God. Jesus recognized it immediately: "Woman, you have great faith! Your request is granted." (Matthew 15:28) She saw the Master, she saw her own heart, she saw the precious value in everything that Jesus did, she saw the inclusion of the Gentiles in the Covenant. In other words, it turned out that here was one of the children of Abraham, not born by physical descent but by spiritual descent from her spiritual father. Because she had *the faith of her father Abraham*, she was an heir of all the promises of the covenant and could rightfully lay claim to any of them — which is exactly what she was doing here.

Jesus granted her request on that basis — legally she had the right to claim something from the Son of God, and legally he had the duty to give it to her. He could not deny her. Until she proved her claim, he was under no obligation to do anything for her; but once she provided proof of her family relationship, he willingly gave her what rightfully belongs only to the children of Abraham.

The switch from physical to spiritual

What confused the Jews the most about Christ was that he was introducing them to a new spiritual Kingdom. They had expected God to preserve, continue, and yes perhaps fix the old physical system that they were so used to. After all, the Temple and its sacrificial system appeared to be working fine after 1500 years, and they saw no reason to introduce anything new. But they missed the point of the old system.

What they didn't understand was that the Old Testament system was *designed* to be replaced, right from the very beginning. Some of their own Scriptures taught this:

> The LORD your God will circumcise your hearts and the hearts of your descendants, so that you may love him with all your heart and with all your soul, and live. (Deuteronomy 30:6)

One of the most physical acts commanded in the Law of Moses was the circumcision of infant Jewish boys; anybody not circumcised had no part in the covenant of Abraham, and had to be thrown out of the community of the people of God. Yet this passage points to what really needs to be circumcised – it's not the cutting of flesh that will make us holy, but cutting sin out of the heart. The Old Testament law was only symbolic of the spiritual reality that God was primarily interested in.

In fact, the entire Old Testament deals with the physical with an eye toward the ultimate spiritual world of Christ's making. During the Old Testament days, the physical takes prominence; there is where God worked with his people, so that they could follow what he was doing and learn the appropriate lessons. The spiritual was there in the background, but only showed between the cracks here and there, so to speak. Here is a diagram showing the two levels of the Old Testament and New Testament.

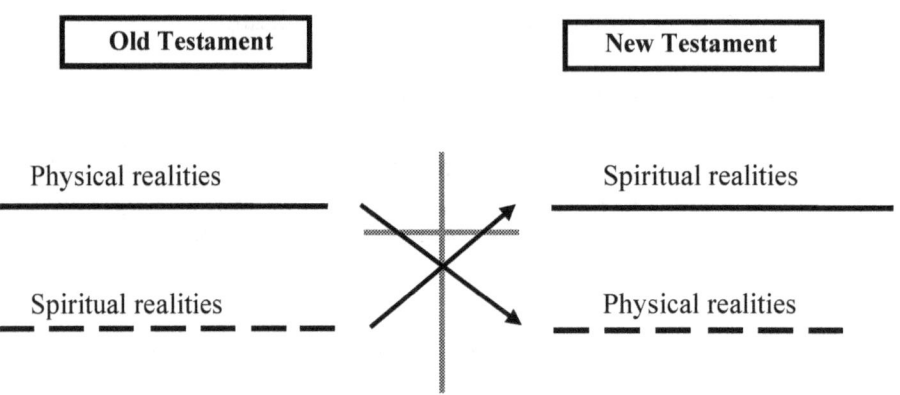

When we get to the New Testament, however, the levels switch. The physical level takes a background position while the spiritual takes prominence. Let's look at some examples.

The Old Testament dealt with physical realities, mainly because this is an easy way to start learning about God. They learned, for instance, these things:

The Creator – God created the physical world, and there are "footprints" that he left behind that tell us some important things about him. He is **wise** to be able to create such a perfect and well-balanced world. He is **powerful** enough to create the universe, and that simply by speaking it into existence. He is the **King** because he created a kingdom full of subjects, well-ordered and designed to serve his purposes. He **cares** about his creation, since he fulfills their needs daily and abundantly.

Death – God made a perfect world for man to live in, but Adam and Eve didn't want to serve God; they wanted to satisfy their own lusts in violation of God's Law. God, of course, being the King that he was, couldn't let this go unnoticed. He condemned humanity to death for its rebellion against him. We know by the context that he imposed a spiritual death upon us by his separating man from access to God and eternal life. But the physical repercussions from God's edict of death have been staggering. Death comes to every human being, and in many forms. Not only do our bodies die and return to the dust, but life is full of disease, suffering, trials, adverse circumstances, wars, jealousy, rage, robbery, setbacks, disappointments, loss of property, emptiness, loneliness – a huge list of failures and painful experiences that are all part of the curse upon mankind.

The Temple – Here is where we learn about God's solution for man's problem. But it's going to be a bloody solution. Someone (or something) has to die for the sin of man. But at least it doesn't have to be God's people! They can present an animal as a substitute to die in their place, and God will accept that death as payment for sin.

Abraham – The Lord made a covenant with Abraham and his children, an agreement that would reverse the curse of death and bless God's people abundantly. Abraham in his own day tasted the fruit of this covenant in having a son born to him, and enjoying the land (at least partially) that was promised to him.

David – When Saul had done as much damage as he could to the cause of the Lord in Israel, and the nation was in abject misery, the Lord chose David to lead the Israelites out of their troubles and into the most powerful and glorious stage of their history. He eliminated their enemies, created and strengthened the government, and laid plans for the Temple that would focus the nation's life around the presence of God.

The Exile – God will put up with rebellion against his rule for only so long, and then he has to do something about it, if for no other reason than his own credibility and glory. He finally, after the Israelites had ignored his warnings through the Prophets to reform, sent the Assyrians and Babylonians to destroy the land – including the precious Temple. And the people of God went into Exile to a foreign land so that the land of Canaan would have a rest.

These are some of the highlights of the Old Testament. Each one deals with issues on a physical level. Compare them with the issues of the New Testament:

The New Creation – In order to fix the problems of the first Creation (due entirely to sin), Christ is going to do away with it and build a new world. The new world of his spiritual Kingdom won't decay, fall apart, or fail like the first one did. It will be a spiritual world, not a physical one. And the people living in it will be remade also – they will no longer sin against God. They won't even think about it! They will have new hearts that love God, and they will be willing and able to serve God forever. The whole thing, of course, rests on the person and work of Christ who can't fail. Build the house on an immovable rock, and the house becomes immovable.

Death and life – Adam and Eve lost their lives when they sinned against God. Their bodies eventually died; but their souls died immediately. We learn this through the account of God putting a barrier between himself and man, a barrier so complete that nobody has ever known God apart from the revelations of himself that God has made through history. But in the new Creation there will be life like no human has ever experienced. We will experience God himself, with no created thing between us. We will hear his voice, we will see him in his pure glory, and we will feel his hand upon us giving us his life. This is what man was designed for, but now we will live *with* God in Heaven instead of living under his rule on earth.

The Temple – Jesus predicted the day when the Temple in Jerusalem would be destroyed. But he didn't seem too worried about it, because he also taught that God wants his people to worship him in Spirit and in truth – not in Jerusalem! Christians all around the world will learn the skill of approaching the throne of grace in Heaven, through the blood of Christ, through the veil that Christ tore aside for us.

The King – David ruled over the Israelites in Palestine, but Jesus (the son of David) rules over his people no matter where they live. His body consists of believers all around the world; he rules by means of his Word and his Spirit. His government rules the heart and mind, not just the actions of the body.

The Covenant – Even Abraham knew that the real fulfillment of the Covenant would be in Christ. It's not as important who inherits the land of Palestine now, but who inherits Heaven. It's not Isaac who inherits the Kingdom of Heaven, but Jesus – and anybody who is one with Christ is also an heir of this same Kingdom.

These are spiritual issues. There's very little evidence of such things in the physical world; we know they are real, and we deal with this kind of currency, through faith, not by sight. Unbelievers think that there are no such things as God, the Covenant, the Spirit, the new Creation, and so on. But believers know they are real because the Holy Spirit has opened our eyes of faith to them. A Christian would rather have the treasures of Heaven than any amount of treasure on earth – a crazy notion to those who can't see Heaven!

What's more important to recognize is that the Jews themselves think that Christians are out of their minds. They still think that their religion consists of physical, material things of this world; they can't see the spiritual world of God that the New Testament describes. You can tell that they are still operating on the Old Testament physical level when you read their sacred literature – the Mishnah and the Talmud.

One aspect of Jesus' mission was to turn or pivot this great Old Testament system around into a spiritual direction. As Paul says –

> Therefore, if anyone is in Christ, he is a new creation; the old has gone, the new has come! (2 Corinthians 5:17)

To do this, he taught on two levels for a while. To the Jews, he did physical miracles and addressed the physical system of the Old Testament. He spoke of the Temple and sacrifice; he fed bread to thousands; he healed the sick and rebuked the Pharisees for not keeping the "weightier matters of the Law." He did this to show that he had the authority to speak of such things, but also the mission to address the weaknesses of that system. He came to change it, and he had to explain to them why it must be changed. To replace the physical Old Testament system he introduced his new spiritual Kingdom. It would be a rule over the heart, governing the "thoughts and attitudes of the heart." The sacrifice for sin would be his own blood, but also the service that God's people would offer to God of their very lives. Repentance doesn't consist of outward prayers and sacrifices, but what comes out of a broken heart before the Lord in secret.

And to emphasize the fact that the day had come to dispense with the old and bring in the new, Jesus sent his Spirit upon his disciples and launched a world wide church. This body of believers would consist of spiritual children (not physical descendants) of Abraham, who had the faith of Abraham. They would have new hearts which would enable them to satisfy the Law's strict demands much more effectively than the Jews themselves could do it. They would worship God wherever they lived, through the Spirit bringing them before God in Heaven. The miracles would go on in Jesus' Kingdom, but now they will be building a spiritual house, not a physical house. Jesus has little use for physical shows of power in a kingdom that consists of hearts reborn, service to God in Heaven, fighting against spiritual enemies, and laying hold of treasures in Heaven. This is, in fact, what he meant when he promised his disciples that they would do greater things than he did. They would be working on a spiritual, eternal Kingdom, solving problems that all of history hasn't been able to address before now.

The new Kingdom

Remember the message of the Prophets? They mourned the long centuries of Israel trying to keep the Law of Moses and failing miserably. The Jews never did get the point that they were supposed to approach the physical shadows and lessons through faith, that the physical realities symbolized the deeper spiritual world of God in which one should hope. When people get so fixed on the shadows and symbols instead of the God they symbolize, they aren't saved – it's that simple. The Prophets shook their heads, so to speak, over the ignorant Jews and longed for the kind of kingdom that would save the soul. They longed for the real kingdom that the shadows promised. The time had come for God's eternal Kingdom to enter into human history.

So what Jesus introduced was the first step toward realizing a religion that is real. He took those first steps in real righteousness that the Law could only long for in a man, and that no man until him had done. He made his peace with God, he loved God and man as the Law required, he set up the foundations of the kind of kingdom that would last forever, and that would completely satisfy the soul that longs for a restored relationship with God. This was the day that the Prophets spoke of when they said:

Behold, I will create new Heavens and a new earth. The former things will not be remembered, nor will they come to mind. (Isaiah 65:17)

The Apostles

The coming of Christ was an event that demanded to be witnessed; it could not have happened in obscurity without someone being there to see it. When royalty goes somewhere – since they are not commoners – everything they do has great significance for the kingdom, even if they just want to get away for a vacation! When Jesus came, it wasn't just a visit – it was the greatest and potentially the most explosive event in the history of the universe!

The problem, however, is that he came almost incognito. Almost nobody knew who he really was. He set aside his glory that he had with the Father in Heaven, and "being made in human likeness" (Philippians 2:7) became one of us: the son of a poor carpenter in an obscure village in Palestine. He did this for a reason, of course: he didn't want to make a physical show of who he was; he wanted us to grasp his greatness by faith, not by sight.

The apostles were witnesses of the life and ministry of Christ. They lived with him, worked with him, listened to him, and watched him as he taught and worked miracles through the countryside. At the time they probably didn't realize the important role they would play in the Church; but actually they were witnesses of the true nature of the Messiah. While everyone else was wondering who Jesus was, the disciples were given a clear vision. For them the mystery was swept aside and they saw his glory.

The definition of the world *apostle* is "the one sent out." But if we use just this definition, then many teachers in the Church today might feel that they are also apostles – which some do. But the Scripture adds another dimension to the definition. Since Judas had betrayed the Lord and killed himself, the rest of the disciples decided to choose another man to take his place. They laid down a certain qualification, however, for an apostle – whoever was chosen *had* to be a witness of Christ's life and ministry.

> Therefore it is necessary to choose one of the men who have been with us the whole time the Lord Jesus went in and out among us, beginning from John's baptism to the time when Jesus was taken up from us. For one of these must become a witness with us of his resurrection. (Acts 1:21-22)

There's a lot of depth to this verse. Essentially the apostles were to testify of Christ's resurrection, which is the central event of the Gospel. But not just anybody who saw the resurrection could be an apostle. It must be someone who also witnessed the entire ministry of Christ. Therefore, only a man who knew the events of the life of Christ would understand the point of the resurrection, and the resurrection would also shed light on the events of Christ's life that he witnessed.

John also describes the unique position of an apostle:

> That which was from the beginning, which we have heard, which we have seen with our eyes, which we have looked at and our hands have touched – this we proclaim concerning the Word of life. The life appeared; we have seen it and testify to it, and we proclaim to you the eternal life, which was with the Father and has appeared to us. We proclaim to you what we have seen and heard, so that you also may have fellowship with us. And our fellowship is with the Father and with his Son, Jesus Christ. (1 John 1:1-3)

The reason they had to be qualified witnesses, as we have seen, is that the life of Christ was so startling, it was so unexpected and mysterious, that there had to be someone who saw it to assure us that it really was the Son of God come in the flesh. We can doubt someone's ideas and opinions, but we can't doubt an eyewitness without calling him a liar. His testimony becomes invaluable if we want to know what really happened.

The Apostles

The disciples spent over three years with Christ. They watched him and listened to him as he did the works of God. They slowly came to understand who he really was; it didn't come to them overnight. This in itself shows us that what they were witnessing was not of this world. Christ was a man, but he was also *the Son of God* – and that means that there are deep spiritual realities involved in his ministry, and we need the Spirit of God to reveal them to us. Understanding Jesus doesn't come easily, as if we only need to put in a little effort to understand the point about him. The Pharisees, for example, also saw things that Christ did, yet *they* didn't see the deeper level at work like the disciples did.

What did the disciples see in Christ?

- **The God of the Old Testament** – Jesus was careful to show the disciples the *same God* that they had learned about from their Scriptures. We often miss this fact, because we think that Jesus came to do a new thing – to show us something different about God that the Old Testament doesn't show us. This is why many people don't bother to study the Old Testament: they think that the New Testament sets aside the Old, as if we don't need the Old anymore.

The disciples themselves realized that they were witnessing the Old Testament God first-hand. Jesus did the same works as God, he taught the same truths, he called his people in the same ways. For example, he kept insisting that he did *the works of God, and that should be proof of who he really was and who was behind his ministry:*

> I have testimony weightier than that of John. For the very work that the Father has given me to finish, and which I am doing, testifies that the Father has sent me. (John 5:36)

> Don't you believe that I am in the Father, and that the Father is in me? The words I say to you are not just my own. Rather, it is the Father, living in me, who is doing his work. (John 14:10)

What were his works? Jesus taught the people of God about the kingdom, and about their responsibilities in the kingdom, just as God had done from the days of Moses, through the Kingdom of David, all through the ministry of the Prophets. Jesus fed his people, just as God had done in the wilderness. Jesus ruled over his people, laying out his laws for them to obey, just as God had done on Mt. Sinai and through the reign of King David. Jesus protected his people from their enemies, just as God did from the Philistines and others. Jesus led his people into the new Promised Land, just as God did the Israelites.

One important point to realize is that Jesus did these things in the *same way* that God did them in the Old Testament. This is the way we can know that we are dealing with the same God. Other gods won't do these things in this way, because they *can't*. The apostles were careful to point out this fact to us – this is what most impressed them during their time spent with him.

To be more specific, there are certain aspects of the God of the Old Testament that the Apostles saw in Jesus and brought to light in their writings:

- *The Ways of the Lord* – God has certain ways of doing things. When you first hear about God you will learn about his attributes, some of his works, the Names that describe him – things that can be known about him right away. But to learn his ways will take some time. His ways aren't like our ways – he's the Creator and

Redeemer, and he can reach his goals by completely different paths than we would take.

The point about learning how God likes to do things is twofold: *first*, he isn't going to do things the way we do them. In fact, we aren't usually going to understand his ways nor will we like them. They conflict with what we want to see! But we've been failing at the job of being righteous all of our lives, so it's time the Lord show us the right way, the effective way, of getting there for a change.

Second, when we learn how he does things, we need to change our ways to fit his ways. We need to fit in with his work, instead of working against him all the time. If he's leading us down a certain path towards holiness, he doesn't appreciate our taking side trails all the time! He wants some cooperation for a change. We may not understand why we have to do what he says, and we may not like what he says, but his ways lead to life and salvation.

The apostles noted that Jesus had the same ways that God did in the Old Testament. This is highly significant, because it tells us that we're dealing with God here. Jesus isn't just a mortal man, but he is God in the flesh doing his work in the way that God always has done his work. He knows what it will take to get the job done; he knows that man's ways don't work and never have worked. So he takes the sure and certain path to Heaven even over the objections of his own disciples who didn't understand his ways! For instance, one of the ways of the Lord is that he wins by losing. We can't understand how someone can deliberately set things up to lose and expect to win in the end; God, however, prefers to work this way – because he knows he can use a miracle to solve the problem in the end. So does Jesus. But Peter couldn't handle it!

> From that time on Jesus began to explain to his disciples that he must go to Jerusalem and suffer many things at the hands of the elders, chief priests and teachers of the law, and that he must be killed and on the third day be raised to life. Peter took him aside and began to rebuke him. "Never, Lord!" he said. "This shall never happen to you!" Jesus turned and said to Peter, "Get behind me, Satan! You are a stumbling block to me; you do not have in mind the things of God, but the things of men." (Matthew 16:21-23)

- ***The Works of the Lord*** – Man is a worker; God made him to work and accomplish things. It's in our hearts to love work. So it's natural that we usually try to find our own way out of our problems and create the kind of world that we want with our own labor.

  But there are certain things that only God can do. He alone can work miracles. He alone can create a spiritual world for man to live in. He alone can forgive sins. Only God can fulfill the Covenant to Abraham and his children. There are two principles about God to learn from this: <u>*first*</u>, this is a good way we can use to find out whether it's really God at work in a circumstance, or whether it's really the works of man (even when done in God's name!). If anybody can duplicate or explain how a certain work is happening, then it's not God at work – only he can do his peculiar work, and nobody can understand how he does it.

Second, it's time we back away from trying to do works to save our own souls and appeal to God to do this work for us. Now is not the time for pride. God has to work miracles in us, and lead us where we are blind, and teach the ignorant the truth. We are helpless, hopeless, weak, ignorant – the book of Revelation describes us well:

> You say, 'I am rich; I have acquired wealth and do not need a thing.' But you do not realize that you are wretched, pitiful, poor, blind and naked. (Revelation 3:7)

So we need to learn about God's works so that we can turn to him for those things and wait on him to do what only he can do.

Again, the Apostles saw in Jesus the God of the Old Testament because of the works he did. He did the same kinds of things, in the same ways, as God has always done for his people. Jesus himself made that claim:

> I tell you the truth, the Son can do nothing by himself; he can do only what he sees his Father doing, because whatever the Father does the Son also does. For the Father loves the Son and shows him all he does. Yes, to your amazement he will show him even greater things than these. For just as the Father raises the dead and gives them life, even so the Son gives life to whom he is pleased to give it. (John 5:19-21)

When we see Jesus doing the works of God, that's the basis of putting our faith in him. He can save us, he can lead us to Heaven. He can and will keep all the promises that he made to us.

- ***The Creator*** – We already looked at the way God created the world, as Genesis records it. I hope you see the importance of understanding his unique Creation work – he did it by the power of his Word, through miracle, and by command. This isn't the natural explanation of the world's beginnings (or a scientific analysis), but it's definitely God's unique way of doing things.

    The story of Jesus gets *very* interesting once we realize that he uses the same methods to do his work of building and ruling his Kingdom. The Apostles didn't miss the point. They show us the Creator at work, using the same creative forces that he used at the beginning. There are reasons for this. <u>First</u>, the Creator has all the power and authority he needs to rule over, and fix, his world – no matter what forces try to stand in his way. Nothing can frustrate the Creator when he resorts to the power of the Spirit to do his work. <u>Second</u>, when the Creator shows up again on the scene, we should be alerted to the fact that something is about to happen – like a *new world*. He isn't pleased with the state of the current one; we've done our best to ruin it. Instead of leaving it in its destruction and misery, he's going to make a "new Heaven and earth" where his original purposes will finally be fulfilled, only now on a spiritual, eternal, and more glorious level than the first Creation.

- ***The Names of Christ*** – The Names of God were important in the Old Testament because they teach us what God is like. Names describe things; in God's case, they describe his nature, his special work, his relationship with Creation

The Apostles

and with us, his goals and achievements. And when we learn his Names, we can use them in prayer to ask for what that Name describes. In fact, this is why the Temple was built in the first place:

> May your eyes be open toward this temple day and night, this place of which you said you would put your Name there. May you hear the prayer your servant prays toward this place. (2 Chronicles 6:20)

The Apostles gave us many names for Christ, for the same reason – to show us the kinds of things that Jesus can do for his people. His names reinforce the fact that we have the Old Testament God in the flesh, here with us, ready to do the same kinds of works that he did for his people in the old days. In fact, one of the names of Christ reflects that very fact – Immanuel, which means "God with us." This fact gives us the freedom to call on our God who has come so close, and the confidence to believe that he will answer our prayers when we call – since that's why he came!

God's most powerful name in the Old Testament is Yahweh – the Hebrew letters for the name are יהוה . We find the Lord's own definition for his special Name in the following passage (The NIV Bible uses the English word "LORD," in all caps, to translate the Hebrew name) –

> The LORD, the LORD, the compassionate and gracious God, slow to anger, abounding in love and faithfulness, maintaining love to thousands, and forgiving wickedness,

rebellion and sin. Yet he does not leave the guilty unpunished; he punishes the children and their children for the sin of the fathers to the third and fourth generation. (Exodus 34:6-7)

Of all the names that God has, Jesus had to demonstrate that he was *this* in his life and work or else the Jews could have turned away from him as an impostor. But in fact this is exactly what Jesus demonstrated to those who came to him for help: the love of God, the great compassion of God, the God who forgives over and over and gives sinners a new chance. And to make sure that we don't miss the point that this God, Yahweh, really has come to earth to call sinners to himself, he is given the same Name:

You shall call his name Jesus, for he shall save his people from their sin. (Matthew 1:21)

The name "Jesus" is a combination of two Hebrew words: "Yahweh [*is*] salvation."

The point is this: the apostles testified that Jesus has the same goals and the same purposes in mind as did the God of the Old Testament.

The disciples carefully noted what Jesus did and how he did it, and recorded these things for the benefit of the Church. They didn't miss the significant details, nor did they create a story to suit their own notions of who Jesus was (as many in our day accuse them of doing!). They were faithful witnesses of the event when Israel's God came to visit them in person. Who will accuse them of lying about what they testify of? Jesus

The Apostles

really is the Son of God; what he said and did is proof of that.

- **Miracles** – The stories of the miracles in the Gospels are an absolutely essential part of the apostles' witness about Christ. Jesus came to do miracles. The job of the apostles was to witness them, and record what happened. Without the miracle stories, we wouldn't have a Gospel to preach.

A miracle is an impossible thing come true. Nobody but God can do miracles (though the devil can fool people with his tricks and sleights of hand). In fact, this is the definition of a miracle:

A miracle is what God does directly, apart from natural means.

For example, we all know how to get bread to eat: We start with last year's grain, plant it, water it, hoe the weeds out, harvest it, grind it up, add other ingredients, bake it, and we have bread. But when God makes bread, he bypasses all the intermediate steps that we rely on and creates it out of nothing. He sent manna out of the sky, for instance, when his people needed bread in the desert. (Exodus 16) How did he do that? *Nobody knows*. It was a physical impossibility; we couldn't do it if we tried. When there's a need that the natural world, and man himself, can't fill, God bypasses the natural means and works a miracle to fill that need.

Jesus' entire ministry was filled with miracles. They were all clearly impossible events. In fact, this is why people don't believe that Jesus did such things – they aren't possible; our world doesn't work like that. Only a naïve child would believe that such things happened. So unless someone was there and actually saw them happen, we just won't believe it.

There's the whole point. Someone *was* there and saw them happen. *We* weren't there, it's true, but the disciples were just as reliable witnesses as we would have been: they too were unbelieving, ignorant, refusing to believe their eyes, self-righteous, thick-headed, self-centered, and highly opinionated! So Jesus worked miracle after miracle, proving to them over and over the divine power behind his work. Gradually they began to understand the point of this man who could do the impossible whenever he wanted – whenever the need arose.

Jesus did astonishing things. We read the Gospels in such a casual way, as if miracles were normal fare in those days. If he were here in our age, the newspapers would cover their front pages daily with the staggering works of Christ. Every person across our nation would be talking about this worker of wonders. That's exactly what happened in his day:

> And when the demon was driven out, the man who had been mute spoke. The crowd was amazed and said, "Nothing like this has ever been seen in Israel." (Matthew 9:33)

> Jesus returned to Galilee in the power of the Spirit, and news about him spread through the whole countryside. (Luke 4:14)

Why are the miracles such an important part of the Gospel of Christ? *Because only God does miracles.* No man, no matter how holy or powerful or wise he may be, can do these impossible things. Man is forced to work under the constraints of the real world. Modern man is very clever, and has found almost "miraculous" ways of controlling his environment, but he still has to work according to physical laws. So when we see Jesus doing what only God can do, this tells us something crucial about him: that he's the Son of God, who does the works

The Apostles

of God and speaks the very words of God. In this respect he is *not* like us.

> Why then do you accuse me of blasphemy because I said, 'I am God's Son'? Do not believe me unless I do what my Father does. But if I do it, even though you do not believe me, believe the miracles, that you may know and understand that the Father is in me, and I in the Father. (John 10:36-38)

We need to know this, because we need to know where to go when we need help – to the only one who can work miracles for us. There is much that we can't do for ourselves: we can't extend our lives, we can't protect ourselves against the world, we can't save ourselves from our sin, we can't reach Heaven – we can't even *see* Heaven! "No one can see the Kingdom of God unless he is born again." (John 3:3) As Jesus said, unless we believe that he's the miracle worker, and go to him for what we desperately need – a miracle of salvation – we will surely die. Many refuse to go to him for this miracle. It was said of people in his own hometown, "he did not do many miracles there because of their lack of faith." (Matthew 13:58)

The apostles, therefore, knowing how crucial it is to our faith to see the true nature of the person and work of Christ, made no mistake in presenting him to us in the Gospels. They showed us his glory in all its majesty: commanding the dead to life, touching and healing, healing from a distance, stilling the storm waves, walking on water, turning water to fine wine, knowing men's thoughts. And they testify to these things as *eyewitnesses*. They were there; they saw these things happen. They were sane, level-headed, practical men who saw Jesus do the impossible. Who will call their testimony into question? Will we? We weren't there! Does our modern scientific outlook deny the possibility of such miracles? That's the very point about a miracle, however – Jesus went *around* scientific laws, something that we can't do, to do his will. We are not dealing with an ordinary man here; the apostles are showing us God at work.

But the lesson about the miracles is not that Jesus did them to impress us with his power. If this is God – and that's what the miracles prove – then the next step in our faith is obvious:

> We must pay more careful attention, therefore, to what we have heard, so that we do not drift away. For if the message spoken by angels was binding, and every violation and disobedience received its just punishment, how shall we escape if we ignore such a great salvation? This salvation, which was first announced by the Lord, was confirmed to us by those who heard him. God also testified to it by *signs, wonders and various miracles*, and gifts of the Holy Spirit distributed according to his will. (Hebrews 2:1-4)

In other words, if Jesus did these physical miracles, then he's the one who can and will work spiritual miracles in our souls. He can do the impossible – like make a sinner into a saint, a rebel into a child of God, and Heaven into the eternal home for man.

- **The fulfillment of the prophecies** – We already looked at how important the prophecies of the Old Testament are as a testimony to Christ and his true nature. It's still possible, however, for people to doubt that the prophets had Jesus of Nazareth in mind. After all, how in the world could a prophet look into the future and utter a prophecy about a single man out of the billions of people in history? Isn't it possible to interpret those prophecies as describing many different men, even the entire nation of Israel? Even if you have never had such thoughts about the prophecies, there have been many others who have.

That's where the apostles come in. In a master stroke of historical documentation, they brought out the hundreds of Old Testament prophecies and proved that they were fulfilled in the words and works of Christ. *This is the man that the prophets spoke of;* here is the proof that he fulfilled those prophecies, one by one, to demonstrate his divine nature and ministry. And they saw the dream of the prophets fulfilled: Here was the King who would sit on David's throne and make the Old Testament shadows real. The old physical system, weakened and made ineffective by the sin of man, is about to be replaced by a spiritual system that will effectively save us from sin and death forever. He will do what his forefather David did, but in such a way that it will never fall into sin and ruin again.

The apostles were well-versed in the prophets, and lost no opportunity to point out when Jesus fulfilled another prophecy. For example, here are just a few of Matthew's testimonies of Christ fulfilling the prophets:

> All this took place to fulfill what the Lord had said through the prophet. (Matthew 1:22)

> And so was fulfilled what the Lord had said through the prophet. (Matthew 2:15)

> ... to fulfill what was said through the prophet Isaiah. (Matthew 4:14)

> But this has all taken place that the writings of the prophets might be fulfilled. (Matthew 26:56)

Sometimes we may wonder why the apostle thinks that Christ's action was a fulfillment of a prophecy. It seems to us that the prophecy could be interpreted in several ways, and what happened to Jesus doesn't appear to be the real meaning of the prophecy. For example, Matthew claims that Jesus' parents moving to Egypt to escape the wrath of Herod fulfilled the following prophecy:

> When Israel was a child, I loved him, and out of Egypt I called my son. (Hosea 11:1, see also Matthew 2:15)

On the surface it appears that the prophet Hosea was talking about Israel in Moses' day – they were an infant nation, a new people that he called out of the slavery in Egypt and brought into the Promised Land. Surely Hosea had that story in mind! But Matthew tells us that it's also about Christ as an infant! No matter what Hosea might have understood in his day, God (who spoke through Hosea by the Spirit) looked *forward* in time to when his *own* Son would come out of hiding in Egypt. Now we have something interesting here: even the Exodus of the Israelites out of Egypt was a type, a shadow, that teaches us about the more important event of Christ coming out of Egypt. Matthew forces us to change the way we have previously understood Scripture, because the point of *all* prophecy is Christ.

- **The Kingdom of God** – The Kingdom of God is one of the most important themes of the New Testament. All that we have said about Jesus so far would be impressive in itself, but nobody would have any reason to believe that it necessarily involves us today. But the apostles saw an amazing thing unfold before them in the ministry of Jesus. They saw a vast spiritual kingdom taking shape that reaches out into all of history, through all nations and cultures. They saw and testified about a kingdom that includes us all.

The Apostles

The Old Testament, of course, is about the Kingdom of God over the Jews. At the very beginning of Jewish history, God announced that he was their God – and he would rule over them, they must abide by his Laws, and he would make them into a kingdom in which there would be peace and justice and righteousness. The kingdom experienced various degrees of success: under Joshua and David, for example, things went very well; but under most of the kings of Israel and Judah, the Israelites basically ignored God and did things their own way – and suffered as a result.

The prophets knew (through the Spirit) that things couldn't go on this way. God hates sin; he simply will not tolerate a world where people rebel against his Law. And it's not as if he's acting like a tyrant! It's to man's benefit to submit to God's Law, and depend on God to provide what he needs. Only when people rebel against the King do they end up with misery and death on their hands. So the prophets spoke of a day when God would put new life into his kingdom – through the work of Christ. We have already looked at some of those prophecies.

The disciples knew, once they realized who Jesus really was, that he was here to work on that Kingdom. They remembered the prophecies. What they didn't realize at first was the true nature of Christ's kingdom! They thought he came to set up an earthly kingdom, with his throne in Jerusalem, ruling over the entire earth with them as his special counselors:

> So when they met together, they asked him, "Lord, are you at this time going to restore the kingdom to Israel?" (Acts 1:6)

It wasn't until after his resurrection and the outpouring of the Spirit that they understood what kind of kingdom he had come to set up. In fact, he had begun the building of the kingdom right under their noses! As they wrote their testimonies of him, they remembered important events that revealed him at his work of building up the kingdom. They remembered that he started out his ministry with these words:

> After John was put in prison, Jesus went into Galilee, proclaiming the good news of God. "The time has come," he said. "The kingdom of God is near. Repent and believe the good news!" (Mark 1:14-15)

They remembered that he described his kingdom as something to look forward to:

> After this, Jesus traveled about from one town and village to another, proclaiming the *good news* of the kingdom of God. (Luke 8:1)

They remembered that he laid the Law down in his Kingdom:

> For I tell you that unless your righteousness surpasses that of the Pharisees and the teachers of the Law, you will certainly not enter the Kingdom of Heaven. (Matthew 5:20)

They remembered that he challenged the kingdoms of this world, that he proclaimed himself King of all other kings:

> You are right in saying that I am a king. In fact, for this reason I was born, and for this I came into the world, to testify to the truth. Everyone on the side of truth listens to me. (John 18:37)

They remembered the King traveling around and making things right in his Kingdom: calling people into it as new citizens, healing the hurts, defeating his enemies, feeding the hungry, lifting up the downtrodden:

> Jesus went through all the towns and villages, teaching in their synagogues, preaching the good news of the Kingdom and healing every disease and sickness. (Matthew 9:34)

They also remembered that he promised a vast spiritual treasury to his followers, part of a world that's not of this physical world:

> Do not store up for yourselves treasures on earth, where moth and rust destroy, and where thieves break in and steal. But store up for yourselves treasures in Heaven, where moth and rust do not destroy, and where thieves do not break in and steal. For where your treasure is, there your heart will be also. (Matthew 6:19-20)

The point is that the apostles realized that Jesus was building a spiritual, eternal, perfect kingdom that was all that the Old Testament kingdom promised to be and never was. It was only the beginning, to be sure, but they alert us to the fact that it exists now, and we are either inside or outside of Jesus' kingdom.

The mystery of the Gospel

In probably the most astonishing move in history, God completely solved the problem of the human race. He had this in mind since before the creation of the world, but he kept it secret even during the Old Testament times when he was working out the rest of the details of the plan of salvation. Not until Jesus came, died, and rose to Heaven did God then unveil his secret – through his servants the Apostles.

The problem is this: how are we, who are so sinful, ever going to become perfect and *stay that way* so that we can live with God forever in Heaven? How can we erase our past so completely that the Law will never have any problem with us? How can we, who have our minds and hearts so fixed on this world, be made to desire only God's world?

God could remake us so thoroughly that we would be righteous once again. A new creation. But haven't we learned the lesson from the first creation that, in ourselves, we will only fall again under the right circumstances? Adam and Eve were righteous – but when God set them on their own feet, they didn't *stay* righteous. Why would God risk another disaster like that by bringing us to Heaven?

God never does things in small measure; he does things out of abundance, full and overflowing. So his idea of how to save mankind from sin and death would be, as expected, rich and satisfying. What God did was to send his only Son Jesus Christ into the world as a human being. Then he would have Jesus fulfill the Law to the letter, as a man is supposed to. Then he would send Jesus to shoulder the sins of the world. Then he would have Jesus die as a sinner, and so satisfy the Law that it would have no more problem with the sinner. Then he lifted Jesus up from the grave into eternal life, seated him at his right hand, gave him authority to rule the nations, and gave him all the treasures of Heaven as his personal inheritance. Keep in mind that God did all this to Jesus *while he was a man.*

Now, the brilliant stroke. He then takes us – we who have no hope otherwise of ever living with the holy God in any manner – and *makes us one with Christ Jesus.* In that one act he takes away our sin, our guilt, our past; he changes our hearts and minds to be pure, as Christ's are; he gives us everything in Heaven; he lifts us up to his side to rule the universe. In a miracle of grace, he takes the broken and impure, brings it into the holy and whole, and achieves his goal of transforming us into his image as he first intended for us.

Nobody expected God to approach the problem like this. The Jews certainly didn't, because they saw their hope in themselves following the Law and satisfying God. The Gentiles, who were probably more open to a metaphysical marvel like this, didn't know anything about this God and his world. It was a breakthrough that astonished the Apostles, and they spent the rest of their ministries spreading the news about this unique salvation in Christ. Notice what Paul says about it:

> Now to him who is able to establish you by my gospel and the proclamation of Jesus Christ, according to the revelation of the *mystery* hidden for long ages past, but now revealed and made known through the prophetic writings by the command of the eternal God, so that all nations might believe and obey him – to the only wise God be glory forever through Jesus Christ! Amen. (Romans 16:25-27)

> Surely you have heard about the administration of God's grace that was given to me for you, that is, the *mystery* made known to me by revelation, as I have already written briefly. In reading this, then, you will be able to understand my insight into the *mystery* of Christ, which was not made known to men in other generations as it has now been revealed by the Spirit to God's holy apostles and prophets. This *mystery* is that through the gospel the Gentiles are heirs together with Israel, members together of one body, and sharers together in the promise in Christ Jesus. I became a servant of this gospel by the gift of God's grace given me through the working of his power. Although I am less than the least of all God's people, this grace was given me: to preach to the Gentiles the unsearchable riches of Christ, and to make plain to everyone the administration of this *mystery*, which for ages past was kept hidden in God, who created all things. (Ephesians 3:2-9)

> Pray also for me, that whenever I open my mouth, words may be given me so that I will fearlessly make known the *mystery* of the gospel, for which I am an

ambassador in chains. Pray that I may declare it fearlessly, as I should. (Ephesians 6:19-20)

I have become its servant by the commission God gave me to present to you the word of God in its fullness – the *mystery* that has been kept hidden for ages and generations, but is now disclosed to the saints. To them God has chosen to make known among the Gentiles the glorious riches of this *mystery*, which is Christ in you, the hope of glory. We proclaim him, admonishing and teaching everyone with all wisdom, so that we may present everyone perfect in Christ. (Colossians 1:25-28)

I have been crucified with Christ and I no longer live, but Christ lives in me. The life I live in the body, I live by faith in the Son of God, who loved me and gave himself for me. (Galatians 2:20)

For in Christ all the fullness of the Deity lives in bodily form, and you have been given fullness in Christ, who is the head over every power and authority. In him you were also circumcised, in the putting off of the sinful nature, not with a circumcision done by the hands of men but with the circumcision done by Christ, having been buried with him in baptism and raised with him through your faith in the power of God, who raised him from the dead. When you were dead in your sins and in the uncircumcision of your sinful nature, God made you alive with Christ. (Colossians 2:9-13)

God is going to use a simple yet mysterious process to make us one with Christ, since that's our ticket to Heaven. Jesus is going to send his Spirit into us, to live in our hearts. This is so that whatever he has been through, we will also experience; wherever he lives, we also will live. We will take on his very life through his Spirit. So the Holy Spirit becomes vitally important to the people of God, which is why the Spirit is another major theme in the writings of the Apostles. It all fits together, once you see the overall picture.

The special work of the Spirit

Usually we think of the Spirit in terms of sanctification — that is, making us free from sin, or holy. "But you were washed, you were sanctified, you were justified in the name of the Lord Jesus Christ and by the Spirit of our God." (1 Corinthians 6:11) "To God's elect ... who have been chosen according to the foreknowledge of God the Father, by the sanctifying work of the Spirit, for obedience to Jesus Christ and sprinkling by his blood." (1 Peter 1:1-2)

But that's not the *primary* work of the Spirit according to the Bible. In a total of over 80 different passages that talk about what the Spirit does, I found only five places where it refers to his work of cleansing from sin, and some of those are marginal. Over half of the passages teach that the Spirit *reveals* the things of God, and the other half talk about the Spirit's *empowering* work.

- **<u>The Spirit reveals the world of God.</u>** " 'No eye has seen, no ear has heard, no mind has conceived what God has prepared for those who love him' — but God has revealed it to us by his Spirit." (1 Corinthians 2:9-10)

    If we want to know more about Heaven, the first hurdle that we have to get over is the fact that we are so earthbound. Since the day we were born, we have known only what we can see, smell, touch, taste, and hear. This world that we live in has been, to us, the *only* real world, as far as we can tell. The things that we put value on and the things that we own are in *this* world; the issues that we consider important are in *this* world; the people we respect are in *this* world; the forces that we fear are in *this* world. Most people live and die knowing nothing more than what is in this physical world, and they really don't care if there is another world — it seems like unrealistic stories anyway, myths and fairy tales.

But there is another world that's different from this one, even if we don't know anything about it: it's the world that God lives in. God is not of this world. That's a fundamental doctrine of Christianity. We have to believe that God's world is a completely different place than this world that we live in, that he can and does exist without any dependence on the physical world. He is the Creator: he made the universe, and he doesn't depend on it in the least — it depends on him. We could all snap completely out of existence and he wouldn't change in the least. He is what he is, and he will always be what he is, without our help or interference.

God's spiritual world is completely different from ours. Whereas ours is always changing, always falling apart and needing to be built up again, his is unchanging. Ours is completely physical, which means that the One who made it can unmake it just as easily (which he intends to do someday, by the way); but God's world is spiritual and therefore eternal. Our world looks good on the outside, and promises to satisfy us — but those are hollow promises, because it can't deliver on those promises (God intentionally made it unable to satisfy us); God's world doesn't look so appealing to our senses but it does satisfy the soul's deepest needs. Our world struggles under the curse of sin and death, and God has already passed judgment on it — its time will come; God's world remains untouched by that stain and therefore remains God's only choice for where spiritual life can thrive.

What about this completely "other" world that we don't know anything about? We can, and do, live our entire lives in complete ignorance that it even exists. The two worlds actually run parallel to each other, like two cities on either side of a railroad track; and if it weren't for certain historical events that forced

The Apostles

a link between the two we would still not know how the people lived "on the other side of the tracks."

One of the most important historical events that forged a bridge between the two worlds was the giving of the Holy Spirit. The Spirit reveals, makes plain, uncovers, makes "see-able" this other world that God lives in. It's like taking the veil away from a statue so that the public can see it for the first time. It's like opening a window into Heaven so that we can see inside.

The first occasion in the Bible where we find the Spirit doing this type of work is in connection with the Tabernacle. God was concerned that Moses and the Israelites build their central place of worship in the right way; not just anything would do. So instead of running the risk that the makers of the Tabernacle would misunderstand his instructions, no matter how plain he made them, the Lord poured out his Spirit on the two men in charge of the building project:

> See, the LORD has chosen Bezalel son of Uri, the son of Hur, of the tribe of Judah, and *he has filled him with the Spirit of God*, with skill, ability and knowledge in all kinds of crafts ... And he has given both him and Oholiab son of Ahisamach, of the tribe of Dan, the ability to teach others ... so Bezalel, Oholiab and every skilled person to whom the LORD has given skill and ability to know how to carry out all the work of constructing the sanctuary are to do the work just as the LORD has commanded. (Exodus 35:30,34-35; 36:1)

And what did the Spirit show them?

> They serve at a sanctuary that is a copy and shadow of what is in Heaven. This is why Moses

was warned when he was about to build the tabernacle: "See to it that you make everything according to the pattern shown you on the mountain." (Hebrews 8:5)

The Spirit showed these men what the Heavenly Tabernacle, in God's world, looked like. To what extent we don't know, but at least we know that they saw the essentials so that they could pattern the earthly tabernacle after it in a way that would satisfy God. The Tabernacle on earth had to be like the one in Heaven, or it wouldn't have served God's purposes of redemption and representing his glory.

In Isaiah there is a prophecy of the Messiah, and it tells us that he will be filled by the Spirit:

> The Spirit of the LORD will rest upon him — the Spirit of wisdom and of understanding, the Spirit of counsel and of power, the Spirit of knowledge and of the fear of the LORD ... He will not judge by what he sees with his eyes, or decide by what he hears with his ears ... (Isaiah 11:23)

In other words, he won't rely on his senses to judge how to work in this world, but by what the Spirit tells him — knowledge from another world than this one.

Jesus said that when we face authorities who persecute us for our faith, the Spirit of God will give us the right words to say — words that we wouldn't ordinarily think of on our own. (Mark 13:11) He also promised to send the Spirit to us, who would "guide you into all truth." (John 16:13) The Spirit of God opened Stephen's eyes to see Christ standing at God's right hand when the Jews were stoning him. (Acts 7:55-56) The Spirit tells us what to pray for and how to pray when we don't know what to say. (Romans 8:26) The mystery of Christ "has now been revealed by the Spirit" to the Church." (Ephesians 3:5) Paul said that whoever rejects the teaching of Scripture isn't rejecting man but the Spirit, who is actually doing the teaching. (1 Thessalonians 4:8) The Spirit gives us a taste of the Heavenly gift, and enlightens us about the world of God. (Hebrews 6:4) The prophets, Peter tells us, always spoke as they were "carried along by the Holy Spirit" — the Spirit told them what to say. (1 Peter 1:21) The Spirit testifies to the cleansing power of Christ's blood. (1 John 5:6) John the apostle was praying in the Spirit when he had his revelation of Christ. (Revelation 1:10) The Spirit says things to the churches of Christ that they need to hear. (Revelation 2:11)

This is just a sampling from the Bible about the work of the Spirit as he reveals the world of God to our minds and souls.

- ***The Spirit gives power.*** "But you will receive power when the Holy Spirit comes on you; and you will be my witnesses in Jerusalem and in all Judea and Samaria, and to the ends of the earth." (Acts 1:8)

The kind of power that this verse is talking about isn't any power that we are familiar with. Simon made that mistake when he saw the apostles working miracles and tried to buy the power of the Spirit from them. (Acts 8:9-24) The power that the Spirit gives is a new thing, something that the mind of man doesn't know anything about.

The first time that we find the empowering work of the Spirit in the Bible is in Genesis.

In the beginning God created the Heavens and the earth. Now the earth was formless and empty, darkness was over the surface of the deep, and the Spirit of God was hovering over the waters. (Genesis 1:1-2)

What exactly was there at the beginning, the building blocks that God used to make the world, we don't know; we do know that it was "without form" and "without substance" (as the Hebrew words mean), which are the two necessary characteristics of matter as we know it. In other words, the Spirit brought non-existence into existence; he gave life and substance to what used to be nothing. The earth and plants and animals and man all exist because the Spirit gave us the ability to exist. Without him we would return to nothingness.

That's what happened to the world when the Spirit moved in the beginning. What happens in men's souls now? Here is where we need the Spirit most of all, because we are all dead to the world of God from our birth. (Ephesians 2:1-3) Even if we see God (the first job of the Spirit), and even if we *know* the truth about God and his world, we still can't do anything about it. God requires obedience from us — but we can't obey him because we are so bound up in our sin, and without power to obey his commands. He requires faith from us — but we can't believe in him because we are so confused, wandering in this dark world. He calls us to live in *his* world, but we can't get out of our world. At the very least we are to "love the Lord your God with all your heart and with all your soul and with all your mind" (Matthew 22:37), but unfortunately we aren't interested — there are other things that we love more.

When the Spirit works on the heart, however, that person wakes up to God's world, like opening one's eyes on a bright morning. "Wake up, O sleeper, rise from the dead, and Christ will shine on you."

(Ephesians 5:14) He can see things now that he hasn't seen before. Even this dark world that we live in gets a new light: the Spirit shines on our lives, on circumstances, on other people, like a spotlight and shows us things that we couldn't see before.

The Spirit not only wakes us up to the world of God, he makes us *able* to live in God's world. "Flesh and blood cannot inherit the Kingdom of God" (1 Corinthians 15:50), simply because the conditions there would kill us. The air is different, the food is different, the light is different (I'm using symbols of the realities, you understand; "air" and "food" and "light" in Heaven are spiritual things, whereas we think of our physical world when we hear those words.) Paul said that before we can hope to rise into Heaven, some things about us have to change:

> So it will be with the resurrection of the dead. The body that is sown is perishable, it is raised imperishable; it is sown in dishonor, it is raised in glory; it is sown in weakness, it is raised in power; it is sown a natural body, it is raised a spiritual body. (1 Corinthians 15:42-44)

In order to live before God and not die, we have to change completely. Our natures as they are now can neither survive before God's glory, nor can we understand or appreciate what we would see there. Our physical senses weren't made to be aware of the things of God. Unless, of course, the Spirit gives life to our souls — our souls *were* made to be aware of God. That's why the Bible talks about having "eyes to see" and "ears to hear." The Spirit makes us alive spiritually (which Jesus called, appropriately, being "born again" — John 3:3) so that our spiritual senses can start picking up on the things of God. In order to pick up the signals from a radio station, you have to first turn the radio on. In the same way, before anybody can hope to know God, their souls must be made alive first.

The Spirit makes it possible for us to obey God's commands; without him we could never do it. (Ezekiel 36:26-27) The Law is spiritual, Paul says (Romans 7:14), and the Spirit shows us what God means by his Law and how he will make us conform to its requirements. The Spirit of God blew over the bones in Israel and made them alive again. (Ezekiel 37:1-14) The Lord will build his Kingdom "not by might nor by power, but by my Spirit" (Zechariah 4:6); because of this, his Kingdom will be eternal and it will consist of things that will satisfy both him and us. Jesus drove out demons by the Spirit of God. (Matthew 12:28) Jesus said that, when someone has the Spirit in him, it will be a spring of water welling up inside to eternal life. (John 4:14) "The Spirit gives life, the flesh counts for nothing" (John 6:63) — and Jesus' words were Spirit because they give us spiritual life, the awareness of God and ability to live for God. Peter, the disciple whom the Jews had last seen denying the Lord, stood up at Pentecost full of the Spirit and preached the eternal Gospel to the Jews — with thousands of conversions as a result. (Acts 2) The Holy Spirit gives joy to God's people. (Romans 14:17) It's because of the Spirit's work that we have faith in Christ — a faith that comprehends the breadth and depth of Christ's person and work. (Ephesians 2:8; 3:16) The Spirit washes and renews us so that we become heirs of God's promises. (Titus 3:5)

Our journey to Heaven

You may have noticed something important in the previous discussion. The Spirit reveals – what? The world of God! He shows us the spiritual Kingdom that God lives in, the one that we've been called to live in ourselves. And the Spirit empowers us – to do what? To live in that Kingdom of Heaven! God's world is of such a nature that the Spirit has to make us *able* to come into God's presence, *able* to take advantage of the treasures that God put in Christ for us. In other words, the primary purpose of the Spirit in our lives is *to make us fit to live in the Kingdom of God.*

When a person becomes a Christian, his heart changes. Jesus described it to Nicodemus (who, by the way, should have known about this already, because he was an expert in the Old Testament!).

> I tell you the truth, no one can see the Kingdom of God unless he is born again … I tell you the truth, no one can enter the Kingdom of God unless he is born of water and the Spirit. Flesh gives birth to flesh, but the Spirit gives birth to spirit. You should not be surprised at my saying, 'You must be born again.' The wind blows wherever it pleases. You hear its sound, but you cannot tell where it comes from or where it is going. So it is with everyone born of the Spirit. (John 3:3,5-8)

Our souls, dead to God at birth and completely unable to sense his presence or feel any inclination to be interested in him, suddenly become alive to God. The Spirit blows from Heaven in a way that none of us can describe or predict and, for some reason, we are suddenly interested in the things of Heaven. We can tell now that there really is a God; we know he's there. More specifically, we find that we fear this God (which means we want to be careful how we act around him), and we hope in this God (which means that we long for the things that he has for us in Heaven).

When this revelation happens, we discover that we have a practical problem on our hands. It's such a precious gift to become a child of God, an heir to the eternal Kingdom, with the right to enjoy our Heavenly inheritance. But we find ourselves still on earth, with physical bodies and physical needs! We would like to leave for Heaven immediately and be done with this world! But it can't be, not yet at any rate. Even Jesus prayed about our problem:

> I have given them your Word and the world has hated them, for they are not of the world any more than I am of

the world. My prayer is not that you take them out of the world but that you protect them from the evil one. They are not of the world, even as I am not of it. (John 17:14-16)

What we have here is a dual-identity problem. In Hebrews we find a description that fits all of God's children, as long as they remain here in this world:

All these people were still living by faith when they died. They did not receive the things promised; they only saw them and welcomed them from a distance. And they admitted that they were *aliens and strangers* on earth. People who say such things show that they are looking for a country of their own. If they had been thinking of the country they had left, they would have had opportunity to return. Instead, they were longing for a better country — a Heavenly one. Therefore God is not ashamed to be called their God, for he has prepared a city for them. (Hebrews 11:13-16)

As long as we remain here, we actually have one foot on earth and one foot in Heaven. Our hearts are in another world, and our eyes are focused on the Throne of God. We know that we don't belong here anymore. We aren't supposed to love the things in this world anymore; as Jesus told us,

Do not store up for yourselves treasures on earth, where moth and rust destroy, and where thieves break in and steal. But store up for yourselves treasures in Heaven, where moth and rust do not destroy, and where thieves do not break in and steal. For where your treasure is, there your heart will be also. (Matthew 6:19-21)

We could go on and on, listing the passages from the Bible about our new life in Christ, our new spiritual inheritance, and God's command to turn our backs on this world. It really is a new life that we've begun because of what Christ did in our hearts.

Here, now, is where the Spirit comes in. Becoming a Christian isn't just a matter of changing from the old way of life to a new way, or holding to a different set of beliefs about God. As Paul says, "If only for *this* life we have hope in Christ, we are to be pitied more than all men." (1 Corinthians 15:19) Our goal now is *Heaven*. We have begun a journey: from the moment that we woke up spiritually and saw our Savior, the rest of our lives will be a steady progress *from* earth *to* Heaven. And the Spirit is doing two things for us: leading us in the right way to Heaven, and slowly making us fit to arrive there in perfect condition and pleasing to our Master. We are making plans for *leaving* this world – and that fact should become more apparent to others as time goes on.

In the Old Testament Temple, there were certain vessels and articles that the priests used for purposes of worship only. The Law strictly forbade anybody from using these articles for common use; the priests sprinkled each article with blood and "set it aside" for sacred use in the Temple. That's exactly what the word "sanctify" means in Hebrew – to "set aside for Temple use." Once a pot, for example, was sanctified, it couldn't be used for ordinary cooking anymore. Even if it was broken by accident, it had to be destroyed – the people were forbidden to use it for any common purpose once it had been sanctified.

That's exactly what the Spirit is doing to us. God is so holy, and the Temple in Heaven is so overwhelmingly holy, that it's forbidden that any common, ordinary, wicked sinner should ever be allowed there. Earth is full of sinners; but Heaven has, and shall have, *none*. There won't even be the hint of sin in the presence of the holy God. But you can probably see the problem here: if God calls us to come up before him, and especially to share the inheritance with Christ as God's children, what are we going to do about our sin? And even if we *were* allowed inside his Temple, what in the world would we say or do there? We know nothing about the place! So the Spirit is going to prepare us for life in Heaven. And here is how he will do it:

- ***Crucify the flesh:*** "Flesh and blood cannot inherit the Kingdom of God, nor does the perishable inherit the imperishable." (1 Corinthians 15:50) We like to pamper our flesh, to line our nests in this world. We want comfortable jobs, respectability in the community, plenty of friends and good times. We also like to indulge in our lusts from time to time.

But there is nothing in Heaven for the flesh to lust for! There are no earthly pleasures, no wealth that we are familiar with, no lusts allowed – or even possible! Remember that Jesus told us that "at the resurrection people will neither marry nor be given in marriage; they will be like the angels in Heaven." (Matthew 22:30) Not too promising for anybody looking forward to pampering their flesh! The pleasures there are purely spiritual. The physical as we know it will be gone, remade, unrecognizable. The physical has to die, like a seed, so that the spiritual can be born and live in a spiritual Heaven.

Now before we can be ready for such a strange place, and before we can even *want* to go to such a place, the Spirit has to work on us and make us into spiritual creatures who love God's spiritual Kingdom. The flesh must die.

- **_Renew the mind:_** "Do not conform any longer to the pattern of this world, but be transformed by the renewing of your mind." (Romans 12:2) Our minds are remarkable tools for enabling us to get along in this world. In fact, we pride ourselves at being "savvy" or intelligent, and we hate to play the fool and show our ignorance.

But when it comes to the world of God, we know almost nothing about it. We don't know what it looks like, we don't know much about God himself, we don't know the immense riches in Christ or how to get at them, we don't know how to act in front of God and Heaven's hosts when we pray – there is so much we don't know about God's world, that the first sight of it will surely humble us!

That's what the Spirit is going to do. He's going to renew our minds, make them able to see and understand spiritual truths and realities, and make us skilled at knowing and using Heavenly treasures.

> We have not received the spirit of the world but the Spirit who is from God, that we may *understand* what God has freely given us. This is what we speak, not in words taught us by human wisdom but in words taught by the Spirit, expressing spiritual truths in spiritual words. (1 Corinthians 2:12-13)

- **<u>Fruits of righteousness</u>:** "But the fruit of the Spirit is love, joy, peace, patience, kindness, goodness, faithfulness, gentleness and self-control. Against such things there is no law." (Galatians 5:22-23)

What naturally comes out of a human being's heart? Read the newspapers! Earth is full of wickedness; it's been that way since the fall of Adam and Eve. None of us can claim moral perfection; even the best of us have failed God at some point in our lives.

But God can't tolerate the least trace of sin! He is so holy – Isaiah said that he is "holy, holy, holy!" (Isaiah 6:3) – that he would sooner have us all put to death than pollute his pure environment with our wickedness. Notice that he didn't have any qualms about destroying sinners in the past! Read the stories of Noah, and Korah, and the Exile, and Sodom and Gomorrah, for proof of his hatred of the wicked.

But the Spirit is going to take care of this spiritual cancer in our hearts. Knowing that we can't appear before God in our own wretched rags of "morality" which haven't made us any more righteous in God's eyes, he's going to replace them with the robe of righteousness that Jesus bought for us with his obedience. Slowly, he's going to *make* us do what pleases God in our lives, day by day. Slowly but surely he's going to remake our hearts in holiness instead of leaving them in wickedness.

- **_True worship:_** "Yet a time is coming and has now come when the true worshipers will worship the Father in Spirit and truth, for they are the kind of worshipers the Father seeks." (John 4:23)

The ways that we invent to worship God in our churches and denominations can be pretty pitiful. We believe firmly that the way *we* worship God is the only right way; but, if you think about it, we can't *all* be right! We all have different versions of how to do worship. But so much of what we do is simply because of our preferences, traditions and culture.

Almost none of it, unfortunately, fits in with the way the servants of God worship him in Heaven. In fact, we probably would feel completely out of place there – we wouldn't know the first thing to do if we were presented to God in person! What would we say? What would we do? Even if we could think of what to do for the first five minutes, what would we do for the rest of the day? For a year? For eternity? Remember that the worship of God is going to be our work in Heaven *forever*. Do we have any idea of how to go about such work?

The Spirit, then, has to train us in spiritual worship. He has to show us what God likes, and what he expects from us. He has to make us skilled at saying and doing things for God that please him. He has to show us the real work going on in Heaven and what our part in it will be.

- **_Walk by faith:_** "For in the gospel a righteousness from God is revealed, a righteousness that is by faith from first to last, just as it is written: 'The righteous will live by faith.'" (Romans 1:17)

The Apostles

What most people mean by "faith" is a poor substitute for the tremendous spiritual gift that God has given us in true faith. Most people think it means believing in some doctrine or Biblical truth. So they think that they have faith when they, for example, believe that there is a God. James ridicules such "faith!" "You believe that there is one God. Good! Even the demons believe that – and shudder." (James 2:19)

What would happen if God would suddenly lift you up from earth and set you in Heaven? Would you recognize anything? Would everything be totally new to you? Would you be like a foreigner, lost and wandering, friendless, homeless, without a clue as to what is going on around you? If God would invite you to share in the spiritual treasures in Christ, which is your inheritance, would you even know what those treasures are? Or where to find them? Or how to use them?

Faith is walking in the light of God's world. It's the result of the light of Christ coming down from Heaven, that the Spirit shines down on us as he reveals to us the things of God. We *know* God, we *see* God, through our faith. We see the riches in Christ; that's why we reach out to *him* when we need help. We see a world that others can't see. That "seeing" is what true faith is all about. With true faith, this physical world means little to us, and the world of God becomes our only hope. Living by faith means we conform our daily lives to spiritual realities – things that other people can't see and don't know. The Spirit, as he reveals these things to us, makes such a faith possible. And now through faith we start making ourselves familiar with the world of God and how to take advantage of our spiritual inheritance.

- **<u>Resist the enemy</u>:** "Put on the full armor of God so that you can take your stand against the devil's schemes." (Ephesians 6:11) The enemy of our souls is desperate to destroy us. Satan has hated God's creation since it was first made. And since we bear the image of God in our very nature, he especially hates us. He does not want us to succeed and live with God forever; he wants to see us dead. This is war, in the worst sense. Our very lives are at stake, and anybody who loses this war will be damned forever.

We need help against this fierce a foe. We need wisdom from God, the power of the Spirit, a clear way that we can follow from this world to the next. We need to learn the ways of the enemy so that we won't be tricked, deceived, or blind-sided by his forces. We need armor that will be effective against his power and weapons. Jesus himself has dealt the enemy a mortal blow that has broken the stranglehold he had on God's people; but now, as our path to Heaven unfolds, we need to take precautions to safeguard ourselves along the way. Even a mortally wounded enemy is capable of doing a lot more damage!

The Spirit gives us the necessary weapons to fight the enemy and his forces. Not only are we fitted with the truth, with righteousness, with salvation, with faith, and with truth – but we're going to get some wisdom on how to use these weapons. One of the things we have to learn is where and when to use these weapons! We have to distinguish between the real enemy and people who simply aggravate us. In other words, the world is full of misguided and ignorant people who are being used by the enemy to get at us, like a front behind which Satan hides and through whom (whether they know it or not) he does his dirty work. Satan we will and must fight; the dupes he uses to pull us down, however, need our pity and love. We were once in their place! They need our help to come to their senses and change masters before Judgment Day comes.

- ***Hope in Heaven:*** "For in this hope we were saved." (Romans 8:24) We hope in whatever we set the greatest value on. If we love this world with all of its "riches" and "glory," and we long to fill our physical lusts with earthly pleasures, then we won't have much interest in a spiritual world where there is none of that sort of thing.

When we are brought before God's judgment seat on the Last Day, it will be plain for everyone to see what we have been putting our hope in. If our hearts have been set on things on earth, we will look with great disappointment and fear at this God that we haven't been paying any attention to. We will cringe before a Heaven without worldly pleasures. We will look back, like Lot's wife, at the earth burning behind us, destroyed by God's punishing hand, wishing that we were there instead of in this spiritual world with God and his people. What will we do if Heaven turns out to be so foreign and offensive to us?

So the Spirit is going to wean us from the world now, and set our hearts on Heavenly things. He works in us to will and do God's perfect will. He helps us pray – for spiritual treasures. He sets our eyes on Christ, seated at God's right hand, above all earthly powers and pleasures. When he gets done with us, there will be nothing on earth that we desire but God, and nothing in Heaven that so wins our hearts but God. (Psalm 73:25) The longer we live with the Spirit, the more we will *long* for Heaven.

Walking with the Spirit

The Israelites were bound to obey the Law that God gave them at Mt. Sinai. The Law was, simply put, a list of rules and regulations that described the government of God over his people. He expected obedience – strict obedience, upon pain of death. There was no leeway in this, either; one single broken Law and they were in trouble. The Law often required death as a punishment.

The key to understanding the Law is that *the Israelites themselves had to keep the Law*. "And if we are careful to obey all this law before the LORD our God, as he has commanded us, *that* will be our righteousness." (Deuteronomy 6:25) They had to *do* what the Law said. When they did, God considered them righteous; if they didn't, God punished them.

The history of the Israelites is a lesson on what happens when God turns us loose with the Law: we fail miserably. None of us can keep the Law as God requires it. The Israelites couldn't. Their sin and ignorance, the temptations of the world, the deceits of the enemy, all of that conspired to trip them up in their attempted obedience to the Law. The only man who ever kept the Law completely, to God's satisfaction, was Jesus – the Son of God.

Jesus did more than keep the Law, however. He bought a righteousness for us that none of us could achieve on our own. Now he is busy applying that righteousness of his to our souls – we're getting righteous the easy way! We are reaching a spiritual level that no Israelite could do on his own. But in order to pull this off, we have to be careful and let the Spirit guide us into that righteousness.

This is a subtle point that many people often miss. Though we claim to be Christians, and we understand that nothing that we do can save us or make us righteous in God's eyes, we still try our best to follow the Law! As if we could do what the Jews couldn't do! It's so tempting to follow the Law that the Galatians fell into that error, and Paul had to write rough rebukes to them for attempting to do what they couldn't do and they weren't allowed, as followers of Christ, to do.

> Are you so foolish? After beginning with the Spirit, are you now trying to attain your goal by human effort? Have you suffered so much for nothing — if it really was for nothing? Does God give you his Spirit and work miracles among you because you observe the Law, or because you believe what you heard? (Galatians 3:3-5)

A Christian isn't obligated to keep the Law; he can't anyway, so it's no use trying. He has a much better approach for becoming righteous: the Spirit of God is going to do it for him. Paul describes it this way:

> For what the Law was powerless to do in that it was weakened by the sinful nature, God did by sending his own Son in the likeness of sinful man to be a sin offering. And so he condemned sin in sinful man, in order that *the righteous requirements of the Law might be fully met in us*, who do not live according to the sinful nature but according to the Spirit. (Romans 8:3-4)

So the result is the same – a righteous man – but the methods are completely different. The Law just stands coolly off to one side, arms crossed, demanding that we obey or be punished. No help, no encouragement, no hope. But the Spirit goes about it in a different way: he gives us three spiritual skills: faith, hope and love. We find these three skills listed in several places in the New Testament.

> And now these three remain: **faith**, **hope**, and **love**. But the greatest of these is love. (1 Corinthians 13:13)

> ... we have heard of your **faith** in Christ Jesus and of the **love** you have for all the saints – the faith and love that spring from the **hope** that is stored up for you in Heaven ... (Colossians 1:4-5)

> ... your work produced by **faith**, your labor prompted by **love**, and your endurance inspired by **hope** in our Lord Jesus Christ. (1 Thessalonians 1:3)

> ... he has given us new birth into a living **hope** ... who through **faith** are shielded by God's power ... though you have not seen him, you **love** him ... (1 Peter 1:3, 5, 8)

Why are these skills so crucial for making us ready for Heaven?

- *<u>He gives us faith.</u>* Faith, as we have seen, is walking in the light of Heaven. By faith we are enabled to see the reality of God, the reality of the treasures of Heaven, the true nature of Christ, the true state of our souls, the true nature of the world that we live in and why we don't want to stay here. Faith opens our spiritual eyes so that we can see the truth, just as the Bible describes it. Without faith we can see nothing.

The Spirit has to open our eyes like this. Faith is a gift from God – Ephesians 2:8. It's the first step toward life. A person who can't see where his salvation is, will remain in darkness and die in his sins, though he might work as hard as he can at being pleasing to God. But the person who sees how to reach salvation, and where it is, can start moving in that direction. We're going to need this gift as the Spirit leads us through life.

- **_He gives us hope._** Hope isn't just wishing that something *might* come true; it's the assurance that it *will* be true. It's what we are waiting for, not wishing for; it's been promised to us, and it's only a matter of time until we receive it. Once we see what God offers us in Christ, we then long for these things – we look forward to them, and put our hope in them. Hope means what your soul longs for.

Only the Spirit can give us this kind of hope. People without hope from the Spirit have no idea how God will receive them at Judgment Day; they "hope" that he will be merciful to them, but they have no reason for their "hope." But a Christian has already heard encouraging words from his Savior. He knows that Jesus went "to prepare a place" for them in Heaven, and the Father is waiting to receive them into an eternal family. Remember, the Spirit reveals the things of God: he shows us the heart of God, the love of God, the certainty of the promises of God. He shows us Christ, who came to save sinners and restore them to a relationship with their Father. When the Spirit shows us how certain these things are, we put our sights on

Heaven now instead of earth. The temptations, the sins, the darkness of this world take on their true light and we willingly turn our backs on all of that. True faith naturally leads us into true hope in the things of God. We're going to need this gift later as the Spirit leads us.

- ***He gives us love.*** There are different kinds of love (in Greek there are *eros* and *philos* as well), but the kind of love that the Spirit puts in our heart is a self-sacrificing love. The New Testament word is **agape** (pronounced, ah-GAWP-ay). John tells us what this kind of love means:

> This is how we know what love is: Jesus Christ laid down his life for us. And we ought to lay down our lives for our brothers. (1 John 3:16)

> Jesus said that our duty is to –

> 'Love the Lord your God with all your heart and with all your soul and with all your mind.' This is the first and greatest commandment. And the second is like it: 'Love your neighbor as yourself.' (Matthew 22:37-40)

To truly love God, we will lay down our lives in service for him. We won't live for our own purposes, but for his will. This means that whatever his commands are, we will do them; wherever he sends us, we will go. If he tells us to crucify our sin and put on righteousness, then we do it without hesitation. If he tells us set our hearts on things above and not on things below, then without looking back we count our lives here as nothing and our only hope to be Heaven with him.

Someone who loves God will also love God's children, because they bear the image of their Father.

The early Church learned the sacrificial love that God requires when they sold fields and houses and then distributed the proceeds of the sales to those in the Church who had need. (Acts 4:32-35) *Agape* love means that we will do whatever is necessary to help our brothers and sisters in need; we will "look not only to your own interests, but also to the interests of others." (Philippians 2:4) We would never think of turning away someone we love! We are going to need this gift later as the Spirit leads us.

When the Spirit gives us these three skills – faith, hope, and love – we are now in the position to start walking with the Spirit and having our hearts changed into the righteousness of Christ.

As we follow the Spirit, he leads us into circumstances that will prepare us for Heaven. Each circumstance is going to require one or more of these three skills that God put into our hearts. Since these are gifts from Heaven, we needn't worry about whether they will help us confront the situation successfully – they are so powerful, so effective, and so satisfying to God's expectations that even a little bit of each will keep us in the right way!

> I tell you the truth, if you have faith as small as a mustard seed, you can say to this mountain, 'Move from here to there' and it will move. Nothing will be impossible for you. (Matthew 17:20)

Remember, because of these skills in our hearts, we will *naturally* respond appropriately to the situation that the Spirit leads us into. We will want to please God and do right, from the heart. The prophecy in Ezekiel will finally come true:

> And I will put my Spirit in you and *move* you to follow my decrees and be careful to keep my laws. (Ezekiel 36:27)

Actually this is Jesus living his life through us, through his Spirit. We can't take credit for our new-found feelings and inclinations, since he is taking control and making us conform to his image.

> I have been crucified with Christ and I no longer live, but Christ lives in me. The life I live in the body, I live by faith in the Son of God, who loved me and gave himself for me. (Galatians 2:20)

Let's take an example from Scripture. In Luke 10:38-42, we are told that Jesus visited Mary and Martha at their home. Martha got busy preparing for a meal, and Mary sat at Jesus feet, drinking in the wisdom of God. When Martha complained about Mary being lazy when there was work to be done, Jesus responded to her by pointing out that Mary was responding in faith, and Martha was not. Mary saw a golden opportunity to get wisdom, which is far more valuable than anything in this world. She longed for this wisdom; she willingly put herself at God's feet in obedience to get it. Her heart was there with Jesus, and she didn't let the world distract her from her hope. This is a perfect example of someone led by the Spirit – the circumstance calls for faith and hope and love, and the person gifted with those skills will rise to the occasion.

New Christians overflow with these spiritual gifts. If you remember back to your first days after conversion, you were captivated by this God you were starting to know. You couldn't get enough of his Word; you loved his salvation; you willingly turned your back on the world (which you saw as empty) and turned your heart to Heaven where your inheritance is waiting. You loved other Christians, and would have willingly laid your life down if necessary for their sake. A new Christian floats in the sea of the Spirit and it's a beautiful thing to behold.

Faith, hope and love are natural "instincts" in the heart of a Christian. Just as a mother finds herself strangely drawn to her newborn, and willing to do anything – even something life-threatening! – to protect it, we find ourselves strangely drawn to the God we once hated. Now we love him, we long for a better world, we hate sin and all its results, we are drawn to others who share our life. Our hearts flow with new emotions that move us toward Heaven, towards God and our Savior, and away from this world.

Over time, however, our hearts start to dull to the excitement of living in the Spirit. The world pulls us back with its pleasures, we lose sight of the God we once knew, and the fire of zeal for the things of Heaven dies down. Jesus predicted this again and again; so did the Apostles. Paul counseled his readers to keep the fires burning:

> Love must be sincere. Hate what is evil; cling to what is good. Be devoted to one another in brotherly love. Honor one another above yourselves. *Never be lacking in zeal*, but keep your spiritual fervor, serving the Lord. Be joyful in hope, patient in affliction, faithful in prayer. Share with God's people who are in need. Practice hospitality. Bless those who persecute you; bless and do not curse. Rejoice with those who rejoice; mourn with those who mourn. (Romans 12:9-15)

When we lose our spiritual zeal, it's hard to imagine being so interested in God and his world that we willingly put aside this world to prepare for the next world. It's hard to accept the responsibility of using our valuable property and time for someone else's benefit. New Christians seem so naïve to us when we've settled back into a comfortable, "reasonable" way of life ourselves.

That's why Jesus had to rebuke his Church in Revelation – they needed to kindle the old fires again and learn to let those spiritual skills in their hearts have their way again:

> Yet I hold this against you: You have forsaken your first love. Remember the height from which you have fallen! Repent and do the things you did at first. If you do not repent, I will come to you and remove your lampstand from its place. (Revelation 2:4-5)

How does one rekindle (or better yet, keep burning) the fire of the Spirit in our hearts? For starters, we have to return to the sources of spiritual strength that God provided for us: the Word, prayer, and Christian fellowship with other believers. By using these resources we can get rid of the world and its troubles and temptations that are filling our hearts. At the sight of Heaven, faith, hope and love will burn brightly again. Then when the Spirit calls for one of these skills in the next trial of life, we will find them guiding and filling our hearts instead of the world turning us away from God and his Kingdom.

We still have to cover one more possibility in the life of a Christian. When the Spirit calls us into faith and we refuse to follow him – that is, we turn to the world and listen to its lies instead – that grieves the Spirit deeply. His job is to get us ready for Heaven; his mission is to get us away from the world and pruning our souls to righteousness. If we refuse to cooperate with him, how is he going to do his job?

> And do not grieve the Holy Spirit of God, with whom you were sealed for the day of redemption. (Ephesians 4:30)

We do this all the time, unfortunately. When the Spirit leads us into getting more wisdom (through preaching, Bible study, fellowship with others) we turn away to entertainment, work, anything but what God wants us to do. We know deep in our hearts that we're disobeying the Lord (remember he puts his Spirit in us, and those spiritual skills that make us know his truth are real and alive in us) but still we turn a deaf ear to the Lord to follow our own paths instead. So, what the Spirit will often do is let us go our own way and let us suffer for a while – because it's still true that the wages of sin is death, even to believers. When we suffer, when we fall into the "tender mercies" of the enemy, and come to our senses (like the prodigal son) we will come running back to God ready to try it his way again. Fortunately he's a merciful God and he will take us back.

Is this the Law?

Following the Spirit is designed to succeed, where the Law failed. Under the old system of the Mosaic Law, the Israelites were commanded to follow the Law and by that process *become* righteous.

This is what I call ***proscriptive*** – the Law tells us what we must do, and now it's up to us to do it. If we don't, we're lost.

Following the Spirit, however, depends on fact that the key ingredients of righteousness are *already planted* in our hearts. Just following their lead, when they naturally rise up in a situation, means that someone else is making sure that I do the right thing. We just have to make sure we don't throw water on the fire and quench the Spirit's leading! This is what I call ***descriptive*** – what we do, by the Spirit's leading through his gifts in us, is righteous. We end up doing the right thing by following the Spirit's leading. And we want to – that's the miracle of it.

This is the answer to how to become righteous when we aren't able to follow the Law. When Christ lives his life in us, the Law is entirely satisfied – it has no problem with us. As Paul tells us in 1 Corinthians 13, love is perfect – it does its work in such a complete and pleasing way that the Law has no cause for condemnation.

> Love, joy, peace, patience, kindness, goodness, gentleness, faithfulness, and self-control. Against such things there is no Law. (Galatians 5:22-23)

Conclusion

Someone recently asked me whether a Christian should be so intense about studying the Bible. Isn't it good enough to know a few of the basics – about how to be saved, about living a holy life, and a few things like that? Won't God accept even the smallest faith and take his children to Heaven, not based on what they know but on their faith?

My answer to this question is that it all depends on what you want from God. It's true that a Christian with a simple faith will end up going to Heaven; they don't have to be Bible scholars to please God. People don't have to go to college either. But if you want a better job than flipping hamburgers at minimum wage, college is a must! And if you want to be able to handle the problems of life, responsibilities of being a Christian, and preparation for your place in the next world, then knowledge is the key to success.

Christians have fierce forces in this world to struggle with – Satan is leading a huge force against us to do whatever they can to destroy us or foul up the work of the Church. Only someone who has the insights of spiritual warfare will be able to push back the enemy, win souls from his camp, and protect himself from harm.

Christians are still plagued with the sins and weaknesses of the old man, the "flesh" as Paul calls it. We are a stench in the nostrils of the Lord with our wayward hearts, unfaithfulness, worldly lusts, shameful thoughts, etc. Only someone with a deep insight into the human heart can know what needs fixing, and only someone who has searched out the available remedies in the great resources of Heaven can skillfully apply those remedies to heal the soul.

God himself deserves all glory for the amazing works that he has done on earth. He has gotten little of the glory he deserves, however. Most people think that he's responsible for little more than making the world (and through evolution at that!). To educate others

Conclusion

about how much God has done here – Creation, redemption, raising and destroying nations, guiding history, putting people and nations where and when he wants them and then demanding an account of their lives – this and much more that God has done has to be *told*. Who knows the story well enough to convince an unbelieving world? We need Christians who have made it their lifelong work to know their God, and know how to glorify him.

In light of all this, I have a feeling that there will be many Christians who arrive at Heaven only to find out that they made a serious mistake taking the easy road there. God has planned great things for his profitable servants, the ones who threw themselves into knowing God and serving him in his Kingdom. Unprofitable ones will be assigned the least important jobs in Heaven (if they are let in at all), which will be far less than they will wish they could do for God in eternity. The ones who showed their love for him the most by devoting their lives to his glory and Word will be lifted up to the position of most honoring him, forever. For that they will be grateful.

Knowing a few Bible verses here and there, and a few of its stories, will make you minimally useful in God's Kingdom. Besides not knowing how to address the serious problems in life with your little knowledge, you probably won't be given much responsible work even in this life – God can't risk the failure by assigning you people in need, and situations that demand skill and wisdom. He will probably bypass you and give it instead to someone who knows what they are doing.

On the other hand, if you search the Scriptures that God gave us for our wisdom and salvation and use it for that, then a deeper understanding of its life-saving message is absolutely necessary. After all, the Bible itself assumes that you will grapple with its message until you get it – the *whole* Bible!

> Therefore every teacher of the law who has been instructed about the kingdom of Heaven is like the owner of a house who brings out of his storeroom *new* treasures as well as *old*. (Matthew 13:52)

Conclusion

But as for you, continue in what you have learned and have become convinced of, because you know those from whom you learned it, and how from infancy you have known the holy Scriptures, which are able to make you wise for salvation through faith in Christ Jesus. *All Scripture* is God-breathed and is useful for teaching, rebuking, correcting and training in righteousness, so that the man of God may be thoroughly equipped for every good work. (2 Timothy 3:14-17)

Notes